THE REIGN OF HENRY VII

The Reign of
Henry VII

R. L. STOREY
Reader in History
at Nottingham University

WALKER AND COMPANY
New York

CONTENTS

Acknowledgments

THE author wishes to record his gratitude to Dr. J. G. Bellamy for kindly reading the proofs of this volume.

Acknowledgment is also due to the following for their permission to reproduce illustrations:

Aerofilms Ltd. No. 22
Bodleian Library, Oxford Nos. 13, 14, 15
Richard Burn No. 21
Central Office of Information, Crown Copyright No. 17
Robert Cooke, M.P. Nos. 30, 31
Country Life Ltd. No. 33
Guildhall Library Nos. 4, 23, 27
A. F. Kersting No. 25
National Monuments Record Nos. 1, 6, 7, 11, 16, 20, 26, 28, 29
National Portrait Gallery Nos. 2, 3,
Public Record Office Nos. 5, 9, 12
Radio Times Hulton Picture Library Nos. 10, 32
The John Rylands Library, Manchester No. 24
Victoria and Albert Museum Nos. 8, 18
No. 19 Photograph supplied by Weidenfeld & Nicolson Ltd. and reproduced with the permission of the President and Fellows of Corpus Christi College, Oxford

List of Illustrations

Introduction

A SMALL fleet sailed from the Norman port of Harfleur on 1 August 1485. The young leader, Henry Tudor, earl of Richmond, had spent the last fourteen years of his life as a proscribed and hunted exile, and with him was a small band of other refugees from the wrath of the English king. Most of the total force of some 2,000 men was a contingent of very dubious quality provided by the king of France. It seemed a pitifully weak army to win a kingdom, for its objective was no less. It lacked even the advantage of being unexpected. For months now Richard III had alerted England against the invader; his ships patrolled the seas, his watches manned the coasts, beacons were ready to blaze the news of Henry's approach; throughout the country men were under orders to march against him whenever he should land, while the king took up his quarters in Nottingham castle to be ready to proceed in any direction 'for the resistance and subduing of his enemies, rebels and traitors'. Yet only three weeks later, on 22 August, Richard was slain at Bosworth and Henry had the crown.

It was an inglorious victory. Both leaders showed courage on the field, but the issue was settled by calculated treachery. Indeed Henry's advance from the beachhead in Milford Haven would not have been possible had the men stationed by Richard to oppose him instead put themselves under Henry's command. At Bosworth his forces were outnumbered, but the earl of Northumberland, commanding Richard's right wing, refused to fight, and Lord Stanley kept his men in the wings until they could be sent to complete the ring round Richard and his bodyguard as they made a last, desperate sally to kill Henry himself.

Bosworth Field, although one of the most sordid battles fought on

1

English soil, has long held a place as a landmark in the history of England. The year 1485 has been enshrined in textbooks and examination syllabuses. The victor became King Henry VII and his family the Tudors thereafter held the throne until its extinction for failure of direct heirs in 1603. The weight given to political events in the study of English history, and the predominant importance of the monarchy in this aspect of national life, has long caused historians to find 'natural breaks' in chronology at the points where one royal dynasty succeeded another; it is only when they come to the nineteenth century that other events, like the Reform Bill, are awarded the distinction of being made boundary posts. We may doubt whether the significance given to the fortunes of royal houses has not tended to distort our picture of England's past. We may well feel that in tracing the changing pattern of life in the whole community events like the Black Death or the Dissolution of the Monasteries were of far greater moment than the deaths of kings.

The year 1485, however, has been accorded yet more importance than that of other milestones in our political history. It has been accepted as the dividing line between medieval and modern times. As the age of the Tudors saw fundamental departures from the medieval patterns of life, innovations which continued to unfold in later centuries, so the establishment of the dynasty has been held to belong to this new age. The battle of Bosworth then ran down the curtain on an era when public affairs were supposedly dominated by the unending struggle of a poorly endowed crown with an overmighty feudal baronage; when the organisation of religious life, and with it education, were kept under the rigid tutelage of a privileged clerical establishment, ultimately obedient only to the pope in Rome; when the daily lives of the general population were closely regulated, the urban proletariat by the restrictive codes of gilds and closed municipal corporations, the more numerous peasantry by the immemorial custom of their native manors. Then when the curtain rises again at Henry VII's accession, we are to witness England on the road to its modern identity: the political order is crowned with the doctrine of the sovereignty of the king in parliament, the church in England is subjected to secular authority, deprived of its privileges and gradually of its monopolies in faith, learning and moral jurisdiction, while private enterprise enriches the kingdom by commerce and industry and transforms the countryside by the enclosure of fields and commons and by the reclamation of fen and forest. The coming of this new period in English history seemed moreover to coincide with dramatic changes abroad—the 'new' monarchies of western Europe, with their policies guided by 'reasons of state', forming international leagues for waging war with professional armies and new-fangled artillery; the discovery of the Americas; the Reformation. The close of the fifteenth century, as David Hume wrote, saw 'the dawn of civility and science', the end of the dark centuries of superstition and barbarity.

We are now aware, of course, that there were medieval antecedents for various once supposedly novel aspects of the age of the Renaissance and Reformation. It is not our concern here however to consider whether it is legitimate to draw a line between 'medieval' and 'modern' times at any chronological point. What is relevant for us is to bear in mind that it has long been customary for our present subject, the reign of Henry VII, to be regarded as falling on the near side of this arbitrary and unreal division. The twentieth-century fashion for general histories in several volumes, each the work of a separate author, has not surprisingly led readers of the parts for 1485–1603 to believe that Henry VII bore a closer resemblance to his successors than to his predecessors. The authors of the appropriate volumes, distinguished scholars in Tudor history, naturally tended to stress elements of continuity throughout their period and often lacked the expertise to distinguish aspects of the first Tudor's government which had been present in earlier reigns; nor could they have received much assistance from the published work of specialists in English medieval history, for the fifteenth century rarely attracted their interest. The period of civil warfare in the third quarter of the century formed a chasm and there were few lifelines between the medievalists on the one side and the Tudor specialists on the other. The latter, then, cannot fairly be censured for dismissing the years before Bosworth as a period of anarchy, of total collapse by the institutions of government, and of writing of Henry VII as making a completely fresh start in the exercise of kingcraft.

The historians of older generations inherited a traditional picture of the fifteenth century which coloured their approach to Henry VII. In 1547 there was published Edward Hall's *Chronicle* which he entitled 'The union of the two noble and illustrious families of Lancaster and York, being long in continual dissension for the crown of this noble realm'; their strife began with the deposition of Richard II in 1399 and it continued until the peaceful accession of Henry VIII who, as the son of Henry Tudor and Elizabeth of York, was 'the indubitable flower and very heir of both the said lineages'. Shakespeare, taking Hall's theme second-hand from Holinshed, has through his history plays given immortal currency to the Tudor myth of medieval England's death-throes in intestinal conflict. And recent historians, taking up the thread from 1485, have rarely failed to hail Henry VII as the saviour of his country from the plague of civil war, and presumed that it was a major aim of his policy 'to unite the white rose and the red' and by other measures to prevent a recurrence of the dynastic strife. We will consider the Wars of the Roses more fully in another chapter. It need only be observed now that since we now realise that both the basic causes and the nature of the wars have been misunderstood, it follows that our assessment of the reign of Henry VII requires modification.

Another preconception about Henry VII to obsess our historians has been his reputation for wisdom. It cannot be denied that contemporary evidence is given by the reports of ambassadors that Henry's mental calibre was high; he was perceptive and well-informed, he could express himself with clarity or conceal his true reactions under graceful language. Polydore Vergil, Hall, Holinshed and other authors of historical literature for the loyal subjects of the Tudors never failed to laud the great sagacity of the founder of their glorious royal dynasty; they could pass over or blame others for the darker episodes of his reign, but it would not have been politic to be lukewarm in their appraisal of the grandfather of Queen Elizabeth I.

The strongest influence in later assessments of the king was *The Life of Henry VII* (1622) by Francis Bacon. Bacon's appreciation of his subject was doubtless stimulated by his desire to recover the favour of Henry's descendant, James I, whose inheritance of the English crown was the outcome of the first Tudor's enlightened foreign policy. One suspects that Bacon designedly fashioned Henry in the same image as James believed himself to be cast. From this biography springs the myth of Henry as 'a wonder for wise men', 'this Solomon of England', the 'arbiter of Europe', the far-sighted legislator whose laws 'are deep and not vulgar, not made upon the spur of a particular occasion for the present, but out of providence for the future', the king with such consummate mastery of affairs, international as well as domestic, that 'what he minded he compassed'. The familiarity of these and other quotations from Bacon's *Life* is the measure of its acceptance almost as a primary authority down to the present century. The fact that Henry ruled for twenty four years, whereas there had been four kings in the equally long period before Bosworth, seemed to provide confirmation of Bacon's assessment: it must indeed have required preternatural capability to hold so treacherous a throne and leave its peaceful succession to the natural heir.

This formidable reputation has proved to be a serious obstacle in evaluating the achievement of Henry VII. The preconceived belief that their subject was a man of infinite ability has led historians to claim for Henry's actions a greater degree of deliberation than is reasonable to expect of any man. When accounts of his reign have been compressed into the opening chapters of a history of the Tudor period this characteristic has been still more exaggerated. We are led to believe that from the very moment his brow is decked with that legendary crown retrieved from the hawthorn bush, Henry realises that to remain king he has to build up the resources of the crown to an extent unparalleled in the past, and at the same time to depress the power of the dangerous feudal nobility; and so he straightway forms a council of subservient yet able officials, establishes the Yeomen of the Guard for his own protection, reorganises the kingdom's finances so that all sources of revenue flow into his private coffers, and legislates for the abolition of 'livery and maintenance' and other adjuncts of baronial might.

In this version of Henry's aims and achievements there are two fallacies. One comes, obviously enough, from compressing the work of his government into too narrow a compass. He was king for twenty four years, and some of his most celebrated 'reforms' were not made until several years after his accession. The act against liveries, indeed, came only in the nineteenth year of his reign. The evil against which it was directed, therefore, had survived Bosworth by this span. The other misconception is the consequence of Henry's reputation for sagacity. Too often is he considered as a ready-made king, fully capable of mastering all the needs and complexities of government from the onset of his reign. We must not forget that Henry was twenty eight years of age when he came to the throne and that he had been in exile since he was fourteen. If he knew anything about the methods of royal administration, he had not learned it in England. Before his exile he had been the ward of Edward IV's trusted councillor, William Herbert, but it is unlikely, to put it mildly, that Herbert saw fit to instruct his young charge in the mysteries of Yorkist statecraft. Whatever Henry discovered in France and Brittany of the administrative organisation of their rulers cannot have been more than a superficial impression, and it was scarcely of much value to him when, as king of England, he assumed the direction of a highly developed governmental system of native growth. In 1485 Henry VII was an apprentice in the art of kingship. The experiences of his exile had an important part in the formation of his character, and the contemporary evidence does permit us to presume that he had considerable powers of understanding. But it is absurd to claim that he ascended the throne with a blueprint for a successful reign. He was still young enough to develop his potential capacity. He had to experiment and profit from his mistakes, he had to adapt himself to meet the stresses and unforeseeable hazards of his new position.

Historians of an older generation, misled by the traditional account of the Wars of the Roses and overawed by Bacon's portrait of Henry VII, attributed to him aims—and consequently achievements—of a revolutionary character. It was his purpose, they claimed, to establish an entirely new pattern of monarchical government in England. Only by abandoning the archaic principles of his predecessors could he hope to save his throne from the disasters they had suffered; only by refashioning the organs of authority could he make England ready to take a dynamic role in the new and expanding world. As the middle ages in England were held to have died with Richard III, it was agreeable to discover that the first king of modern times was an innovator in the art of government. The origin of this thesis was the work of a German scholar. James Gairdner's *Henry the Seventh* published in 1889 was a workmanlike survey based on the available literary evidence and sparing in its attention to constitutional and administrative aspects of the reign. One cannot say this of a book which appeared in Germany three years later and was published in an English translation in 1895. This was the first volume of a projected *History of England under the Tudors* by Professor Wilhelm Busch. Busch propounded the argument that what Henry VII accomplished was nothing less than the establishment of a despotism under which all aspects of national life were subjected to royal control. This view was accepted by English and American scholars, and propagated and developed in the following thirty years. A more readable biography was produced by Miss Gladys Temperley in 1917 and she enthusiastically upheld the doctrine of the 'new monarchy' of Henry VII.

In the existing state of medieval studies, the exponents of this thesis appeared to have a strong case. No precedents were known, for instance, for a council like Henry's, large in membership yet enjoying no more influence than he gave it. The famous act *pro camera stellata* of 1487 could be directly linked with the conciliar jurisdiction exercised by his Tudor and Stuart successors. This, like his muzzling of parliament by the use of official bills for legislation, revealed the despot's preference to dispense with the limitations imposed by common law and constitutional precedent. The magnificence of his court, moreover, and his patronage of artists seemed to denote the Renaissance prince no less than the insincerity of his diplomacy and the methods he employed against his domestic enemies. While he retained the old machinery of government, his fiscal organisation, as Professor Dietz showed in 1921, largely dispensed with the ancient Exchequer and made a new branch of household administration, the chamber, the effective centre for national finance.

A subsidiary myth was added to this interpretation of Henry's reign. This was that although a despotism, his monarchy was popular. It won public approval because Henry's subjects recognised that the enhanced authority of the crown was their guarantee against a renewal of civil war. To no section of the populace was the new monarchy more welcome than to that perennially rising body, the middle class, by which we are to understand the smaller landowners, merchants, lawyers and members of other professions. They shared the king's distaste for the baronage, and while he desired stability for the establishment of his dynasty, they wanted it so that they could grow rich by the pursuit of trade and other lawful activities. The middle class therefore put its heart into seconding the royal programme, dutifully accepting his control over parliament and, as justices of the peace, vigorously enforcing public order and undertaking a great range of duties laid upon them by the king's social and economic legislation; while some members of this class even served in the council, so giving it a unique character, for these humbly born councillors, we are told, owed everything to their master and therefore gave him devoted and expert service.

Now the argument about the 'new monarchy' of Henry VII has already gone by the board, thanks to the work of both medievalists like Professor T. F. Tout and Tudor specialists headed by Professor A. F. Pollard. As more was learnt about the administrative organisation of medieval kings it could be shown that Henry's financial arrangements were not an innovation but a return to methods practised in the thirteenth and fourteenth centuries. The interpretation of the act *pro camera stellata* was radically amended and Henry's conciliar jurisdiction was likewise shown to have had medieval precedents. More recently still, the researches of Professor J. R. Lander and Dr. B. P. Wolffe on the council and financial system of Edward IV have revealed that both institutions then had the features once regarded as novel in Henry's reign. In both these and other aspects of his policies Henry can be shown to have made no decisive break with the past. Above all else, however, in so far as he exercised constant personal oversight of his government, permitting nothing to be done without his express command, Henry conformed to the medieval pattern of kingship.

The reappraisal of Henry VII has hitherto largely been confined to the central institutions of his government. The secondary argument concerning Henry's relations with the middle class has not been seriously re-examined. It is difficult to ascertain what positive contemporary evidence supports it save the employment of middle-class councillors. It is the outcome, we may suspect, of reading history backwards and it was welcomed because any discovery that the virtues of this class were recognised in earlier times was congenial to modern liberal sentiment; while Henry's despotism became more respectable to modern English eyes when it was seen to have enjoyed public favour. We will consider this question more fully at a later stage.

Many aspects of national life under Henry VII still require fresh investigation. The amount of surviving contemporary record evidence in national and local repositories is enormous. Professor Busch asserted that all the unpublished official records of Henry's reign were contained in two boxes in the Public Record Office. In fact, not only are the rolls, files and boxes of records relating to the reign and known to working historians numbered in thousands, but there are several hundred files of documents which the Office is still unable to make available for public inspection.* Many years will pass before it is permissible to assert that we have a comprehensive knowledge of Henry's reign. The present study cannot claim to be more than an interim report.

* References to authorities, signalled in the text by small raised numbers, are listed on pp. 223–8.

1

The Governance of Medieval England

FIFTEEN years before Henry Tudor embarked for England, another English prince was preparing to end his exile in France. This was the seventeen-year-old Edward, prince of Wales, the only son of the last king of the house of Lancaster, Henry VI, and his queen, Margaret of Anjou. After the victory of Edward IV at Towton in 1461 had secured the throne for the house of York, Prince Edward's parents had taken him to Scotland, and two years later, when the last embers of Lancastrian resistance had been extinguished, he settled with his mother at the castle of Koeur in the duchy of Bar, in Lorraine. Among the members of their small court was Sir John Fortescue, formerly chief justice of England. Fortescue was the most outstanding English lawyer of his day; he had been appointed to this office at a comparatively early age, in 1442, without previously holding a lower rank in the judiciary. He was undoubtedly the most distinguished member of the court at Koeur and he was the chancellor of this government in exile. Queen Margaret and her followers never abandoned hope of a Lancastrian restoration and Sir John consequently felt it necessary to instruct the prince about the nature of the kingdom which he might yet rule. Thus there came to be written the only known contemporary account of the constitution of fifteenth-century England, the *De laudibus legum Anglie*.

The king and the law

The work is cast in the form of a dialogue between the prince and chancellor. The boy was devoting himself to military exercises, for which Fortescue commended him, but he pointed out that a king's duty was not only to fight his people's battles but also to judge them rightfully. It was essential therefore that a future king should study his subjects' laws while he was still young, as the proper apprenticeship for his calling, so that by learning justice he himself would become just. As a lawyer, Fortescue naturally esteemed his profession before all others, but in placing this emphasis on the responsibility of the king as a dispenser of justice he was adhering to contemporary opinion about the duties of the monarchy. Indeed, from the earliest times kings had been expected to act as law-givers to their peoples, and it was through the exercise of this recognised charge that the monarchies of England and other West European kingdoms had established sovereign authority over their subjects. At his coronation, every English king swore to keep the peace for his people, judge them in mercy and truth, and uphold their laws. This function made the office of king indispensable: Bracton in the thirteenth century could say that the law makes the king, and in 1470 the royal justices agreed that 'it is necessary for the realm to have a king under whom the laws shall be held and maintained'. The commons in the parliament of 1449–50 held the same belief in the purpose of monarchy when they declared:

'The honour, wealth and prosperity of every prince reigning upon his people standeth most principally upon conservation of his peace, keeping of justice, and due execution of his laws, without which no realm may long endure in quiet or prosperity' [1]

The prince was persuaded that he should study law but he suggested that it might be better if he studied the civil law of Rome which was highly respected throughout the world. No, replied Fortescue, he should study the laws of England, for the king of England had to keep those laws and was not able to change them; he was no absolute prince enjoying the kind of dominion indicated by the civil law when it states 'what pleases the prince has the force of law'. Fortescue now made a distinction between two kinds of monarchy. There was one, of which France was the best example, where the king had purely regal power and so could make or change laws at his pleasure and also impose taxes on his subjects without their assent. It was otherwise in England, for here the king's dominion was political as well as regal, and the consent of his people was required for both legislation and taxation.

There were undoubtedly features common to both English and civil law which sprang from natural law, but in addition England had customs of great antiquity and statutes enacted in parliament by the assent of its members and which could not be amended or annulled without their approval. There had been English kings, said Fortescue, who had tried to free themselves from the restraints of political dominion so that they could enjoy the unfettered use of solely regal power. He doubtless had in mind Richard II who, at his deposition in 1399, was accused of breaking his coronation oath and of declaring that the laws were in his mouth and breast and that the lives and property of his subjects were at his absolute disposal. Though kings might regret the denial to them of such unlimited discretion, the English were inestimably fortunate in the security of their persons and property thus safeguarded by law, and their resulting prosperity really brought advantage to the king: it was far better to rule over a contented and high-spirited people than over a race of wretched slaves, as did the king of France.

Yet, Fortescue said, a king ruling politically had no less power than one who ruled regally; only the nature of his authority was different. As he wrote elsewhere, both kinds of king were equal in the sight of God. They were, in fact, accountable only to Him: the king ruling politically, just as much as the king ruling regally, was not answerable to his people or any group of them; the obedience they owed him was absolute. Admittedly the king of England was obliged to respect the laws of the land, but he was not a constitutional monarch. Fortescue believed that kingdoms originated in contracts between kings and subjects, but the latter had not united themselves by a previous act; they came together only when they chose a king, under whom they were thereby associated. He could not conceive of any body politic but a kingdom, and there could be no kingdom without a king. The purpose of the contract was the introduction of law to regulate the relationships of people previously without law and, again, there could not be law without a king to enforce it. But the king was not above the law, he could not change it at pleasure or violate it by seizing the property of his subjects whom it was designed to protect; for the reason for there being a king was the preservation of the law and it was to enable him to carry out this supreme duty that he was endowed with otherwise absolute authority. Fortescue was not original in holding these views on the kingship: they had a long history in medieval political thought and the value of his writings to us now is that they reflect contemporary opinion on the purpose and authority of the medieval English monarchy.

Royal powers and resources

When we turn from theory to practice it becomes a more complex task to piece together the various attributes and privileges which a medieval king actually exercised. He held the highest rank in secular society and, indeed, the anointing of his person in the coronation ceremony gave him a partially sacerdotal character. He recognised no superior authority in temporal affairs, not even that of pope or emperor, for, as Richard II said, the king of England was 'emperor in his realm'. The monarchy was his property; so high was his 'estate', the judges said in 1460, that they were not competent to determine claims to the crown. He was habitually addressed in terms of the utmost respect, most commonly as 'the king our most sovereign lord'. This was a hallowed custom: in 1423 the mayor and commons of London petitioned 'the king our most sovereign and most gracious lord', 'your most high and most gracious lordship', when this exalted being was not yet two years of age. The terms 'your highness' and 'your majesty' were also employed as a matter of form.[2] The use of such high-sounding titles to emphasise the surpassing eminence of the royal person was certainly not a Tudor innovation, nor was the pomp and circumstance of religious festivals celebrated at court or solemn state occasions attended by the king.

The laws of treason were designed for the king's protection and they best exemplify the unique legal standing of his person. There was then no conception of the body politic which did not embrace the king. A treasonable offence like conspiring with external enemies was regarded not as a crime against the English people but as an act against the king, and the accused would have been put on trial for conspiring with 'the king's enemies', the term used to describe all subjects of a country with which England was at a war. An act of rebellion was termed, in legal phraseology, as 'raising war against our lord the king'. The statute of treasons of 1352 did specify certain acts against the king as being treasonable, but besides these the courts of common law interpreted it so that other kinds of offence could be regarded in the same light, such as spoken or written criticism of the king's person or government; then those on trial would be accused of conspiring to seduce his subjects from their allegiance. What is more, the king by his own proclamation could declare certain persons to be traitors, and call on his faithful subjects to oppose and destroy them; while if these rebels were taken alive, they would be tried and sentenced in a court specially constituted by the king under the presidency of his most trusted noble followers. For all these offences classed as treasonable the penalty was the ferocious sentence of hanging, drawing and quartering, and it was reserved solely for traitors against the king.

The king was endowed with the material means to uphold his 'estate': these included not only the lands belonging to his predecessor or which may have otherwise come to him by the laws of inheritance, but the right to possess the land and other property of any tenant of the crown who died without heirs and of any subject who was condemned for treason or felony. As feudal overlord of England, he received oaths of homage from all his immediate tenants, whether they were great magnates or petty squires; when they died, he had the profits of their lands until the heirs were of age to enter into possession, and he could dispose of the marriages of widows and wards to his advantage. As king, moreover, he possessed numerous other revenues: the traditional issues of the shires, the profits of justice, the taxes and customs duties granted by parliament. In times of peace, he was expected to 'live of his own', that is, to make his regular revenues suffice for the costs of his household and administration. In the event of national danger, however, he could call upon all his subjects to place both their services and their belongings at his disposal, for the common good.

The defence of the realm was another primary regal responsibility; as in the administration of justice, here the king had to perform a duty for which his monarchy had been instituted, the protection of his people. He was the supreme captain in war, and if he did not lead an army, he commissioned a lieutenant to take charge as his representative. In times of public danger, all private interests could be overridden, otherwise the king's ability to defend the country might have been jeopardised. In more peaceful circumstances, however, the king could circumvent laws and statutes which were binding on his subjects. Henry IV, for one, could quote the well-known dictum, 'necessity knows no law', and decide for himself when to act in its spirit. It was allowed that the king had various attributes, expressed in somewhat nebulous terms like 'liberty', 'will', 'grace', 'prerogatives'. He could dispense from the requirements of statutes: for instance, he gave licences to subjects to grant their lands to others or to religious foundations, or, to the clergy, permission to accept benefices from the pope, although these practices were forbidden by statutes. He exercised a prerogative of mercy, pardoning subjects felonies and misdemeanours which they might have committed, even if they had been formally charged. The king could not be called upon to answer plaintiffs in the law courts against his will, though he often gave his licence for such cases to proceed, though not to judgment without his further assent. This privilege extended to defendants who could invoke the king's protection. As the fountain-head of justice, the king exercised equity, providing remedies in cases where the common law was unable to do so, and numerous subjects addressed petitions to the king praying for him to relieve their hard cases.

Beginnings of royal administration

The multifarious duties and requirements of the king were, by the fifteenth century, being performed by a complex of judicial and administrative bodies, with central departments at Westminster co-ordinating and supervising the operations of his agents in the shires. The oldest agencies of royal government in England, as elsewhere, were those which had been devised to collect his revenues. Most ancient of these offices was that of sheriff, the successor of the Anglo-Saxon shire reeve, whose original function had been to take charge of the royal demesne lands in his shire. These early sheriffs had once come to the king's court to render their accounts and deliver their profits, but from early in the twelfth century the members of the royal household who specialised in this financial business were detached and formed the first English department of state, the Exchequer; the earliest of its surviving pipe rolls for recording sheriffs' accounts belongs to the year 1131.

Another county office, that of escheator, was subsequently established to collect the revenues accruing to the king as feudal overlord, and they likewise made an annual account at the Exchequer and produced the revenues they had gathered from estates between the deaths of the king's feudal tenants and the grants of livery to their heirs. Numerous other offices for receiving money came into existence: there was the mint, there were special custodians of large royal or feudal estates, there were collectors of taxes in the counties and of customs in the ports, there were the more recent central departments which made a profit in the execution of their duties. In addition, other branches of the administration had to make account at the Exchequer for the money they had spent. The Exchequer was more than an office for receiving the king's revenues: it was a court of law, with authority to summon and examine debtors to the crown, and to compel them to make satisfaction. It was the king's treasury, and it either supplied cash to meet his requirements or arranged for these to be paid from particular sources of revenue.

Courts of law

The reign of Henry II (1154–89) witnessed a great extension of royal justice at the expense of baronial courts, which were gradually driven out of business. Subjects discovered that the quickest and most sure way to obtain remedies for their wrongs was to be obtained by making application for relief to the king. His local agents, the sheriffs, were then required to assemble juries and compel defendants to come before his justices and, after judgment, to ensure that the courts' decisions were observed. The growth in the volume of judicial business brought to the king's presence and heard in the *curia regis* led to the detachment of a number of legal specialists from the household, and in compliance with a clause of Magna Carta, this court which entertained pleas between subjects, Common Pleas, was permanently established at Westminster.

A court of law remained attendant on the king to determine pleas in which he had an interest and it was not until the close of the thirteenth century that this body, as the court of King's Bench, became a separate institution with its regular home also in Westminster. The two central courts had largely parallel jurisdictions over subjects' pleas for recovery of lands, rents, services and debts, but King's Bench only dealt with cases in which the king was a party and exercised an immediate criminal jurisdiction by trying indictments for felonies; it also exercised supervision over proceedings in lower courts, calling records of proceedings begun elsewhere for determination before its justices. Despite this establishment of specialised judicial organs, the king did not abdicate his own inherent judicial authority and he continued to exercise a supreme jurisdiction in his council and parliaments. The justices of the two benches were frequently commissioned to go on circuit in order to try the inmates of county gaols, but from 1361 their work in this connection was supplemented by the activities of justices of the peace in every county.

Secretarial departments

The second administrative section of the royal household to go 'out of court' was the office of the chancellor. The early administrative history of England centres to a large extent on the fortunes of the king's seals. All original documents had to be sealed in token of their authenticity as expressions of the wishes of their authors. The chancellor, as the custodian of the king's great seal, therefore, was responsible for the preparation of royal letters; and whether these were charters conferring privileges or possessions in perpetuity or short notes—writs—giving orders to officers or subjects, all bore a wax impression of the seal in token of the king's will. From the reign of King John (1199–1216) copies of many of these letters were entered on a number of series of rolls according to their nature, whether they were charters, or closed or open ('patent') letters. With the development of the royal law courts, subjects came to apply in increasingly large numbers for the writs necessary to initiate legal proceedings.

The chancellor's office also attended to much of the business concerning the king's feudal rights: it ordered escheators to take possession of lands when crown tenants died and ordered reports to be sent to it concerning the services attaching to these lands and their values; heirs subsequently came to Chancery to ask for livery, and after further enquiries as to whether these heirs were of full age, it arranged for the taking of homage and issued letters granting possession. All these activities led to the accumulation of large numbers of records—rolls, writs and reports of inquisitions—more than could conveniently be carried round the country as the chancellor attended a peripatetic king, and in the thirteenth century a permanent home was found for them in the Rolls Chapel in Chancery Lane, the site of the present Public Record Office. Since Chancery had ceased to be solely the king's secretariat and had become a department with important facilities for his subjects, it was clearly also advantageous to them that it should have a fixed abode in the capital.

From the close of the twelfth century English kings are known to have used a smaller seal for attesting correspondence on matters of more personal concern to themselves. The medieval king was frequently on the road, in England and often abroad in his French possessions, and arrangements for the supply and accommodation of this itinerant court were made by the officers of his household. As he travelled he obviously required a supply of money to be at his immediate disposal, and he also took valuables like jewels and gold and silver plate, and the servants of his chamber were responsible for their safe-keeping and use. This domestic organisation required a seal, and with the detachment of Chancery from the household, the king made increasing use of this seal in his general correspondence because it was available for immediate employment: wherever he might be, he might need to issue orders in haste. A second royal secretariat thus developed in the household for preparing letters to be sent out under the privy seal. These privy seal letters became the regular means of communication between the king and the departments in the capital, even when he also was there, because these offices made it their regular practice to keep written instructions for their acts; thus Chancery kept files of the privy seal warrants which authorised the issue of letters under the great seal, and the Exchequer retained similar warrants for its disbursements and its allowances to accounting officers. The privy seal thus held a key place in royal administration. Moreover, it was employed by the king in correspondence with foreign princes, and he used it when sending written commands to his subjects.

The importance of this personal instrument of royal authority brought it attention from baronial groups who sought to reform the king's government to their own liking. There was little need to make regulations for Chancery and the Exchequer to prevent their becoming tools of an arbitrary-minded king in the fourteenth century; both were sufficiently restricted by their own bureaucratic nature, by the traditions and practices which had developed in the centuries since they achieved their separate existence; their functions were defined and their methods well known. The omnicompetence of the privy seal, however, enabled a king to circumvent the restrictive practices of the two great departments. Attempts were occasionally made, therefore, to detach the privy seal from the household, to deprive the king of ready access to it. The office of keeper of the privy seal, established by the Lords Ordainers in 1311, was thus from time to time taken 'out of court'; but although the keeper, with a sizeable staff of clerks, found it useful to maintain a separate establishment in London, he generally continued to be one of the closest and most regular members of the king's entourage.

In the periods when the king was without direct access to the privy seal, he made use of a third and still smaller seal, the signet. Although holders of the office of king's secretary, who had charge of this seal, are known from the reign of Richard II (1377–99) the signet office had a spasmodic history until the time of the Yorkist kings. It then achieved permanence as an administrative institution, for it remained in being during the brief reign of the boy king Edward V (1483); previously it had gone underground when the king was incapable of ruling, as its existence was dependent upon his personal activity. The king's secretary was now an important officer of state, frequently employed as the personal representative of the monarch in his foreign diplomacy; while his clerks wrote the warrants and other letters which directed the other branches of the royal administration. The signet office, in fact, had taken over the part of the Privy Seal Office as the mainspring of government, and the latter now became little more than a post-box for the warrants under the signet.

The civil service

These administrative departments, and the various lesser offices such as the great wardrobe for providing the king and his officers with robes and hangings or the privy wardrobe for keeping his arms and ordnance, employed several hundreds of clerks and other servants; his household had a large establishment of knights, squires, yeomen and menials, and throughout the kingdom there were numerous offices at the king's disposal, for the custody of his castles and estates and for the collection of his revenues. From the earliest times in the history of medieval government, work which required a basic education could only be undertaken by members of the clergy. As these clerks proceeded to take Holy Orders they qualified to hold benefices in the Church and the king was thus able to provide them with salaries without any expense to himself. As the greatest of landowners he had the patronage of many rectories and minor benefices; he could also bestow livings in the gift of bishops and secular tenants when these were in his hands by virtue of his feudal rights; and through a work-

1 St. Ursula and Henry VI

2 Henry VII

3 Elizabeth of York

4 Richmond Palace

REWARDS FOR SERVICE · 21

ing agreement with the pope, he was usually able to nominate bishops. The highest offices in the Church were, therefore, available for the senior members of the king's administration; this was a strong inducement for faithful service and made royal employment the most attractive of careers to ambitious clerks.

For the layman in the king's service, besides wages and prospects of promotion, there were opportunities to benefit from royal favour by making claims for consideration when their master had a wardship, for instance, or a rich widow or a profitable office at his disposal. Many of the positions in the king's administration were of ancient origin, but although they lost their original utility they still carried salaries; while others had become so profitable that their holders could afford to leave the work to deputies. Like benefices in the Church, these sinecures formed an economic way for rewarding good service. Thus Henry VI's doctor became chancellor of the Exchequer and the treasurer of his household was keeper of the writs of the court of Common Pleas.

The king's council

This then was the king's government; through the agency of these departments and offices he made his will felt throughout the kingdom. It was a highly developed machine, normally adequate for ruling a country of between two and two and a half million inhabitants. Some parts of the system were ancient by the fifteenth century, some even obsolescent, some fulfilling their purpose by methods established in an earlier age; while others were more recent, some still in the process of growth. Each had its particular purpose and a staff of specialists. The king was their employer; they were answerable only to him. But no king, even the most capable, could have been conversant with all the details of this complex organisation. He needed expert advisers who could tell him, at need, how his policies could be carried out, whether the means existed, what parts of the administration should be employed. The growth of royal administration, in fact, made it essential for the king to have a council. Here again, he had complete discretion in choosing his advisers; there was no means short of armed rebellion or financial blackmail of compelling him to admit men to his council against his will. The normal king's council of the later middle ages was composed of men selected by the king because he believed their counsel would be profitable to him.

B

He was not obliged to accept this counsel, the final decision always rested with him. Nor need the king admit his council to his confidence on every matter, and he could and did exercise his powers on his sole and immediate initiative.

It is unlikely that any medieval king was ever without a council in the sense that he regularly had with him a small number of men whose opinion he sought on the business of his government. Until the fourteenth century, however, it is difficult, for lack of records, to trace the history of the king's council as a continuous institution. The absences of Edward III (1327–77) on the continent, followed by his incapacity and then by the minority of Richard II, led to the council gaining not only a permanent character but an almost autonomous existence and the possession of powers to direct the king's government. The measure of its development was signalled in the constitutional crises of these years. Now the king's critics realised that the council was the kernel of his government: if his despotic tendencies were to be restrained, or the country to be rescued from administrative incompetence, it was at this strategic point that a remedy had to be provided. Richard II's opponents therefore packed the council with their nominees in order to prevent him acting against their interests; while the parliamentary critics of Henry IV required him to disclose the names of his councillors and made regulations for their conduct of business so that, fearful of being called to account, they should animate the whole administration with a desire for economy and efficiency.

Except in circumstances like these, the king's council of this period was a small body without a defined or constant membership or formal constitution. Appointments in general appear to have been made informally, probably by the king's word of mouth. The senior member was the chancellor, almost invariably a prelate and eventually often an archbishop; as his department could function without his regular personal oversight, the principal reason for his appointment as chancellor was presumably the king's esteem for his counsel. The same is true of the treasurer, another regular councillor, now more often a secular peer than a prelate. The keeper of the privy seal, another cleric destined for the episcopate, was a frequent member of the council, whose decisions were usually given effect by letters written in his office. Apart from these three great officers of state, there were rarely more than four or five councillors in regular attendance; they would include one or two lords, possibly royal kinsmen, as many bishops who had experience as civil servants or diplomats, and a few of the leading officers of the household, the steward and chamberlain in particular.

The council sat almost daily; sometimes it went with the king about the country, sometimes it remained at Westminster in his absence. Much of its work was of a routine, administrative character, taking care of the king's financial interest, drafting letters of appointment, contracts for military service or instructions for ambassadors, and whatever else the king chose to refer to its attention; his approval to their proposals was essential, but so also was their expert knowledge and advice. The most important single function of the council was as a judicial body: it took particular interest in serious breaches of the peace by nobles and other men with considerable means, citing disputants to its presence and trying to ensure their future good behaviour, but it also considered pleas from humbler subjects with injuries for which they could not obtain remedies in the courts of common law. Complaints of this kind had become so numerous in the later fourteenth century that the council made a practice of referring them to the chancellor with such regularity that plaintiffs began to take their pleas direct to Chancery. As the volume of petitions mounted in the course of the fifteenth century Chancery developed its function as a court of law, providing a valued supplement to the existing common law system.

Personal responsibility of the king

With this network of organised talent at his command, the English king of the late middle ages appears to have been well placed to provide effective government. But, of course, this was rarely achieved. The quality of every administration is naturally decided by the calibre of its leading personnel, and above all on that of its supreme director. The succession to the English crown passed from father to son, and there was no guarantee that every king would have all the qualities required for his office. A king of mediocre talent was unlikely to recognise suitable candidates for responsible positions in his government; a king without a serious will to rule would fall under the influence of self-seeking favourites: our history provides these and other kinds of examples of kings whose errors and shortcomings brought about political crises of varying degrees of gravity.

Kingship was the most exacting of all offices: apart from political and military expertise, it called for constant application and a high degree of physical energy. No day passed without the king being required to attend to the work of government. By a fortunate chance a very high proportion of the records of the Privy Seal Office survive from the years 1404–5. They show that Henry IV had to take a decision on at least four or five items brought to his attention every day. Of 2,500 letters issued from Chancery, more than half were ordered by his warrants, and he would also have sent hundreds of similar written instructions to other departments. Each year he received between two and three thousand petitions for grace and favour. Despite the assistance of a council, a king could not escape having to take decisions on many of the trivia of day-to-day administration.[3] Yet at the same time he might be, as Henry IV was in those years, constantly on the move, leading forces to suppress rebellion, pacifying disaffected areas, showing himself to his people to impress his authority and allay their grievances. Uneasy indeed was the head that wore a crown.

Taxation and parliament

The personal qualities of a king were thus a vital factor in medieval administration. There was a second major consideration, the adequacy of his material resources to sustain effective government. The regular revenues of the crown may have sufficed for the king's domestic expenditure and the routine costs of his administration, but they left no margin for extraordinary expenses like the prosecution of a war overseas. Yet English kings had done this regularly since Edward III claimed the French crown in 1340. Taxes were granted by parliaments to support this military expenditure, but they did not carry the whole burden, and as the Hundred Years War dragged on the enthusiasm of parliaments waned and they became increasingly reluctant to vote supplies. This was serious enough, but the crown's financial difficulties were made desperate by a simultaneous decline in its customary sources: the revenue from crown lands dwindled as the agricultural population was decimated by plague; a recession in overseas trade reduced the yield from customs duties; while both factors caused the tax-paying classes to seek exemption from, or reduction of, their contributions to the king's extraordinary revenue. Richard II had an average annual income of £120,000, but by 1450 the total coming to the king had slumped to £50,000. In these conditions it was difficult to pay the wages and other costs needed in regular administration, let alone pay off debts or find the means to continue the war with France.

Even before the crown reached a state of bankruptcy in the fifteenth century, the straitness of its means had brought about a curtailment of royal authority. Kings had been compelled to make frequent resort to national taxation since the thirteenth century, and for this relief it had to pay a price. The costs of the wars waged by Edward I (1272–1307) in Scotland, Wales and France occasioned many assemblies of parliaments when subsidies were granted. He was obliged to recognise the principle that he could not impose widespread taxation without first obtaining the consent of some body representative of his subjects. Edward III's constant need for money for his continental wars led to a stricter definition of this rule; reluctantly and with much hedging, Edward came to accept that all taxes and customs duties required the prior consent of lords and commons in parliament. Sir John Fortescue had implied that the restraints on royal authority in the sphere of taxation had been an immemorial feature of the English constitution. In fact they only achieved permanence in the form he knew in the course of the fourteenth century as the outcome of Edward III's financial difficulties and their exploitation by his parliaments.

The same is true with regard to legislation. Edward I had made statutes on his own authority and there was not always a parliament in being at the time they were announced; but a hundred years later the accepted method of enacting statutes required the advice of the lords and the consent of the commons, and they could only be made in parliaments where these representatives were present. In many individual statutes, moreover, the initiative for enactment came from below; they were the result of petitions from the commons applying for remedies from administrative oppression and the inadequacy of the existing legal system. Again it was the crown's dire need for taxation which obliged it to give way before such pressure. Among the measures enacted in these circumstances was the statute establishing justices of the peace (1361); despite the wishes of Edward III, country gentry were declared eligible for this new office. Another was the act of 1340 which forbad the retention of sheriffs in office for more than one year. Thus the parliamentary commons were responsible for important modifications in the pattern of the local administration of the law. Parliamentary pressure also from time to time constrained the king to dismiss ministers or appoint councillors or accept regulations for their conduct of his business.

Legal restrictions on royal authority

The picture drawn by Fortescue for his royal pupil was a static one, describing conditions at one particular time. The pattern of government in England, however, had only arrived at this stage after a long process of evolution, and there was no guarantee that the movement had come to a full stop. The constitutional practice of the past hundred years undoubtedly supports his belief that the authority of the English crown was unable to surpass certain bounds, but earlier precedents would have allowed the king a less circumscribed power. If we were to single out one outstanding reason why the English monarchy, instead of extending its authority to the status of a 'lordship purely regal', as in France, had to accept conventions limiting its freedom of action, it might well be that Edward III involved himself in an endless and expensive war for the conquest of France. Another major reason was the complete ineptitude of Edward II (1307–27), an outstanding example of the dangers inherent in hereditary succession. But there were more basic reasons for the limited nature of the English monarchy. Fortescue points to the laws and customs of the country, and the reason for these being as they were, he stated, was sociological. There were in England, he rightly said, many men of adequate substance who could therefore be entrusted to act as jurors. This, to his mind, was the explanation why the English common law flourished: there was no jury system in France, because there the average subject was miserably poor, and so their king was able to impose the practices of Roman law and enjoy the enhancement its precepts allowed to the powers of the monarch.

There was a second reason for the continuity of common law in England which Fortescue overlooked. In 1292 Edward I made the judges responsible for the education of advocates in the common law courts. As the central courts where the judges sat were in Westminster, their academies were established in London. These inns of court, as they became, thus had a monopoly in professional training: they were the only gateway to a lucrative career at the bar. As judges were appointed from the ranks of the serjeants-at-law—

the medieval equivalent of our Queen's Counsel—this meant that the whole profession was animated by the principles and practice of common law. It therefore largely escaped being seriously influenced by the ideas of Roman law being taught at the universities.

Future members of the legal profession were not the only ones to attend inns of court. The sons of gentry were also sent there, to acquire, among other assets, the learning necessary to manage their estates and to take their place in the local government of their shires. It was from this class that sheriffs, justices of the peace, and parliamentary representatives were chosen. The unpaid services of these gentry were indispensable to the king's local administration, and they could bring the experience they gained in it when, in parliament, shortcomings in the legal system and loopholes in the law were under discussion. The shire knights with a legal training were well-fitted to organise the business of their house, and as parliaments were frequent and the re-election of former members was common, the parliamentary commons were able to sustain their corporate sense and cherish and exploit the precedents being established. Here was a well-equipped and well-entrenched source of potential opposition to any king who proposed to abridge the liberties of his subjects.

The lords

More formidable still was the English baronage. They formed the real effective deterrent against royal absolutism. The true interests of the nobility were, no doubt, invariably selfish, confined to preserving the privileges and possessions of their own class. They had already, however, with Magna Carta, and in the course of the thirteenth century, forced the king to accept the supremacy of the rule of law. Once more Fortescue has nothing to say on this vital topic. He believed that the right of English subjects to their possessions had always been defended by law. Yet King John and his immediate forbears had acted as if they had an undoubted right to seize their subjects' estates at will; if any subject incurred the wrath of an Angevin king he was pursued with countless vexations until he submitted to the king's grace, and this would have been a ruinously expensive favour to buy. It took military rebellion to force the king to renounce these capricious modes of government, to win his assent that no free man could be endangered by the king in life, liberty or fortune without due process of law; and further shows and threats of armed resistance were needed to retain the crown's adherence to the concessions enshrined in Magna Carta.

The nobility, like other institutions of English public life, was gradually transformed as the centuries passed. The feudal basis of society gave way to a more recognisably constitutional form, with personal rank rather than tenure of land determining a man's standing. It was undoubtedly true that a lord in the fifteenth century was still a feudal tenant-in-chief of the king, in that he held his lands by fealty and nominal military service at the royal command, but he was never called upon to perform this duty and his political pre-eminence before other landed men arose from his being called in person to parliaments. The only nobles actually having titles before the fourteenth century were the earls, but then the king began to confer new titles such as duke and marquess. The other families in the peerage, as we should call them, had merely acquired during the course of the same century a hereditary claim to receive writs of summons to parliament, or had been raised with this intention. They owed their distinction, in fact, to royal favour. The same must be said of nearly all grandees in the fifteenth century who did have titles, even ancient comital ones, for these were only still in existence because they had been resurrected and conferred by the crown. The total number of lords with and without titles generally remained between fifty and sixty, for although some noble families died out the king was constantly adding new creations.

The fact remains that the nobility was important because of its material resources. Its total landed wealth in 1436, it is known, was equal to the gross annual revenue of the crown; the lords' strength in manpower, whenever they acted in unison, was invariably greater than that of the king. The king lacked the means to keep more than the nucleus of a standing army: if he ever required an army, he was dependent upon the readiness of the lords to put their contingents under his command. For this reason it was always advisable for the king to foster harmonious relations with the lords. This was not an impossible task. As landowners the lords had a strong vested interest in the preservation of public order and competent government. The wealthier nobles, with properties dispersed throughout the country, had built up their own private administrative systems to bring in their revenues. They enjoyed the highest style of living the age allowed; they built for themselves in the fourteenth and fifteenth centuries palaces rather than fortresses; they kept large retinues of servants, spent lavishly on clothing and imported luxuries, and dispensed hospitality on the great scale expected of their rank. The dearest wish of these lords was to preserve their inheritances for their heirs, if possible enlarge and embellish their properties; for these ends they made marriages for their children inside their own class and created entails to safeguard descent in the male line. Military glory, a reputation for chivalrous conduct, public esteem and local superiority were also dearly held prizes. Royal favour opened the gate to all these aims. A king like Edward III who fostered the lords' dynastic ambitions and offered them opportunities to prove their martial prowess had little difficulty in retaining their loyalty; if the king himself possessed all the martial and other virtues they admired, their fidelity was assured.

The lords were held to be the king's natural councillors. Their claim to be so was usually raised when they rose in rebellion against a king of whose person or policies they disapproved. The assertion that they had this right to advise the king, they thought, cast a cloak of constitutional legality over their manifest acts of disobedience against their monarch; he was put in the wrong for preferring the counsel of unworthy favourites to themselves. But it was not only the lords who believed in their natural right to counsel the king: the townsmen and peasants of Kent who revolted in 1450 protested that Henry VI had been estranged from the great lords, in whom the rebels put their hopes for political reform. The king generally did recognise this special constitutional standing of the baronage. Its members were called to parliament 'to advise and assent on the business of the king and kingdom', unlike the commons, who merely had to assent; such is the wording of the writs of summons. The lords were also called to great councils when no representatives of the commons were usually present. Even so authoritarian a king as Henry V held these great councils. This method of consultation, however, was generally sufficient; provided that the king consulted with them in these periodic gatherings, the lords were content to leave the regular direction of government in the hands of the king and his chosen ministers and regular councillors.

The internal peace of medieval England hung on this thread of harmony between king and lords. It was broken from time to time, but it had to be repaired before normal government could be resumed.

The personal relations of the king with the nobility formed the keystone of the medieval political order. The king's authority was sometimes challenged by popular risings on a large and widespread scale, but these posed no serious threat to the stability of his throne since the lords would rally to his support in such crises. He was in serious peril only when they formed a common front in opposition. The nobility, however, did not normally act as a united body. They generally came together only when summoned by the king, and the interests and ambitions of individual peers often conflicted. It took royal ineptitude or unpopular royal policies to cause the lords to sink their differences in order to oppose real or supposed threats to their whole class. Recent developments, however, were furthering the cohesion of the nobility. Various great houses became extinct in the male line and their estates passed by inheritance to the heads of other houses which were more fortunate. There thus emerged a small group of magnates, men whose estates comprised several inheritances, and the lesser lords accepted the leadership of these men of surpassing wealth. A small caucus of such overmighty subjects was able to humiliate Richard II in 1388, and his final destruction in 1399 was largely achieved by three great families—Lancaster, Percy and Neville. But a capable and personally acceptable king could still keep his head above the waters of baronial hostility if he provided firm government; at the worst, he could take advantage of the private divisions among the lords. The history of the Wars of the Roses reveals the severity of these baronial feuds as clearly as it underlines the personal responsibility of the king for the preservation of law and order.

2

The Wars of the Roses

BETWEEN 1455 and 1487 armies of Englishmen fought against each other on at least seventeen occasions and the crown changed hands five times. This civil warfare has been known as 'The Wars of the Roses' since the expression was, apparently, first coined by Sir Walter Scott in 1829. There is no historical foundation for this title. Scott was presumably inspired by Shakespeare. In his *King Henry VI, Part I*, the two principal adversaries, the dukes of York and Somerset, pluck roses and adopt them as badges in token of their mutual hatred: York's white rose then symbolises the claim of his house to be the true heirs to the English crown, while Somerset's red rose is the emblem of loyalty to the reigning house of Lancaster. This dramatic scene, unfortunately, was a complete invention on Shakespeare's part. There is no report on such an encounter between York and Somerset in the annals of their own time or even in the histories of the Tudor period. Nor is there any evidence that the forces of Lancaster and York marched into battle decorated with these emblems. The white rose was undoubtedly one of the emblems of the York family, but the favourite device of the duke of York was a fetterlock, while his son Edward IV adopted the badge of the rising sun. The red rose was likewise one of several traditional Lancastrian badges, but Henry VI made no use of it and it came to the fore only with Henry VII. But historically justified or not, it is convenient to have a term to identify a unique period in our history. 'Wars of the Roses' is certainly not the only modern name for past events to have achieved currency.

The use of this name, however, does carry certain dangers. It over-emphasises the significance of the struggle for the crown. It gives a

31

completely false picture of the issues at stake. We are led to think that the only reason why men took up arms was to defend the right of one or other dynasty to the English throne. This is demonstrably untrue. The word 'wars' suggests continuous fighting, long campaigns, sieges, devastation. Again, this is a mistake: it has been calculated that in the whole period from 1455 to 1487 there was active campaigning for a total of only three months. Moreover, by giving our attention to these battles and their political results, we may tend to overlook or treat as mere background the general condition of English society at the time. It is true that the populace in general suffered little direct harm at the hands of the belligerents, but they were still the victims of the same unhappy circumstances which caused the war to break out and continue.

The traditional cause

The customary explanation for the outbreak of the Wars of the Roses is that Richard, duke of York, and his friends took up arms to put him in possession of his birthright, the English throne. In *King Henry VI, Part II*, Richard Neville, earl of Warwick, says:

> 'Sweet York, begin: and if thy claim be good.
> The Nevils are thy subjects to command.'

York's case was that the house of Lancaster usurped the crown in 1399, when Richard II was deposed. The duke of Lancaster who ascended the throne as Henry IV was not Richard's rightful heir. This title belonged to the earl of March, as the representative of an older son of Edward III than Henry's father. Richard, duke of York, was the heir of that earl of March and so inherited his claim to the crown. Overcome by these arguments, Warwick and his father, according to Shakespeare, promised him their ardent support. Although York was killed while Henry VI was still king, his son soon afterwards deposed Henry and became King Edward IV. In his first parliament, Edward condemned Henry IV for his usurpation and attributed all the tribulations England had suffered since then to this act of impiety. Tudor historians likewise turned to the events of 1399 as the beginning of a century of intestinal strife, although to them its happy end came with the victory and marriage of Henry VII. In fact, England was not divided into two hostile camps from 1399 to 1485. There were dangerous plots on behalf of the earl of March in 1403 and 1415, but after that this rival claim found no active supporters. Henry VI succeeded his father Henry V without any protest, and his right to the crown was not openly challenged until 1460. Two major battles had already been fought by then, but on neither occasion did the victorious friends of York seek to make him king, and they showed no enthusiasm when he made his claim in parliament in 1460. They had fought against Henry VI, but without any intention of deposing him.

In later stages of the civil war, the crown was the prize aimed at by the combatants, but even then it cannot be said that their sole ambition was to uphold the title of Lancaster or York. When we examine the careers of some prominent warriors it becomes clear that lasting attachments to either royal house were less common than the pursuit of more private aims; for the sake of their personal interests, combatants were fully prepared to transfer their allegiance. In the context of the Wars of the Roses, the saying that 'nothing succeeds like success' was frequently vindicated, because it is remarkable how many sometime adherents of one cause were converted by the victory of the other. For this reason it is unrealistic to describe participants in the wars as 'Lancastrians' or 'Yorkists'.

Henry VI

The principal cause for the outbreak of civil war was the personality of Henry VI. In him England had a king who was entirely incapable of discharging the great responsibilities of his office. He was not hated, he was without any vice or guile; his faults, in fact, were negative. Henry was described as a simpleton in chronicles written in the reign of Edward IV, and there is evidence that his subjects had the same opinion about him: they spoke of him as a fool, remarking on the childishness of his face when he was nearly thirty years old. In 1453 he became insane for a period of eighteen months, with symptoms suggesting a form of schizophrenia. His French grandfather, Charles VI, had suffered a similar malady and presumably Henry's heredity to some extent accounts for his condition. No doubt he was the victim of some kind of mental illness all through his life, but there is insufficient evidence for diagnosis now. Whatever its nature, the consequence was that Henry was unable to give English government the leadership it required.

As a result of Henry's disability, the direction of his government fell into the hands of the leading members of his court. Had Henry been completely and recognisably insane all his life, the lords could have taken it upon themselves to establish a permanent king's council and appoint the great officers of state, who would have been answerable to the council for their conduct. This is what had happened in 1422 when Henry ascended the throne at the tender age of nine months. The lords in parliament appointed twenty-one councillors to take charge of the king's government during his minority: there were six prelates, two clerical ministers of state, eight dukes and earls, one other lord and four knights. The group heavily represented the upper ranks of secular and ecclesiastical peers, but several of the latter, as well as the humbler laymen, represented a great wealth of experience in government. Similar arrangements were made following Henry's breakdown in 1453; again, a large council was set up, including representatives of all sections of the peerage.

Whenever Henry was in a tolerably balanced state of mind, however, there was no constitutional means of compelling him to accept and retain any advisers against his will. He was then fully entitled to please himself in the choice of advisers. As he did not—perhaps could not—apply himself to the business of government, he left it to those who already had positions in his immediate entourage, his relatives and the senior officers of his household. They were answerable only to him for their conduct, and as he did not concern himself with these mundane affairs, they enjoyed a free hand. This was the basic reason for Henry's eventual deposition. The civil war was really begun on the issue of the king's choice of councillors; the conduct of the faction controlling Henry's government was responsible for creating the parties prepared to join battle.

Corruption of justice

The first favourite to dominate Henry's government was William de la Pole, duke of Suffolk. His influence over the king began with his appointment as steward of the household in 1433. After Henry came 'of age' in 1436, the arrangements for the minority of government by council lapsed, and thereafter business coming to the king's attention was handled by Suffolk and two or three close associates. An attempt was made by the great council in 1438 to impose a substantial standing council on the king, but Suffolk was able to frustrate this scheme to control the administration. The privy seal records of the time—the equivalent of 'cabinet papers'—show that only Suffolk and his few colleagues were present when petitions to the king were granted and drafts of letters received the royal approval, often in Henry's absence. Suffolk derived great profit from his exploitation of crown patronage, but a far more serious matter was his influence in the administration of justice. We know from the *Paston Letters* how dominant Suffolk's influence became in East Anglia. Here his territorial resources were supplemented by a manipulation of the processes of justice through his selection of sheriffs and by issuing royal orders to impede actions in the courts. He did as much on behalf of his clients elsewhere, and an instance is known of his shielding a homicide from trial with the outcome that the victim's family tried to take vengeance by direct action. In 1450 Suffolk was banished after a furious parliamentary outburst against his incompetent direction of the French war and his misgovernment at home. His successor in the king's favour was Edmund Beaufort, duke of Somerset, and with him the same misuse of royal authority was continued.

The way Suffolk and other members of the king's household misdirected the legal system was one of the principal grievances of the Kentish rebels who rose under Jack Cade in 1450. The jurors of the county provided considerable evidence of oppression and perversion of legal processes by these people. Their selfish aims, dishonestly pursued, were depriving the king of his subjects' loyalty. The king, as the fountain-head of justice, had to be above his subjects' quarrels, but Suffolk and company, through their abuse of royal authority, were involving the crown as a party in private suits. This was a grievance held by great as well as humble subjects. The earl of Devon had a dispute with a neighbouring landowner, William, Lord Bonville, dating from 1440 at the latest. The king's council intervened from time to time in an attempt to preserve the peace. Its efforts were unavailing. Devon, naturally, suspected that it favoured his enemy, who was a close associate of the court faction. There was a simultaneous dispute between two other west country landowners; these were the earl of Wiltshire, another courtier, and Edward Brook, Lord Cobham. In 1451 Devon and Cobham pooled their resources and raised an army, allegedly nearly six thousand strong, which they led through Somerset in pursuit of their enemies.

Baronial feuds

Other parts of the country were disturbed by baronial quarrels. In Gloucestershire, Lord Berkeley contended with the countess of Shrewsbury for possession of the Berkeley estates. The senior and junior branches of the Nevilles mustered big followings in their argument over the division of the family property. The duke of Exeter and Lord Cromwell disputed possession of various manors in Bedfordshire. From about 1450 the junior Nevilles, headed by the earl of Salisbury, fell out with the other great northern house of Percy; in Cumberland, 'one half of the shire was divided from that other' under their rival patronage, while in Yorkshire raids, ambushes, destruction of property and eventually, in 1453, a great assembly of forces marked the progress of their dispute. Salisbury's son, the earl of Warwick, quarrelled over the right to hold certain estates with the duke of Somerset to such a pitch that, also in 1453, 'great' forces were collected in Glamorgan and Cowbridge castle was manned 'as if it were in land of war'. These baronial hostilities all reveal the absence of strong monarchy. It was because they had no fear of the king's displeasure that these magnates carried their quarrels beyond the brink of private warfare. Even in Henry VI's minority, the council had sufficient authority to compel disputing lords to accept its mediation. The partisan quality of the council in his later years, however, lost it the respect necessary for it to fulfil its traditional function as the tribunal where baronial quarrels were appeased.

Bastard feudalism

These unruly peers were able to call out private armies against each other, and they were to lead these forces to the battlefields of civil war. It used to be said that these retinues were the same contingents as the lords had raised for service in the French wars and were subsequently, after the final expulsion of the English from France, kept by the lords ready for employment in warfare at home. This was not the case. Apart from the fact that few of the lords who figured in the Wars of the Roses had recently served in France, we know that the number of troops who could have survived the French wars was much smaller than the total forces engaged in the first battles in England. There may have been as many as 50,000 men at Towton in 1461, but there cannot have been a tenth as many able bodied ex-soldiers from France then in England. No doubt there was usually a small proportion of these men in several baronial companies, but the greater part of these bodies were formed by the members of each lord's household and his retainers. The latter were not domestic servants. In medieval terms, a retainer was a man who had been engaged by contract with a lord who thereby retained him for service. This service was occasional. The retainer engaged 'to ride and go with the same lord . . . upon reasonable warning'. Otherwise he lived on his estates and busied himself with the normal pursuits and duties of the country gentry to whose ranks he belonged.

This practice by the lords of retaining country gentry has, since 1885, been known as bastard feudalism. The adjective suggests illegality, but here it would be better to read it as meaning 'imitation'. In the original form of feudalism, service in a lord's armed company was the condition by which men held their lands; feudal retinues were composed of baronial tenants. The members of a bastard feudal retinue, however, were present because of their written undertaking to serve. Their bond to the lord was personal, unconnected with their tenure of land. Some members of a retinue might have been their lord's tenants as well, but they followed him in compliance with their contracts. The fact that tenants were engaged in this way emphasises how moribund the purely feudal conditions of tenure had become: the requirement to perform knight-service was purely nominal by the fifteenth century. Many retainers, in fact, held their lands of lords other than the leader of their retinue. Thus in the 1450's the king's tenants of his duchy of Lancaster estates in Derbyshire contracted with the dukes of York and Buckingham.

These contracts were drawn up in the form of indentures, for the indented deed was the normal type of document on which agreements of all kinds were made in medieval England. By an indenture of service both parties, lords as well as retainers, undertook to perform certain conditions. The retainer promised to attend the lord, under arms if necessary and with such following as he could muster, whenever the lord ordered him to do so. Thus the latter could uphold his 'estate' with a sizeable company wearing his livery when he went to attend parliaments or great councils, wished to make a show of strength locally, or provided a contingent for a royal army defending the realm. In return, the lord undertook to reimburse his retainers' expenses for this service and to pay an annual pension: this rarely exceeded £20 and was often considerably less. To a substantial knight or esquire, this monetary consideration was of less value than the further promise of 'good lordship'. By this the lord undertook to protect the private interests of his followers. Indentures were supposed to bind retainers for life. They also contained clauses saving the retainer's loyalty to the king.

In recent years we have been told that bastard feudalism was not necessarily a danger to English society; indeed it provided a new kind of cohesive organisation to remedy the dissolution of the old feudal structure. It was not illegal: an act of parliament in 1390 had forbidden men below the rank of banneret to give liveries, but this meant that lords were fully entitled to do so. The king did not oppose the creation of baronial retinues; on the contrary, he welcomed this formation of a sort of territorial army which would be prepared to answer his summons to serve against foreign foes or native rebels. A lord could be expected to keep the peace among his retainers, settling their quarrels by his arbitration, and provide a police force for preserving order in his locality. To ensure these beneficial results, however, it was essential for the king to be on good personal relations with the lords and have the strength of personal authority necessary to restrain any lord who showed a tendency to employ forcible or even illegal methods in the pursuit of local supremacy.

Collapse of public order

This vital safeguard disappeared with the death of the masterful Henry V in 1422. In the minority of his son, the lords of the council seized the opportunity to build up their own retinues and extend their areas of influence in the absence of a jealous royal eye; they did not, as councillors, attempt to curb each other, and their example was followed throughout the country. The commons in parliament deplored the upsurge of illegalities committed under the protection of 'good lordship'—the protection of criminals, forcible seizures of property, intimidation of juries. The end of the minority saw no halt in this slide to anarchy, for Henry VI was utterly incapable of bringing the lords to heel. His own chief councillor, the duke of Suffolk, was himself one of the most notable exponents of the arts of 'good lordship', to the great comfort of his clients and dismay of their opponents. The most important of his rivals in East Anglia, the duke of Norfolk, was confined to the Tower of London when he threatened one of Suffolk's local agents, and again when he battered his way into a manor house belonging to another of his rival's protégés. Norfolk's behaviour undoubtedly merited such treatment, but Suffolk's own minions had no reason to fear official displeasure.

The forces of disorder were clearly waxing during Henry's minority and the collapse of law and order continued thereafter. Without firm royal oversight, bastard feudalism easily corroded the legal system, with lords using their influence to suborn sheriffs and pack juries to favour their clients, or employing their retinues to intimidate the courts and enforce dubious claims to property. In these circumstances country gentry even of considerable means could not afford to live without the patronage of some 'good lord'. 'Go get you a lord, for thereby hang the law and the prophets', John Paston was told. Only by engaging himself to some noble champion could a man hope to have some measure of protection for his family and possessions in those troubled times. The law could not defend him; he had to look elsewhere for support, and he found it in the company of the bastard feudal retinue. Thus the system of retaining grew apace, as a snowball, creating by its illegalities the conditions which prompted increasing numbers of men to seek retainder. We must not be too ready to condemn their lords, either, for they were only living up to their promises of 'good lordship' when they took the law into their own hands on behalf of their clients; a noble was expected to champion his dependents.

We have also been shown that some retainers had a light regard for their promise of life-long service: individuals are known to have transferred their loyalty when it suited their turn. If a retainer felt that his present lord was unable to serve his interests, he attached himself to one of whom he had better expectations. An important point here, however, is that even the most fickle of retainers was always at the command of some lord. There are, moreover, many cases of men who faithfully adhered to the one lord. Some had good reason. In several counties there were feuds between families of country gentry which, in the absence of adequate government, led to breaches of the peace involving considerable numbers of men. Sir Nicholas Longford was said to have raised a thousand men by enlisting his friends and their followers for an attack on the house of his Derbyshire neighbour, Walter Blount. In Westmorland, county gentry were able to muster about two hundred men apiece when treating their neighbours' estates in the manner of a foray into Scotland. These quarrelling gentry naturally chose different lords to have the protection of their retinues and the influence required to save them from the consequences of their misdeeds. The Parrs and Bellinghams of southern Westmorland were at loggerheads for many years; they became retainers of the earls of Salisbury and Northumberland respectively, and attended these lords in both their private wars and to the battlefields of the civil war.

Gentry of this kind desperately needed 'good lordship', and if the price was participation in war, they had no choice but to follow their protectors. It did not matter to them whether their lord was a 'Lancastrian' or a 'Yorkist'; if he changed sides, so did they; if he was killed or became ineffectual, they found a new master irrespective of his politics. When the Longfords' champion the duke of Buckingham was slain by the 'Yorkists' at Northampton, they engaged themselves to lords high in favour with Edward IV and fought for him at Tewkesbury.

Richard, duke of York

The alignments of the lords themselves were likewise made for the sake of self interest. Once Richard, duke of York, emerged as the chief opponent of the group around the king, he attracted the support of nobles with enemies in that group. The process by which a 'Yorkist' party evolved was slow and erratic. York made his first challenge in the autumn of 1450, when he demanded the formation of a new council and the trial for treason of those responsible for the English defeats in France. He attracted a fair measure of general support at first, for his demands were said to be 'much after the commons' desire'. York's real motives were probably more limited. He wanted to prevent his enemy the duke of Somerset from being recognised as Henry's heir and he was also extremely anxious to secure payment for his own military services in France. The best way of securing both aims was to exclude Somerset from a position of influence near the king and obtain a place for himself in the royal council. As the greatest of landowners and as the presumptive heir to the still childless king, he felt himself entitled to a position of favour; but first Suffolk, and now Somerset, tried to keep him at a distance from the court.

York's strongest allies in 1450 were the duke of Norfolk and the earl of Devon, who both had good personal reasons for wanting to see the king's council re-formed; then their opponents would lose the advantage of official favour. Devon and his local ally Cobham assisted York in a more forcible attempt to seize power in 1452, but this likewise failed because the remaining great peers, the Nevilles included, brought their retinues to defend the court against York's rebellion. Then Somerset fell out with the earl of Warwick. The Nevilles consequently came to an understanding with York, and their enemies the Percies then naturally joined forces with Somerset. At the next trial of strength, therefore, York had a more formidable backing, for his new allies had far greater resources of manpower than his erstwhile supporters of 1450. On 22 May 1455, they intercepted the king's company at St. Albans and demanded that Somerset and unnamed others should be committed for trial. Only after spending several hours in parley did York and his supporters force their way into the town. The casualties in this skirmish probably numbered no more than sixty, but they included Somerset, York's (and Warwick's) principal enemy, and the earl of Northumberland and his adherent Lord Clifford, who were the chief opponents of the other Neville earl, Salisbury, in his contest for dominance in northern England.

Queen Margaret

In the following weeks, an attempt was made to write off this fracas as an accident best forgotten; it is unlikely that York and his allies had come to St. Albans with murderous intentions, and in an account sanctioned by parliament the blame was laid on Somerset. But this so-called battle set the course for the future. The well-meaning king besought the lords to live at peace, but his queen took over the place vacated by Somerset. Margaret of Anjou reasonably suspected York's ambition to control the government and she had no intention that her husband and son should hold a throne stripped of its prerogative authority. In 1456 she secured the appointment of dependable ministers of state. She gradually rebuilt the court party shattered at St. Albans. The heirs of the victims were ready for recruitment and through her exercise of crown patronage their strength was augmented. Lord Bonville had deserted the court for York and the Nevilles and consequently his enemy the earl of Devon was easily persuaded to join Margaret's party. By these means she hoped to secure the monarchy, but by so doing she was driving York and his allies to the point of challenging Henry's right to the crown.

In 1459 the queen was strong enough to proceed against York and the Nevilles and force them to take refuge abroad, but in 1460 the Nevilles returned unexpectedly, destroyed a depleted royal army at Northampton, and captured the king. On his return, York claimed the crown as rightful heir of Edward III. The lords in parliament reluctantly admitted the strength of his arguments, but persuaded him to leave Henry as king for the rest of his life. Soon afterwards York was killed at Wakefield (30 December 1460) and on 17 February 1461 Henry was restored to his wife by her victory at the second battle of St. Albans. Meanwhile York's son, Edward, earl of March, had defeated a 'Lancastrian' force at Mortimer's Cross. He made for London in haste, for the city refused to admit Margaret's unruly troops. On 1 March a small council of 'Yorkist' leaders agreed that he should become king and on the 4th the reign of Edward IV officially commenced.

Deposition of Henry VI

Events alone had converted these lords to the doctrine of Yorkist legitimacy; they were, for reasons of political and personal advantage, making capital of Edward's claim to the crown. Since they had lost control over Henry VI, they could no longer claim to act as the legal government of England. Henry could now, at Margaret's bidding, revoke all the appointments he had made since his capture at Northampton; he could order all subjects to enlist in his service to destroy the rebels holding London. But with Edward as king, his adherents could lawfully employ the administrative machinery still at Westminster. These men were desperate and had to use every means to hand for their own preservation. Margaret and her followers had shown no mercy in their victories, executing their noble captives on the battlefield. There was no hope for a peaceful compromise now. But even if Edward, Warwick and their supporters were again to defeat and capture Henry, there still could not be a permanent settlement in their favour. Experience had taught them that it was impossible to retain positions in the king's council. York and the Nevilles had been appointed when Henry went mad in 1453, but their dismissal speedily followed his recovery. They had recovered this ground by their victory at St. Albans in 1455, but within a year Henry had been prompted to assert himself and control had passed to Margaret and her partisans. And, finally, the advantage gained at Northampton was in jeopardy with Henry's third escape from restriction.

What these factions were fighting for in the Wars of the Roses was control of the king's council. As the result of Henry's inabilities, dominance in his council gave mastery over the organs of government, the enjoyment of its patronage, but still more important, the use of its influence in administrative and judicial processes. Since the council, unrestrained by the king, had directed his authority for partisan ends, private disputants had gravitated in one of two directions; some were attached to the king's immediate entourage, their opponents joined forces with York. Thus there developed two pyramids of patronage: the bottom tier was formed by the country gentry and others retained to lords, who made the second stage under the leadership of the court of Henry VI or its principle opponent, the duke of York. Both gentry and nobles pledged themselves because of their private need for patronage, the former in county society and the common law courts, the latter in the king's council. Since medieval government was the king's government, and because the king had an absolute right to select his own ministers and advisers, it was the final, logical step in the development of these networks of patronage that they should fight to keep or put their leader on the throne.

It was in this way, and for these motives, that the 'Lancastrian' and 'Yorkist' parties were formed. Now it cannot be denied that the majority of the population, and even some of the lords, took no active part in the civil war. This fact alone is strong evidence of the decline of the monarchy in popular esteem. We may pity Henry VI for his grievous misfortunes and miserable fate, or admire the purity, even the sanctity, of his private life, yet the mere fact of his being king was a disaster to his country. Law and order collapsed because of his incompetence. 'The realm of England was out of all good governance, for the king was simple.' Henry was unable to discharge the duty for which, as Fortescue tells us, the monarchy had been established, the protection and administration of justice to his people. They were indifferent to his deposition in 1461, and there is some testimony of burgesses and peasants welcoming the accession of Edward IV. The majority of the politically articulate classes soon accepted the new king after his crushing victory at Towton (29 March 1461). Justices of the peace, professional judges and civil servants largely continued at their posts; lords who had risen to rank and wealth in the service of the house of Lancaster likewise accepted its overthrow. The small hard core of 'Lancastrians', the personal enemies of Edward and his closest adherents, was preserved by his acts of proscription. He was generous in his restoration of property to those who submitted to his authority, but the irreconcilable rump, exiled and deprived of their estates, alone had a vested interest in the Lancastrian cause.

'Lancastrian' restoration

Their chance came in 1470. The downfall of Edward IV owed more to personal initiative and international complications than to the existence of any residual national loyalty to Lancaster. The events of this year, indeed, provide a conclusive illustration of the absence of dynastic devotion among the most prominent men of the time. Richard Neville, earl of Warwick, had been one of the small junto who had first accepted Edward as king. After taking a vigorous part in the destruction of York's enemies, Warwick eventually became discontented with the new regime. His first coup d'état brought short-lived success. Warwick tried, as he and others had done in Henry VI's reign, to rule by placing the king under restraint; but Edward broke free and Warwick had to flee abroad. Now a landless exile, his only prospect of recovering control in England and possession of his estates was to arrange the removal of Edward. The king of France, thanks to Edward's relations with his enemy of Burgundy, was ready to back Warwick's scheme. The earl made his peace with Queen Margaret and put Henry VI back on the throne after Edward had been driven into exile. Warwick was a 'kingmaker' by necessity, both in 1461 and 1470.

This readeption of the Lancastrian king lasted a bare six months. As France favoured Henry and Margaret, Burgundy helped Edward to return to England. He owed his unimpeded journey through Yorkshire to the inactivity of Henry Percy, fourth earl of Northumberland. Percy's grandfather and father had both been killed under Henry VI's standard, but now as then, the only enemies whom the Percies really hated were the Nevilles. The fourth earl would not lift a finger to save a king who was used for the enhancement of the Nevilles' power in northern England. Edward was consequently able to rally his partisans in the Midlands, defeat and kill Warwick at Barnet (14 April 1471) and enter London in triumph. Here Henry VI was captured for the last time; Edward made sure he would not be restored again. He completed the destruction of his enemies at Tewkesbury (4 May 1471), where Margaret was captured and the remaining leaders of her party were either slain in the battle or executed afterwards. Among the victims was Prince Edward; his death extinguished the royal line of Lancaster.

Edward IV

The second part of Edward's reign passed without any recurrence of serious domestic strife. He was ruthlessly vigilant in crushing any suspected source of treason, as his own brother the duke of Clarence learned to his cost. Under his firm direction, the government of England retrieved its internal authority and developed its resources; once again the king was master in his own council, what is more he was no longer hamstrung by the spectre of empty coffers. His confiscations of the lands of attainted nobles and the efficient management of these and his own estates not only increased the crown's wealth; they also increased Edward's strength in relation to the lords, making him the predominant territorial power in the country. He took a close interest in the preservation of public order and by his vigilance and active intervention did much to restore respect for the law.* Had Edward not died in 1483 at the early age of forty, but survived for another twenty years, it is likely that the crown would long have remained with the house of York and the Tudors would have been lost to history.

Richard III

Edward's heir was a boy of twelve. For the third time in a century, there rose the question of how the king's government should be carried on in a minority. In 1377 and 1422, the assembled peers had set up continuing councils for this purpose; on both occasions they had refused the claims of royal uncles to assume viceregal powers. In 1483, however, as the result of the civil wars, the peerage was no longer sufficiently powerful and united to act as the supreme constitutional authority. The field was open, therefore, for rival factions to

* For Edward's government, see chapters 5 and 6.

compete for control of the young king's person, and thus of his government, with all the means at their disposal. Rightly or wrongly, Richard, duke of Gloucester, the brother of Edward IV, suspected the queen and her relatives, the Woodvilles and Greys, of scheming to monopolise the crown's powers. With the support of the duke of Buckingham, he forestalled his rivals, arresting Lords Rivers and Grey and taking Edward from their charge. Gloucester was then proclaimed protector of the realm. Next he summarily executed Lord Hastings, arrested other former councillors of Edward IV, and ordered the execution of Rivers and Grey. Then after reports had been published that Edward IV had not been lawfully married so that his children were bastards, an assembly of a quasi-parliamentary nature invited Gloucester to assume the crown as the only true heir of his father Richard, duke of York. The next day, 26 June 1483, he began to reign as King Richard III.

The story that Edward IV's marriage was illegal was obviously a fabrication for Richard's benefit. Otherwise it would have been a most remarkable coincidence that it was discovered only after Richard had prepared his position to take advantage of it. It is more credible to presume that he had set his sights on the throne from the beginning of Edward V's reign, since he secured the boy in his custody, and then prepared his ground by crushing potential opponents. The success of his schemes reveals not only that Richard was a brilliant and ruthless opportunist; it shows also that political circumstances favoured his ambition and must have encouraged him to make the attempt.

Richard's actions in 1483 are understandable, if not excusable, when we consider the conditions in which he had grown up. From his boyhood, when his father and brother Rutland had been killed in battle, he had lived in the centre of a storm of violence, treachery and suspicion. Richard's seizure of the throne was prompted by more than ambition, for we may well believe that he felt his own future to be in peril when Edward IV died. His loyal and able services to Edward had earned wealth and authority; next to his brother, he was the greatest man in the kingdom. But this eminence might have been threatened if the government of Edward V fell under the control of the queen mother's jealous and grasping kinsmen. Richard of Gloucester cannot have forgotten the fate of the previous royal uncles who had held his title—Thomas, put to death in 1397, and Humphrey, widely believed to have been murdered in 1447. The Wars of the

Roses had become a struggle for the crown because its possession was the only means of retaining hold of the government of the country. The stark alternatives for Richard were the crown or nothing.

As king, Richard III's record is in many respects no worse than that of Edward IV or his Tudor successors. Like them, he strove to give England the blessings of strong government, enforcing the law, fostering trade and efficiently nursing the financial resources of the crown. But beneficent as his reign may have been to ordinary subjects, its character was tainted by the manner in which it had begun. He had shown no regard for the processes of law when he ordered the summary execution of his suspected opponents. His subjects cannot have felt secure under the rule of a king ready to dispense with the law when his immediate interests were at stake.

Still more disturbing were the rumours about the deposed Edward V and his brother Richard, duke of York and Norfolk. The princes had been lodged in the Tower of London in May 1483 and never emerged; an Italian visitor who left England on 6 July believed them to be dead and on the 8th the title of duke of Norfolk, previously held by the young Richard, was conferred on John Howard, the constable of the Tower. Naturally there is no direct documentary evidence of the death of the princes, but neither is there any proof that they were still living after 1483. On the other hand, both in England and abroad it was being put about that Richard had caused his nephews to be secretly slain, and he did not disprove these rumours by producing the boys in public. Yet again, his subjects had cause to believe that Richard was a king who considered himself *lege solutus*, the medieval definition of a tyrant against whom it was lawful to rebel.

Richard did not rule like a lawful king. His usurpation would not have been possible without the support of the duke of Buckingham, and he had to pay for this aid; already an 'overmighty subject', Buckingham was richly rewarded, becoming a virtually independent ruler of Wales. Buckingham was soon tempted, however, to aspire to the crown himself. Then, as he was persuaded that he had little chance of success on his own, he entered into negotiations with Henry Tudor and other 'Lancastrian' partisans. The plot failed dismally and Richard was able to capture and execute his former confederate on 2 November 1483, while other accomplices were imprisoned or fled abroad.

Richard's success did not make him feel secure. He continued to buy loyalty where he thought it might be found. In many shires trusted men were endowed with lands so that their neighbours could be restrained. The one magnate on whose fidelity Richard could rely because of his implication in—and profits from—the death of the princes was the duke of Norfolk, and Richard's dependence on his services was revealed by his appointment to the head of the commission of the peace in every county. The notorious trio, Lord Lovel, William Catesby and Richard Ratcliffe—'the Cat, the Rat and Lovel the dog'—were likewise given authority in a score of shires, while the commissions were purged of all suspected of disaffection, among them men who had given stout service to Edward IV. In times of crisis, Richard took hostages as guarantees of loyalty. These were not the acts of a king who was convinced of his right to wear the crown and believed that his subjects had accepted his title. They were the desperate measures of an adventurer who had destroyed the country's newly restored unity and lived in constant dread of insurrection. The outcome justified Richard's fears, for even prominent servants of York under Edward remained aloof or joined Henry Tudor in 1485.

3

King Henry VII

HENRY TUDOR had become the figurehead of opposition to Richard III because better qualified candidates had been eliminated. Henry VI had been the last surviving descendant of his grandfather Henry IV. This extinction of the main line of Lancaster was due not only to recent violence but possibly also to a disease inherited by Henry IV and transmitted to his six children, of whom only two had each one legitimate child; Henry VI was the only grandson to have issue. Little better fortune attended the Beauforts, the second family established by the Lancastrian progenitor, John of Gaunt. The sons of the second and third generations had perished, mostly in the civil warfare, so that only one legitimate male of the house survived after 1471.

The head of the Beaufort family had carried the title of earl or duke of Somerset, and he had enjoyed a richer endowment in lands and revenues than the junior members of the clan. When John, the third earl—and the first duke—died in 1444, however, the title was conferred on his brother Edmund, although his lands were inherited by his only child, Margaret. Despite the loss of the Somerset title, therefore, Margaret Beaufort represented the senior line of her house and had the means to support a dignified station. As she was, in 1444, only one year old, she became the king's ward, and Henry VI soon granted her wardship to his favourite, the duke of Suffolk, together with licence to arrange her marriage. Suffolk apparently considered marrying her to his own son, but then discarded the idea when a much wealthier heiress came into his charge. In 1450, his enemies accused him of planning Margaret's marriage to his son with the intention of putting them on the throne in Henry's place. Henry

Select Genealogy

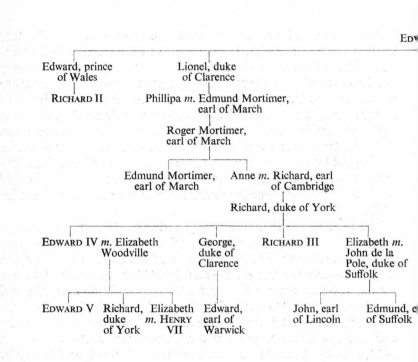

Edward, prince
of Wales
|
RICHARD II

Lionel, duke
of Clarence
|
Phillipa *m.* Edmund Mortimer,
earl of March
|
Roger Mortimer,
earl of March

Edmund Mortimer,   Anne *m.* Richard, earl
earl of March   of Cambridge
|
Richard, duke of York

EDWARD IV *m.* Elizabeth   George,   RICHARD III   Elizabeth *m.*
Woodville   duke of   John de la
Clarence   Pole, duke of
Suffolk

EDWARD V   Richard, Elizabeth Edward,   John, earl   Edmund, e
duke   *m.* HENRY earl of   of Lincoln   of Suffolk
of York   VII   Warwick

ancaster and York

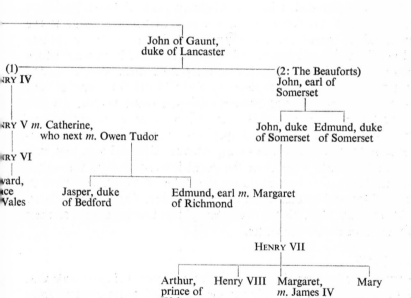

John of Gaunt,
duke of Lancaster

(1)
ᴎʀʏ IV

(2: The Beauforts)
John, earl of
Somerset

ᴎʀʏ V *m.* Catherine,
who next *m.* Owen Tudor

John, duke   Edmund, duke
of Somerset   of Somerset

ᴋʀʏ VI

vard,
ᴄᴇ
ᴠales

Jasper, duke
of Bedford

Edmund, earl *m.* Margaret
of Richmond

Hᴇɴʀʏ VII

Arthur,   Henry VIII   Margaret,   Mary
prince of   *m.* James IV
Wales

IV had declared that the Beauforts were not to succeed to the crown, but it is questionable if he could, of his sole authority, lawfully exclude anyone from a rightful inheritance. The malicious charges against Suffolk in 1450 certainly suggests that people considered Margaret Beaufort as a possible heir to the throne.

Lady Margaret's hand was now given to the king's half-brother, Edmund Tudor. King Henry VII was later to have a pedigree drawn up which traced his descent through the Tudors to ancient Welsh princes and eventually to the mythical first king of Britain, the Trojan Brutus. More fittingly in view of his record as king, sober history finds his earliest known ancestor to have been a capable administrator in the service of Llewelyn the Great in the early thirteenth century who founded a line of Anglesey gentry.[1] Owen Tudor, a younger son of this family, became a page and next a squire in the household of Henry V. He secretly married his former master's young widow, Catherine of France, and four children had been born before the scandalised king's council forcibly parted them. Owen escaped further prosecution for his temerity when Henry VI came of age, and thereafter the Tudor children enjoyed royal favour. To this Edmund owed his bride and the subsequent grant of the earldom of Richmond, while his brother Jasper was given the earldom of Pembroke. After the first battle of St. Albans, Edmund was sent into Wales to establish control in the royal interest, but he was taken prisoner in Carmarthen castle by the duke of York's followers in August 1456 and he died there on 3 November. Three months later, on 28 January 1457, his fourteen-year-old widow gave birth to their only child in Pembroke castle.

Early years

Henry Tudor was certainly the child of civil war. It is probable that he was early parted from his mother, for Lady Margaret was soon found a second husband in Henry Stafford, second son of the duke of Buckingham. Jasper, earl of Pembroke, had charge of his young nephew until 1461, when the troops of Edward IV took Pembroke castle and with it Henry Tudor. At this time, and as long as Henry VI and his son Edward were living, the young earl of Richmond was a comparatively unimportant person and not a potential source of danger to the Yorkist king. Edward was not vindictive and did not pursue vendettas against the young heirs of his fallen enemies. The

His indenture
scriptyre made betwene
the moost cristen king
Henry the vij by the grace
of god king of Englond
and of ffraunce and lord
of ireland the xvj day
of Juliij the ixteuth
vere of his moost noble
reigue of the con partie
and the moost Reuerend
ffader in god William archebisshop of Caunterbury of the secound
partie and the moost Reuerend fader in god Richard Busshop of
Wynchestre of the thirde partie and John Islip Abbot of the monastie
of sainte Peter of westm and the Priour and Couuent of
the same place of the fourth partie and the Deane and Chanons
of the king fre chapell of oure lady and sainte Stephen the
furst martir within the king palois of westm of the vth partie
and the Deane and Chapitre of the Cathedrall chirche of sainte
Paule in the Citie of london of the vj partie and the maire
and Comialte of the Citie of london of the vij partie witnesseth
that wheir by iudentures made bitwene the said king j soueraiu
lord and the said Abbot Priour and Couuent for them and
thair Successours being date the date of these iuseut
¶ The saine Abbot Priour and Couuent haue couenaunted
and graunted and bounde them and thair Successours to the
said king oure soueraiu lord his heires and Successours that

5 Ordinances for Henry VII's Chapel

6 Henry VII's Chapel, Westminster Abbey

7 Prince Arthur's Chantry, Worcester Cathedral

boy, as a future tenant-in-chief, was a valuable ward, but as yet no more than this. His wardship and marriage was granted, at a price, to Edward's most trusted Welsh marcher follower, William Herbert. Herbert was also granted Pembroke castle, and consequently the change in guardians did not bring about any move to a new home. At Pembroke, Henry was brought up as an honoured member of the new countess's household, given the education appropriate for a boy of his rank, and, indeed, considered as a prospective son-in-law, for Herbert intended to marry him to his eldest daughter. This was an entirely normal upbringing, and if Henry's boyhood was at all unhappy, it was no more so than that of other scions of the nobility who were customarily sent to learn their manners under strange baronial roofs. Had there not been a renewal of the civil war, Henry would in all probability have settled down as a faithful member of the Yorkist peerage, possibly attaining through his practical gifts some high office like that of treasurer of England.

Henry lost his guardian in 1469, when the earl of Warwick had Herbert executed after the battle of Edgcott. Warwick was for a while master of the kingdom, but Edward's reassertion of authority led to his exile, the alliance with the Lancastrian queen Margaret, and the 'Kingmaker's' restoration of Henry VI. Jasper Tudor returned from exile and is said to have presented his nephew to King Henry who thereupon declared, 'This truly, this is he unto whom both we and our adversaries must yield and give over the dominion.' Prophetic words indeed, but they are known only from accounts written after their fulfilment. Could Henry VI have foreseen that his own line was doomed to early extinction? This came about in May 1471, and now Henry Tudor could be regarded as the residuary heir of Lancaster. His uncle Jasper, at least, decided that the boy should not again fall into Edward IV's charge. His object was to preserve Henry from danger; the fate of Prince Edward, struck down after the battle of Tewkesbury, must have been in Jasper's mind. There is no reason to suppose, however, that he proposed to make Henry the central figure of a Lancastrian revival. Henry went into exile as earl of Richmond, and he did not claim to be anything else. He did not assert that he was the rightful king of England. At no time, either before Bosworth or afterwards, did Henry Tudor deny that the Yorkist Edward IV was lawfully king of England.

C

Exile

Duke Francis II of Brittany received the two Tudors and permitted
them to remain in his almost independent French duchy. For five
years he refused Edward's requests to send his guests to England,
but in 1476 his resolution wavered and an English embassy was
actually conducting Henry to the Breton coast when the duke was
persuaded to connive at his escape. Edward had professed only the
kindest of intentions, saying that he would marry Henry to one of his
daughters. He may have been sincere. Although the king had taken
charge of the Richmond lands, he was quite entitled to do this as long
as Henry was a minor. He did not, however, have Henry condemned
and proclaimed to be a traitor and so forfeiting his life and possessions. Henry abroad may have been a potential nuisance to Edward,
and could have been a serious problem if the king of France had
championed him. At home, Edward had good reason to feel secure.
Former servants of Henry VI, among them Sir John Fortescue and
Dr. John Morton, recognised the completeness of his victory, submitted to his authority and received pardons. This magnanimity was
itself a sign of confidence. There remained the danger of French
hostility, a cause of Edward's downfall in 1470, but in 1475 he had
come to terms with Louis XI. There is a further reason for supposing
that his plans for Henry were honourable. Margaret Beaufort now
had a new husband, her third. This was Thomas, Lord Stanley, who
had a good record of loyalty to the house of York and had from 1471
held the senior office of steward in the king's household. With her
husband so well entrenched at court, it is hard to believe that Margaret's son would have been murdered on his return to England. But
this, apparently, is what Henry believed: he is said to have nearly
died of terror while he was with the English embassy.

Henry therefore remained in Brittany, with Edward paying the
duke to keep him there. This arrangement was also agreeable to
Richard III. The latter, however, greatly improved Henry's prospects
by his murder of Edward's sons and disruption of the Yorkist ruling
class. The growing number of men who hoped to overthrow his
throne had to consider the claims of the young earl of Richmond.
Richard's sometime champion, the duke of Buckingham, seemingly
cherished ambitions of his own to be king. Then he was persuaded
that a revolt in the name of Henry Tudor was more likely to raise

the following needed for success. Buckingham's adviser here was John Morton, now bishop of Ely thanks to his services to Edward. Morton was one of the councillors of the late king whom Richard thought it essential to remove when preparing his seizure of the throne, and Buckingham was his gaoler. Margaret Beaufort was drawn into the conspiracy and approached Edward's dowager in her sanctuary at Westminster. The two mothers agreed that Henry should marry Edward's daughter Elizabeth, so that the rebellion should attract adherents of York as well as Lancaster. Messengers were sent to Henry to bid him come to win a bride and a kingdom. Then the conspiracy collapsed. Buckingham, rising too soon, was captured and executed on 2 November 1483, while Henry's fleet provided by his host was scattered in a storm and he ignored enticement by royal troops to land in Devonshire. Richard routed out the remaining conspirators: some were executed, others—including Henry—were sentenced as traitors in their absence, while Lady Margaret was strictly confined in the house of her husband, who professed ignorance of her treasonable designs. Henry had a further escape in September 1484, when Richard suborned one of the Breton councillors, by dashing into France in disguise.

From this time Henry began to look like the head of an alternative English government. The regency council of Charles VIII, the new French king, gave orders that he was to be received hospitably when it learned of an agreement between Richard and Brittany. Various English fugitives began to gather round him. The earl of Oxford, imprisoned since he commanded part of Warwick's army at Barnet, escaped to join Henry. Bishop Morton came by way of Flanders. Richard Fox abandoned his studies in Paris to begin his lifelong service to Henry. Edward Poynings was another attendant destined for high office. Kinsmen of the queen-dowager Elizabeth Woodville, knights and squires from Devon, Kent and other counties involved in the abortive rising of 1483, helped to swell Henry's court.

With the counsel of men of outstanding administrative ability like Morton, Fox and Poynings, Henry was able to plan a fresh invasion with care and foresight; in Oxford and his uncle Pembroke he had tried commanders to remedy his own lack of military experience; while the company in general could provide valuable information about conditions and sympathies in many quarters of England and

Wales. This was indeed a government in the making, at present more a general operational staff than a civilian administration, but in command of talents which could manage the affairs of a kingdom. Their immediate programme was clear and urgent. Deprived of all their possessions in England, these exiles had to live on the generous if interested hospitality of the French council, and the internal politics of France gave little reason for confidence that this would continue indefinitely. On the other hand, they had adequate information to believe that Richard's command of English loyalty might well crumble if put to the test soon, but further delay might allow him to strengthen his hold.

The kingdom won

These calculations were justified. Henry's march through Wales to Shrewsbury in August 1485 was an unopposed procession; a few bands of Welshmen joined him as he advanced and companies came from the midland shires as he neared his adversary. Bosworth has often been claimed as a 'Welsh victory', but both in accounts of the battle and in the list of rewards for services on the field English names form an overwhelming majority; and the decisive contribution to Henry's victory was provided by the men of Lancashire and Cheshire under the Stanleys. The battle was scarcely over, and Richard's naked corpse still on its way to exhibition and burial in Leicester, when Henry issued a proclamation forbidding robbery and violence. Its opening words were 'Henry by the grace of God, king of England and of France, prince of Wales and lord of Ireland'. Already he was king and requiring his subjects to keep the king's peace.

The battle had settled the question of who was the rightful king of England. As contemporaries believed, God had revealed His Will in giving Henry the victory; as Richard had lost the day, he had also lost the kingdom. His proven death fortunately put this beyond all doubt. Henry's title to the throne was as simple as this: having been accepted as leader by Richard's rebellious subjects, he automatically became king after their victory at Bosworth. This consequence of the battle received immediate general acceptance. With the exception of Richard's most committed adherents, every Englishman now regarded Henry Tudor as king; the organs of government carried on their accustomed duties in his name; his commissions and appointments gave full and accepted authority to his nominees.

Writs for a parliament were issued in Henry's name on 15 September. The response of spiritual and temporal peers to their personal summonses, the compliance of county freeholders and municipal corporations in meeting to elect their representatives, were in themselves recognition of Henry's royal authority. Before parliament met, moreover, the new king was crowned with splendid ceremony in Westminster Abbey on 30 October. The opening of parliament on 7 November followed the traditional forms. There was an address by the chancellor, wherein the members were reminded of their duties as subjects to their king, who was upheld as a second Joshua, sent by God to rescue his people from misery. Then the chancellor announced the names of the lords whom Henry had appointed to hear petitions. The commons next elected their speaker and presented him to the king.

If the order of entries on the parliament roll reflects the course of business, the next measure was the grant to Henry of customs duties. It was followed by a petition from the commons: this asked, that to remove all doubt, it should be enacted by authority of the present parliament that the inheritance of the crown with all its appurtenances was and remained in the person of Henry VII and the heirs of his body. Then, with the assent of the lords, Henry gave his consent. The fact of Henry's accession was thus registered on the parliament roll. This did nor mean that the parliament had given Henry a title to rule nor that it had legalised or in any way qualified his status as king. Parliaments did not make kings: only the reverse was true, for there could not be a parliament without a king. Since the initiative in having this declaration made did not, apparently, come from the king, it would seem that he had not called the parliament for the purpose of making it. His object was to secure a grant of revenue, and the commons had used the opportunity to clarify the matter of the succession.

It was the accepted view that the king was the person in whose name government was conducted. However dubious his title to be crowned, the acts of his government were valid and binding on the people of the realm. The Lancastrian kings were denounced as usurpers by Edward IV, but the statutes of their parliaments remained in force and the judgments of their courts of law were accepted. The same doctrine was proclaimed in Henry's *De facto* act of 1495, which declared that subjects were obliged to obey the king for the time being. We might observe, moreover, that this principle is the same as one of the guiding rules in British foreign policy down to the present day: the criterion for British official recognition of a foreign regime has not been its legality but whether it was the effective government of its country.

For this reason it is unprofitable to debate the merits of the various grounds on which Henry VII could have based his title to be king. It was irrelevant that his hereditary right to the crown was so flimsy, that if it did have any validity his mother Lady Margaret had a claim one degree stronger. The doctrine of royal legitimacy was a parvenu in English constitutional ideas. It had been invented by Richard of York in 1460, for his own purposes, and adopted by his adherents in 1461; but we need not doubt that if the enemies of Lancaster had been unable to forward this argument on behalf of their leader, they would have found some other reason to justify the deposition of Henry VI. Henry VII's parentage and background distinguished him as being recognisably the male representative of the family of Henry VI, and he was thus qualified to emerge as the natural leader of the enemies of Richard III. He was chosen, one might say, as the anti-Ricardian candidate by the fact that refugees from England came to gather round him in France; and as this party triumphed at Bosworth, so its leader became king.

The new government

The first acts of the new reign followed the conventional pattern: offices had to be filled, the faithful rewarded and active adherents of Richard punished or at least removed from power. At the highest level, Henry aimed to preserve continuity by enlisting former officers of Edward IV. His first chancellor was Thomas Rotherham, archbishop of York, who had held this position from 1474 to 1483. Rotherham's chancellorship was brief (18 September to 7 October) but he was retained as treasurer;[2] and the next chancellor, John Alcock, bishop of Ely, was another former councillor of Edward. The privy seal was given to Peter Courtenay, bishop of Exeter, once Edward's secretary but later imprisoned by Richard for complicity in Buckingham's rebellion. The most confidential of the secretarial offices, however, that of king's secretary, went to Richard Fox. In local as well as central government, Henry retained the services of 'Yorkist' officials as well as bringing in former fellow exiles.

There is, as usual, no record of a formal appointment of a king's council. Henry already had advisers before leaving France in Morton, Fox, Jasper Tudor, Oxford and Poynings, and he continued to keep them near him, adding to the close circle his mother's steward, Reginald Bray, who had acted as her agent in the abortive conspiracy of 1483. Henry was lavish in his grants of pensions and offices of profit to those who had been abroad with him or had given notable service at Bosworth, and titles were conferred on his foremost supporters: Jasper Tudor became duke of Bedford, Thomas Stanley earl of Derby, and the earldom of Devon was revived for Edward Courtenay. The formation of the yeomen of the guard to provide for Henry's personal protection has often been considered as an innovation, but there had in fact been similar bodies in previous reigns; they had then been called by other names, such as yeomen of the crown.

The condemnation of Henry's defeated enemies had to be done in parliament. Attainder for high treason, whereby dead and fugitive opponents were stripped of their property, titles and other legal rights and possessions, had by this time become an established parliamentary process. On this occasion a new departure was made in that Henry, by dating the beginning of his reign from the day before Bosworth, claimed that Richard and his companions were waging war against their lawful king. There were some protests in parliament against this transparent chicanery, but Henry had his way and thus laid his hands on the private estates of Richard, the duke of Norfolk, four other peers and some twenty knights and squires. At the same time victims of Yorkist acts of attainder had their sentences revoked and thus recovered their legal rights and possessions. Henry himself had been attainted but there was no need for his sentence to be reversed: the judges had ruled that the king regnant could not be an attainted person.

The most important function of Henry's first parliament, from his point of view, was that it endowed him with the means to keep his estate as king. He was granted, for his lifetime, the revenues of the customs, and extensive estates—crown lands and the duchies of Lancaster and Cornwall as well as the forfeitures of his attainted enemies. An act of resumption was passed, recovering for the crown all revenues and properties gifted away since 1455. Its effect was reduced, however, by the great list of exemptions, which permitted not only Henry's recent beneficiaries but many of Edward IV's to retain their grants. Another significant financial measure was the assignment of various crown revenues for the maintenance of the king's household. There is no sign here of new ideas on royal finance. All three of these devices had been employed from over thirty years earlier. From other evidence to be discussed later it is clear that Henry had at this time little interest in the organisation of his revenues and was unaware of the advantages of the financial practices of the Yorkist kings.

The other legislation of this first Tudor parliament confirms this impression that Henry had not yet any specific plans for the reform of English government and society. The economic measures appear to have been initiated by the commons, not by the king. Apart from an act against poaching in royal forests, there was no addition to penal legislation. The lords present were required to take an oath that they would not uphold wrongdoers, or otherwise disturb public order and pervert justice. All these actions were already forbidden by statutes and similar oaths had been taken before.

Henry's marriage

On the day this parliament was prorogued for Christmas, both lords and commons urged Henry to marry Elizabeth of York. He had in 1483 publicly undertaken to do so, and had subsequently renewed the promise. It has often been said that he delayed the marriage because he wished to make it clear that he did not owe his crown to his wife. There was in fact another very good reason for this delay. This was that Henry and Elizabeth were related sufficiently closely for their marriage to be unlawful according to the regulations of the Church: John of Gaunt was their great, great grandfather.* Consequently a dispensation from the pope was essential, and this could not be obtained immediately. Fortunately a papal legate empowered to grant dispensations for marriage arrived in the country. He gave Henry and Elizabeth this licence on 16 January 1486 and they were married two days later.[3]

This marriage was a vital act of policy. Although Henry was undoubtedly king from the moment of Richard's death, Elizabeth was the eldest daughter of a king who had enjoyed full authority and, for

* Edward IV's mother, Cecily Neville, was the daughter of Joan Beaufort, countess of Westmorland, who was Gaunt's daughter.

his last twelve years, unchallenged recognition as sovereign. Henry obviously could not have dared to allow her to have any husband but himself, for she would otherwise have made a respectable figurehead for any future sedition. He stood on his own right to be king, but he did not deny the legality of Edward's reign, and Richard's allegations about Edward's marriage were properly ignored: no one dared to suggest that the wife of Henry VII was a bastard. Her marriage to Henry helped to cement the loyalty of Edward's former servants and faithful supporters to the new regime; they could feel assured that their past conduct in the Yorkist cause would not prejudice them with their new monarch. Henry was realist enough to employ officials who had served York. He really had no choice, for his own following from France was too small to staff a national administration, and had he removed all officials with a Yorkist past his government would have been seriously undermanned and inexperienced. Besides, many of these tried magistrates and administrators had already adjusted their loyalty once in entering Edward's service and had few qualms in doing so again; they were ready to serve the king who governed, be he Lancaster, York or Tudor.

When Henry sought the pope's confirmation of the marriage, he stated that its object was to unite the families of Lancaster and York and end their ancient strife. This it did, but only in a limited sense. Later writers have claimed that this union healed a deep, bitter schism in English society; it saved the nation from further agonies of intestinal strife begotten of incompatible loyalties to the rival dynasties. This is doubly false. The last battle of the Wars of the Roses was still to be fought, and the final rumblings of the conflict did not die down in the mind of Henry VIII until he had bloodily removed other descendants of Edward IV. More to the point in 1485, however, was the fact that English society as a whole had not divided itself into two hostile camps; most had viewed the conflict with little warmth and had accepted every victor as king. The marriage of Henry and Elizabeth had personal significance only to the nobility and others of the governing class who had been directly involved in the civil war, and men who had served York by holding office. Henry hoped, no doubt, that there would be children of the marriage to engage the loyalty of former partisans, but he did not stake all his hopes on this prospect. He contemplated the possibility of Elizabeth dying childless, and declared that in this event he would marry again and then the offspring of this marriage would be heir to the throne. Henry alone would be the founder of the royal house of Tudor.

Personal

When analysing the reign of any medieval king, we always come to the problem of his personality. Since so much depended on his own part in government, diplomacy and war, we have to search for information which will illustrate his qualities of mind and character. In Henry VII's time, writers were beginning to pay some attention to individuals; they now made a point of observing people and recording descriptions. For the most part, such eye-witness accounts as we have of Henry belong to his later years, and we cannot put too much weight on them in trying to visualise what he was like at the outset of his reign. For his appearance we know from Polydore Vergil that he was above average height, and slender, although well built and strong, with golden hair which went thin in his later years. Actual portraits offer conflicting testimony: the noble austerity of Torrigiano's bust is entirely absent from the mean, crafty face of Sitium's painting,* although both have the same high cheekbones, hooded eyelids, high bridged, pointed nose, and thin lips. In neither portrait can it be said that 'his face was cheerful', as Polydore wrote, 'especially when speaking', an observation confirmed by Bishop Fisher who said, in 1509, that Henry was in 'his person goodly and amiable'. Spanish ambassadors in 1498 likewise speak of his cheerful aspect.[4]

These impressions hardly accord with the traditional assessment of Henry as a grave, suspicious, somewhat sinister figure, a king who had no pleasures but preferred book-keeping, who attended tournaments only to pass the time writing memoranda, a husband whose relations with his wife were warped by hatred of her father's house. Such flights of Bacon's fancy deserve no credence. There is good reason to believe that Henry was not only a faithful but an affectionate husband. He was not too austere to bicker with Elizabeth in the presence of Spanish envoys.[5] There is a moving account of how they consoled each other when the news came of the death of Prince Arthur in 1502. First Elizabeth fortified Henry, then he went to re-relieve her 'and showed her how wise counsel she had given him before, and he for his part would thank God for his son, and would she

* See plates 2 and 8.

do so in like wise'. When she died in childbirth two years later, Henry 'privily departed to a solitary place, and would no man should resort unto him'.

Henry's piety must be emphasised. It is a commonplace that religious beliefs and practices had an inseparable place in the lives of all people at this time, but Henry's devotions went far beyond those of his contemporaries. He heard two or three masses daily, wrote Polydore: one daily attendance would have been held a sign of grace in a layman. The king's alms-giving was frequent and extensive. He visited famous English shrines like Canterbury and Walsingham. He founded convents of strict Franciscans at Greenwich and Newark and completed the chapels of St. George at Windsor and King's College, Cambridge. His greatest foundation was the chapel in Westminster Abbey; between 1502 and 1505 he spent £9,650 on its building, provided for its completion in his will, and gave crown properties and paid at least £30,000 in buying further lands to a total annual value of £668. The object of this massive endowment was to provide for the ceaseless repetition of masses and prayers for the well-being of the king and his family while they lived and for their felicity hereafter. Henry also made arrangements with nearly a hundred religious houses so that they should perform services for his benefit,[6] and in his will bequeathed money for 10,000 masses to be said within a month of his death. The scale of these provisions surpasses those made by any other English monarch since Henry III, and they reveal Henry Tudor's excessive, even morbid, preoccupation with his spiritual welfare. His contemporaries who were benefactors on a considerable scale did make provision for similar services, but the establishment of educational institutions was the most prominent feature of their endowments. When compared with his bishops, Henry appears to have had little interest in the spread of learning among his subjects; he was more concerned with his own well-being. From his expenses, however, we know that his compassion could be roused by the misfortunes of others: he gave money to 'one that had his hand smitten off', 'for the healing of four sick men'.

Like his fellow-monarchs abroad, Henry preferred to live outside his capital city, staying in the palace of Westminster only in times of parliament and other important official occasions. Richmond, where he built a new palace, was his favourite resort, but he was often at Windsor, Eltham and Greenwich; here again there were new buildings, more commodious than old castles or the cramped palace of Westminster, and in their neighbourhoods were ample parks for hunting deer. In the summer, Henry would go to Woodstock, near Oxford, or more rarely to the New Forest. Though he did not shirk long journeys when treason or discontent demanded a royal progress, he needed such cause to give up his seasonal recreation. He hawked as well as hunted, kept horses, greyhounds, spaniels, falcons and other birds of prey. He indulged, too, in more popular sports like coursing hares or watching bull-baiting; he played tennis and competed at archery; his other pursuits included chess, cards and dice. We know of these pastimes, for Henry played for stakes, and his losses were recorded in his chamber accounts; presumably he sometimes won, but his gains are not mentioned. Once he lost £47* at cards, another time £12 in camp the night before his army faced Perkin Warbeck. He enjoyed the antics of fools and tumblers, 'a priest that wrestled', 'a fellow for eating of coals'. There was 'guising' in the court at Christmas, and the 'abbot of misrule' presided on Twelfth Night.

Henry also had more cultivated tastes. His court was magnificent in both ceremony and decor; such pomp was designed to impress subjects and foreign embassies. His clothing was rich and expensive, as was that of the attendant nobles. Despite the myth that Henry showed a predilection for men of 'middle-class' origin, the records show that he lived in the company of earls and other peers, some his kinsmen, but others descended from the established aristocracy, such as the earls of Oxford, Surrey and Northumberland; these magnates not only frequented the court, they accompanied the king in his pastimes, even competing with him in sport. On great festivals, a large gathering of lords would attend him; for instance, when he kept the feast of All Souls at Windsor in 1488, five earls and seven barons were with him. From time to time lists were set up to entertain courtiers and populace with the pageantry of a still revered chivalry and the skill and valour of mounted combat. It was not, however, a court of the age of feudal chivalry, a kind of glorified military headquarters. Poets, scholars and above all musicians had their places there. Besides keeping his company of minstrels, Henry bought new instruments from time to time—flutes, pipes, organs,

* To appreciate the value of money at this time, we should recall that the average daily wage was 5d.

clavichords—and rewarded those who wrote him songs and ballads. His enjoyment of music is obvious: while passing through Canterbury on his way to invade France, he overheard children singing in a garden and gave them forty pence. Purchases of books, in French as well as English, and for their binding and decoration, give further evidence of Henry's educated tastes. He had a poet laureate and rewarded other poets from Italy, Wales and Scotland; the last was probably William Dunbar.[7]

It is clear enough that Henry was entirely human in his private life, moved by the same beliefs, sorrows and joys, even the simplest, as were his subjects. He was sufficiently conventional in his pursuits to be acceptable as a person, while the pomp and noble company he cultivated conformed to popular notions of what befitted a king. Yet he never won the hearts of his people. There was, obviously, something wanting in his personality; he lacked that indefinable quality which commanded instant devotion, which kept loyalty in spite of unpopular actions. It was noted in 1498, again by a Spaniard, that the king was little loved, but his wife and son Arthur were warmly esteemed, Arthur because in him people saw the image of his grandfather.[8] Edward IV was guilty of many bloody deeds, including the murder of a helpless, 'simple' king; but there was no doubt of his martial prowess, his physical valour and powers of generalship, and these Henry VII made no pretence to possess. Nor had he Edward's robust masculine charm which won the affections of the wives of London and thus the financial aid of their husbands. The same quality which marked 'Bluff King Hal' and his daughter Queen Elizabeth was clearly inherited from their Yorkist forbear, not from the first royal Tudor. Fortunately Henry was well-endowed with qualities of mind and character which enabled him to hold his own despite this disadvantage.

4

Diplomacy and Sedition

HENRY owed a great deal to fortune in the first year of his reign. Both at home and abroad circumstances favoured a king who had newly won his throne. In England there was an absence—at least for the time being—of 'overmighty subjects' with the resources to make a serious challenge to his authority. There was a similar situation among his closest European neighbours. Neither in France, the Low Countries or Scotland was there a government in sufficient command of its dominions to attempt an aggressive foreign policy. James III of Scotland tried to profit from the upheaval in England in the autumn of 1485, but his schemes came to nothing and the endemic disorder of his kingdom soon compelled him to make a truce with Henry. In 1488 James was murdered by a faction of his nobles and Scotland again suffered the hazards of a royal minority. Louis XI of France had died in 1481 and was succeeded by Charles VIII, a boy of thirteen. His sister Anne of Beaujeu became regent, and showed considerable skill and determination in preserving the crown's authority in the face of dangerous if incoherent opposition from the duke of Orleans and other grandees. The ruler of Flanders was also a minor and his father, the Emperor Maximilian, provoked revolt in the great towns by his clumsy attempts to govern.

The first revolt

The youth of a number of baronial heirs was a valuable political asset to Henry in England. He forestalled a Yorkist reaction by arresting the only direct male representative of the family, Richard III's nephew, the earl of Warwick. Richard's declared heir, the earl of Lincoln, however, apparently ingratiated himself with Henry and not only kept his liberty but received office and other marks of favour; while his father, the duke of Suffolk, likewise reconciled himself to the new regime. The earl of Surrey, Norfolk's son and heir, was kept in prison from the time of his capture at Bosworth until 1489. Another captain in Richard's army, the inactive earl of Northumberland, was likewise arrested and kept in the Tower of London until the end of 1485, when Henry decided that he was sufficiently reliable to resume his essential services in the north. The loyalty of northern England was very problematical. Richard had been Edward IV's lieutenant there for a dozen years, besides being a great landowner in Yorkshire, and had won considerable local goodwill. When Henry appointed commissioners to organise resistance against the Scots in September 1485, their first charge when enlisting men was to take from them oaths of loyalty to their new king. Two northern lords had their wings clipped in December, Viscount Beauchmont by giving financial security for his good behaviour and the earl of Westmorland by placing his heir in Henry's charge.[1]

In March 1486, after parliament had been dismissed, Henry set out for the north. Although he had to borrow money from the city of London for his expenses, this was not a large scale military expedition, but rather a progress so that, by showing himself to his people, he could try to win their loyalty and obedience. While at Lincoln, he learned that Lord Lovel, one of Richard's closest adherents who had disappeared after Bosworth, was scheming to waylay him. A body of armed men was hastily assembled and sent against the rebels. This show of force and a promise of pardon were enough to disperse the gathering. Lovel again escaped capture. Henry now went on to York where the inhabitants forgot their devotion to Richard and gave their new monarch a resounding welcome. Henry then turned southwestwards to receive further demonstrations of loyalty and civic pageantry in Hereford, Worcester, Gloucester and Bristol. There had been another abortive rising in this part of the country. The ringleaders, Thomas and Humphrey Stafford, were removed from sanctuary at Abingdon, Humphrey to suffer death as a traitor while his younger brother was pardoned. Only in the far north-west were there known to be any rebels still at large.

None of those who had conspired against Henry in this year were men of great substance or influence, and the rapid collapse of their efforts was a gratifying sign that the country had no mind for another king. Henry's prompt measures, tempering severity to the leaders with clemency for the rank and file, had soon snuffed out these damp squibs of revolt. By showing himself in the disaffected areas he had applied the traditional remedy, publicly making clear his intention to uphold the 'king's peace' and emphasising that he was the fountainhead not only of government but also of justice and mercy. The first anniversary of Bosworth saw Henry in full command of his kingdom. What is more, his wife gave birth to a son on 19 September, Arthur, whose name evoked the ancient glories of Britain celebrated in the most popular secular book of the day, *The Brut*. It must have seemed that the dynasties of Lancaster and York were now securely knit together. But Henry had enemies abroad ready to blow new life into the seemingly dead embers of the Wars of the Roses.

English diplomacy in the later middle ages

There had been three main strands in the foreign policies of England's medieval kings. They had, from 1066, held lands in France as feudal vassals of the French crown. Although Normandy was lost in 1204, Gascony remained in their possession for a further 250 years, valuable both to the king for its revenues and to his English subjects for its wine. The king's interest in Gascony was the principal cause of the Hundred Years War, for Edward III assumed the title of king of France after the French king had confiscated the duchy 'for acts of rebellion'. Thereafter all English kings claimed to be the lawful king of France, and their embassies refused to renounce the title even when military disasters compelled them to abandon the war. After 1453, only Calais remained of the sometime English conquests, but Englishmen thought poorly of a king who made no attempt to vindicate his French title. When the restored Edward IV proposed to attack the French king who had played a large part in his recent discomfiture, parliament readily granted supplies for war. In the event, Edward contented himself with a military excursion and soon returned home after Louis, at the bridge of Picquigny (29 August 1475), concluded a treaty of truce for seven years and promised to pay an annual pension. This undertaking was soon forgotten, as was a second for a marriage alliance, but the truce was continued and subsequently renewed.

England's hostile involvement in France obliged her to make

alliances with other powers which had reasons of their own for anti-French policies. The principalities of the Rhineland and the Low Countries, threatened by French expansion, long proved a fruitful recruiting ground for English allies. When English embassies came armed with promises of gold, even emperors were occasionally found ready to join an anti-French league. In the Spanish peninsula, the kingdom of Aragon tended to side with England as a result of French rivalry in Naples; while her hostile neighbour Castile followed a pro-French policy. The perpetual alliance made between England and Portugal in 1386 was a consequence of an attempt to strike against France by placing John of Gaunt on the Castilian throne. England's strongest continental link, however, was with Flanders. Its durability despite sporadic political breaches arose from common economic interests. The cloth industry of the Flemish towns depended on the supply of wool from England, and nowhere else was the latter assured of a comparable market for this, her greatest export; any interruption to this vital trading link resulted not only in serious social unrest but also severely reduced the revenues of the rulers of both countries. The acquisition of Flanders by the French dukes of Burgundy generally strengthened the connection with England, for the dukes aspired to an independent position in European politics and found in the English king a ready partner in opposition to Burgundy's overlord the king of France. The Anglo-Burgundian political alliance was not stable, because the dukes had too many interests and resources to accept a subordinate role. Charles the Bold married Edward IV's sister Margaret and in 1470 helped his brother-in-law to destroy the pro-French party of Henry VI; he made an agreement with Edward to partition France, but he failed to support his English ally in 1475.

The third persistent element in England's external relations was the state of war with Scotland. There had been no abiding peace on the northern border since Edward I's attempts to impose his sovereignty over the Scots. The independence of Scotland had been reluctantly recognised in 1328, but English kings periodically found occasion to resurrect the claim to overlordship. The Scots had in self-defence made an alliance with France in 1295, and both parties had from time to time felt it necessary to refresh this alliance during the course of the Hundred Years War; Scottish armies crossed the border when the English invaded France, Scottish troops occasionally joined the fight on French soil, more rarely French contingents served in Scotland. But although both the people and the geography of Scotland were too unyielding ever to be conquered, the Scottish king was incapable of inflicting a mortal blow on England's defences. His invading armies were regularly defeated, if they ever stood to fight, but more frequently his effectiveness was destroyed by the anarchical condition of his own country. A regular sequence of royal minorities and the restiveness of Scottish magnates, sometimes in English pay, virtually neutralised Scotland as a source of danger.

As long as England was at war with France, there was no prospect of a treaty of peace with Scotland. The Scottish kings, however, on account of their internal difficulties, were often prepared to make temporary truces with England. Although this meant that the two governments were then on civil if not amicable terms, their subjects in the border counties persistently ignored the official cessations of hostilities; raids and counter-raids, mounted by private enterprise, were a constant feature of border conditions, taking a steady toll in lives, burnt villages, ruined crops and stolen cattle. Neither king was able to give adequate protection to his border subjects, and it was thus scarcely remarkable that they should show little respect for his authority or loyalty to his person.

In recent years, Scotland had assumed greater importance in English eyes, less on account of her own strength than as a consequence of England's internal discord. James II had offered to help Richard of York to become king several years before he made his formal claim in 1460. In that year, the Scots were able to take and destroy the English fortress at Roxburgh. When Edward triumphed in England, the Scots took up the cause of Lancaster, sheltering Henry VI and his court. In return for promises of help, Henry surrendered Berwick-upon-Tweed and the Scots might have had Carlisle as well had they been able to take it. Edward in return fomented disorder by sheltering or pensioning Scottish rebels. Towards the end of his reign, the claim to supremacy over Scotland was brought out of the cupboard and in the course of a full-scale war Berwick was finally recovered for England in 1482. The border was thus restored to its pre-1461 limits.

The transformation of Western Europe

The pattern of European power was dramatically altered in the second half of the fifteenth century. In 1450 the French completed the subjugation of Normandy, thus finally erasing Henry V's conquests and in 1453 the last embers of resistance in Gascony were stamped out. There now remained to England of all her kings' ancient French territories and more recent gains only the strongly fortified port of Calais with its immediate hinterland. Then in 1477 Charles the Bold of Burgundy was killed in battle with the Swiss. As he left only a young daughter, Louis XI took possession of his lands in France, including Artois and the Somme towns ceded to Charles in 1468. The third member of the Anglo-French–Burgundian triangle had been dissolved. The French monarchy was the most authoritarian in Europe: it had a standing army, equipped with artillery; it could raise taxes and enact laws without the consent of national assemblies; it presided over a bureaucratic network giving effective control of the kingdom. There still were great magnates able, if united, to pose a serious challenge to royal authority, but the days of their political significance were numbered; only the duke of Brittany remained outside the full jurisdiction of the French crown. This compact, well-organised kingdom had resources in manpower and revenue three times as great as those at the disposal of the king of England. Only if he had a rush of blood to his head would the latter now consider mounting a single-handed effort to realise his pretensions to be the rightful king of France.

The part taken by the king of England for four hundred years as the principal adversary of France had to be abandoned as he was now outclassed. His place was to be taken by the ruler of Spain. Hitherto the mutual hostility of the kings of Aragon and Castile, their difficulties with their own subjects and preoccupation with the infidel presence in southern Spain, had effectively neutralised the Iberian peninsula in the power politics of western Europe. The two kingdoms were now joined by the marriage of Isabella of Castile and Ferdinand of Aragon (1469), and in 1492 their capture of Granada completed the ancient crusade against the Moors. The two monarchs established firm control over their kingdoms by reducing the power of the nobility and the privileges of constitutional assemblies. Aragon and Castile were not, however, united into a single kingdom until both Isabella and Ferdinand were dead. Only then, in 1516, was their grandson Charles sole monarch of both realms. He was also the heir of his father Philip of Hapsburg, son of the Emperor Maximilian and Mary, the daughter of Charles the Bold. Despite Philip's marriage to a Spanish princess, both he and Maximilian naturally pursued independent policies. In the time of Henry VII, Spain was not the colossus she was to become after his death; nor had the wealth of the Americas yet been exploited to fill the Spanish treasury. Henry had good reason to consider the king of France with apprehension but he cannot have regarded Ferdinand, still less Maximilian or Philip, as being in the same category.

An aggressive French king might easily have chosen to push forward his north-eastern frontier. The recovery of Calais for France was an obvious ambition. He might also have been tempted to resuscitate the former French suzerainty in Flanders, although the great cities there were notoriously difficult to rule. Fortunately for Henry VII, Charles VIII chose to turn to Italy to assert a claim to the kingdom of Naples. His Italian ambitions were doubly welcome to the English king. They meant, obviously the diversion of French military forces from the Channel coast; Henry had good reason for knowing that the sea was no sure defence against invasion. In addition, by involving himself in Italy, Charles challenged the Neapolitan claims of Aragon. Ferdinand had little immediate interest in the preservation of England's possession of Calais or her immunity from French invasion, but he recognised that England could be a serious nuisance to his enemy of France and accordingly decided that her new king's friendship was worth cultivating. The Italian wars, we might say, made Europe smaller. With all the great western powers having close interests in the peninsula, the scope of European diplomacy was extended to a scale unknown in the later middle ages. It was inevitable that efforts should be made to involve England in the network of anti-French alliances, even though their chief concern was with events on the other side of the continent, nor could Henry VII afford to remain entirely aloof and risk being left isolated against France.

'The new diplomacy'

The relations between European powers were now being conducted by methods almost unknown before the fifteenth century. In some accounts of this 'new diplomacy' its hallmarks are said to be insincerity and guile; kings and their envoys deliberately deceived their audiences, made promises which they had no intention of performing, while the treaties they made were broken as soon as 'reasons of state' made them inconvenient. It is undoubtedly true that diplomatic morality was not high in Henry VII's time, but we cannot pretend that deceit was unknown in earlier international dealings, nor that all treaties were faithfully observed: the treaty of Brétigny (1361) is a case in point here. What was really novel in late fifteenth-century diplomacy lay in its methods of communication. Princes made a practice of accrediting representatives to foreign courts, where they resided, sending back to their governments long, detailed reports on conversations with kings and their councillors, describing these persons, particularly their characters, and also conditions and events in their country. These envoys were personal representatives of their monarchs, known to have their employers' confidence. They engaged agents to provide information, they even arranged to pay pensions to influential members of the courts where they resided in order to attach their interest and favour. This was a great change from the temporary arrangements of medieval diplomacy, with its large 'solemn embassies' appointed and despatched when occasion arose, acting in accordance with the terms of their commissions and detailed instructions, and—for less formal purposes—the employment of heralds to deliver written messages. The 'new diplomacy' was much more flexible, more rapid in communication, and its purposes were wider than those of the cumbersome, *ad hoc* embassies of medieval kings.

Despite these innovations in diplomatic practice, we cannot say that foreign affairs were now conducted on a 'modern' basis. In the most developed royal governments, kings still stood at the centre of affairs. They were their own prime ministers and commanders-in-chief. They were also their own foreign secretaries. Their envoys to foreign courts were their personal agents, chosen and instructed by themselves; when embassies visited a court, they addressed the king and he replied. As we know from reports by ambassadors to England, Henry himself decided what answer he should give, and his own skill in the arts of diplomatic conversation was one of his most useful assets in the conduct of foreign affairs. The fact that international diplomacy meant the personal relations between different princes is best illustrated by their use of matrimony as an instrument of foreign policy. Treaties of alliance included provisions for marriage between children of the contracting parties. Often enough the children in question were too young to be married and could only be betrothed, and their parents might call off the match if the alliance had served its purpose or broken down. These dynastic marriages were so commonplace that their significance was often transient. They could lead to the union of crowns when death removed older brothers and sisters, but in general they only marked temporary rapprochements and were no guarantee against fresh outbreaks of hostilities.

Lambert Simnel

After his first year as king, Henry may well have felt his position at home to be assured. Throughout the country government in his name had been accepted; in all branches of national and local administration, his nominees had been performing their enjoined tasks without challenge. The diehard adherents of Richard III had shown their hand and had failed ignominiously. It must have seemed to Henry that the irreconcilables had now revealed themselves and had been dealt with; those still beyond his reach could do him no serious harm. If he did so assume, he was being sanguine enough to mistake acquiescence for loyalty. The English had become too accustomed to dramatic reversals of royal fortunes, too resigned to expecting little general benefit from the hands of their king for the time being. They were submissive enough when there was no rival claimant to their obedience, but when one did appear, their loyalty turned to apathy, and they awaited the denouement with Anglo-Saxon phlegm. If Henry had indeed become complacent about his subjects' devotion, he was to be unpleasantly awakened.

From the end of 1486 rumours of some new conspiracy in favour of the earl of Warwick began to circulate. The earl was, of course, in the Tower of London, but there seems to have been some idea that he had disappeared. This belief was seized upon by an Oxford priest called Richard Simonds who had been educating the son of a local tradesman. The boy, Lambert Simnel, seemingly bore some resemblance to the sons of Edward IV and Simonds had thought of grooming him so that he might pass for one of the murdered princes.

Now he decided that his ten-year-old protégé should impersonate Warwick. He took him to Ireland, where the imposture was accepted. Henry had left the government of the country in the hands of the earl of Kildare, a great landowner who had first been appointed deputy-lieutenant by Edward IV. Ireland's attachment to the Yorkist dynasty dated from the time Duke Richard had been Henry VI's lieutenant there. Whether or not the Irish leaders genuinely believed Simnel to be a scion of that house, they showed little hesitation in having him crowned. The pretender was equally promptly recognised by Edward IV's sister Margaret, the widow of Charles the Bold of Burgundy. When messengers from Ireland solicited her support, she eagerly seized the opportunity to strike at Henry, whom she hated, and provided a force of 2,000 German soldiers under the able command of Martin Schwarz.

There were ramifications of conspiracy in England itself, but Henry was slow to discover them. In February 1487 a judicial commission was sent into Devon and Cornwall and local gentry were named as traitors. Edward IV's dowager and his stepson the marquess of Dorset were placed in detention, Elizabeth being deprived of her lands on the authority of an assembly of peers. To expose Simnel's imposture, the real Warwick was exhibited in London. Among those attending the council of lords, however, was Richard III's nephew and acknowledged heir, the earl of Lincoln. Henry believed that he had won Lincoln to himself, but he was abruptly undeceived when the earl precipitately made for Flanders to join his aunt Margaret and the elusive Lord Lovel. Lincoln then went with Lovel and Schwarz to Dublin, arriving on 5 May, shortly before Simnel's coronation on 24 May as King Edward VI. Lincoln certainly knew that the genuine Warwick was in the Tower, but he became the leader of the pretender's forces. Possibly his plan was to use Simnel as a figurehead, because the Irish had accepted him, and then to discard him when the time was ripe to advance his own claim to be king.

Henry meanwhile had betrayed his unease by offering a pardon, even to proscribed rebels like Thomas Broughton. He expected a landing in East Anglia, from Flanders, and went there to keep watch. Local arrays were ordered on 7 April, but a week later he turned towards the midlands to await developments from the royal fortress at Kenilworth. Lincoln landed his men in Furness on 4 June, crossed the Pennines to the vale of York, and then rapidly moved southward. Henry struck his camp on the 8th, and after a forced march to Lough-borough advanced more slowly along the south bank of the Trent with his forces drawn up for battle. Lincoln crossed the river above Newark and the two armies met south of the town, at East Stoke, on 16 June. Although outnumbered, Lincoln decided on instant attack, and the experienced valour of his German mercenaries and the wild courage of the unarmoured Irish severely tested the royal front line. After three hours, when Lincoln's resistance cracked, his lines were overrun with such speed that the earl himself, Schwarz, Broughton and other leaders perished in the slaughter. Others fled, among them Lovel, who was never seen again. Simnel and his tutor were captured; both were spared, the boy becoming a turnspit in the royal kitchen, while Simonds, out of respect for his holy orders, was confined to a bishop's prison. The majority of the 4,000 slain at Stoke were Lincoln's followers, perhaps nearly a half of his army.[2]

The last battle of the Wars of the Roses cannot have given the victor unmixed cause for satisfaction. It was no credit to his rule that it had happened at all. Moreover, the first severe crisis of his reign had shown Henry how slender was his hold on the throne. Gentry in Norfolk had shown little enthusiasm in putting their swords at his disposal and quibbled over the *bona fides* of his commissioner of array. Rumours of his death went about before the battle and caused reinforcements to turn back. On the field, the wings of his army had not entered the fray, holding back, perhaps, to await the result; had Henry been struck by a chance shot, they would doubtless have declared for 'Edward VI'. Henry is reported to have ordered Lincoln to be taken alive so that he might discover the earl's sympathisers, the royal soldiers to have killed him lest the sparing of one life might lead to the loss of many others. There had even been a case of treason in the king's own household, as an act of the next parliament revealed. It must have been impressed upon Henry that he had to take more positive measures to secure his people's goodwill. One step in this direction was taken on 25 November, when Elizabeth of York was belatedly crowned as his queen. Another was the measure against lawlessness known as 'the Star Chamber Act'. A second lesson should have been that the moment was not opportune for an active part in foreign affairs. As he returned from a progress to Northumberland, however, Henry was visited by French ambassadors whose message tempted him to intervene in the affairs of their country.

Brittany

The news from France was that the royal forces had repelled attacks from the east by Maximilian and had also achieved some success in Brittany. The duchy's aging ruler, Francis II, had no son, but two daughters, and it was the aim of the French government to absorb Brittany into the kingdom through marriage of the heiress to Charles VIII. The Breton nobles wished to preserve their independence, but they were divided and variously attempted to enlist Maximilian or other potential champions by making offers of marriage. As Henry told a papal ambassador, he could not idly watch France assume control of the duchy; he professed bonds of gratitude to the duke for his long hospitality, but he also, and more credibly, said that such an eventuality, giving France complete master of the whole southern shore of the Channel, would pose a serious threat to England. In February 1488, Henry sent a force of three ships to sea against his 'enemies', and a body of volunteers under his wife's uncle, Lord Scales, crossed over to aid the Bretons. An envoy was also sent to both the French and Breton courts; at neither was his reception cordial and Henry was obliged to disown Scales and renew the truce with France. Then a crushing victory by the French led to the treaty of Sablé on 20 August 1488, whereby Duke Francis promised not to marry his daughter without permission from the French king. Two weeks later he was dead.

France claimed the custody of the young Duchess Anne, but the Bretons established a regency. Henry now took the initiative in organising the defence of the duchy. Preparations were made for military action, but understandably in view of his uncertainty about his own subjects' loyalties, he preferred to proceed by diplomatic means, by offering his offices as a mediator to France, by seeking to recruit allies to deter the French government. In February 1489, treaties were made with Maximilian, restoring the Anglo-Burgundian accord of Edward IV's time, and at Radon with Brittany, with whom Henry was able to dictate terms: he undertook to provide 6,000 troops upon the Bretons giving security to pay their wages. Then on 27 March his envoys at Medina del Campo drafted the articles of a treaty with Aragon and Castile.

This came a year after Henry's first overture to the Spanish court that his son Arthur should marry Katherine, the daughter of Ferdinand and Isabella who, at three, was six months older than her proposed husband. The family connection was to crown a political alliance. The Spanish monarchy, with its grievance at the continuing French occupation of Roussillon and Cerdagne, was an appropriate source for a wife for Henry's heir. The same consideration brought Ferdinand, once he was assured of Henry's stability in England, to give his agreement in principle to the alliance. The terms were now hammered out. Ferdinand gave way to Henry's demands about the size of Katherine's dowry, but on the political side of the treaty the two monarchs undertook, in the event of war with France, not to make peace unless England was ceded Normandy and Gascony or Spain was restored Roussillon and Cerdagne. As France would be little harmed by the latter concession, but would obviously never yield such extensive territories to England unless defeated in war, Ferdinand appears to have gained an excessive advantage over Henry; nor did he agree to a date when Katherine should go to England. Henry took this as a pretext for not ratifying the treaty for eighteen months, and when he did so, in September 1490, he added terms which the Spanish sovereigns are not known to have accepted. The treaty of Medina del Campo thus became no more than a scrap of parchment, as far as plans for war against France were concerned, although the association of England and Spain was to be continued and confirmed by the marriage.

Henry sent the promised force to Brittany in April 1489. He was then immediately distracted by a serious insurrection in Yorkshire. The earl of Northumberland, attempting to overcome opposition to the parliamentary tax for the war, was killed by a mob, which then remained together, tried to raise the north and actually took possession of York city. Again the king had to send an army against his subjects and make another northern visitation to subdue and punish rebels. His soldiers in Brittany were less successful, but one continental victory was won for English arms when the garrison of Calais rescued Maximilian's garrison at Dixmude from Flemish rebels. Maximilian showed scant gratitude for this service when he made peace with France six weeks later, on 22 July. The French, seconded by the pope, now tried to persuade Henry likewise to abandon Brittany, but although he entered into negotiations he was not yet prepared to risk the consequent loss of face with his subjects. Their attitude was made clear in parliament, when Henry's reports on the inadequate offers by the French prompted the members to grant further supplies for war. Abroad, he strove to rebuild the anti-French coalition. The volatile Maximilian, having subdued the Flemings, was again drawn in and in December 1490 married the duchess of Brittany by proxy. In the following April, however, Breton resistance was wrecked by treachery, and with Maximilian engaged in Hungary and Ferdinand against Granada, Henry was unable to answer the duchess's desperate call for aid. She therefore accepted Charles VIII's offer of his hand in marriage, and the independence of the duchy was no more.

The invasion of France

Henry's reaction was to prepare for a full-scale war with France. So far, he had operated under the pretext that he was not a principal in the Breton war of independence; he had provided the duchess with troops, but like a mercenary captain, in the expectation of pay. He had thus been able to keep diplomatic links with France. His intervention in Brittany had been fruitless and his costs had not been paid; he had been hurt in both pride and pocket, and he recognised the greater peril of French enmity, now that the Breton ports commanding the western approaches were in French hands. A parliament was called for 17 October, and the commons, stirred by the chancellor's denunciation of French deceits, recalled England's former victories and granted two subsidies so that Henry could recover his forbears' ancient rights in France. All through the winter, preparations were made for the coming invasion, with men, ships, guns, tents and supplies of all kinds being brought together.

How serious were Henry's military plans? It would seem incredible that he believed that England could on its own hope successfully to wage war against the mightiest kingdom in Europe. When we consider the outcome, how Henry consented to be bought off, we readily conclude that his sole object was to make a show of force to achieve a settlement on a cash basis. Yet we may doubt if this was persistently his aim from the time he held the war parliament of October 1491. It took him a whole year after that actually to begin his invasion. When he did leave for France on 2 October 1492, he crossed from Sandwich to Calais. Yet earlier in the year, he had arranged to assemble his men at Portsmouth and erected breweries there to stimulate their valour. He had a plan to seize Brest with the help of disaffected Bretons, and Portsmouth was the most suitable base for an army for Brittany. The French government unearthed the plot and considered attacking England. Henry then had to look to his own defences until this threat evaporated. The summer thus passed away and Henry, with an army gathered and paid for, now had to settle for a last fling to win something with it.

The campaign was soon over. The English left Calais on 18 October to lay siege to Boulogne. Nine days later Henry received an offer of terms from the French, and on 3 November a treaty was concluded at Étaples. The two kings were to be at peace and not support the other's enemies, their subjects might trade on equal terms. Charles also undertook to reimburse Henry for his expenses in Brittany and make up the arrears of the pension due under the treaty of Picquigny; the total of 745,000 gold crowns was to be paid at an annual rate of 50,000 crowns (a little under £5,000). This would still have left Henry the poorer for the past year's military expenses, but he could look forward to this much additional income for fifteen years. Like Edward IV, he had preferred peace with cash to military glory, but he had saved his dignity from the Breton débâcle. He had, undoubtedly, abandoned his continental allies, but they had deserted him in the recent past. The treaty of Étaples was the most realistic conclusion to Henry's French adventures. It was more important for England to be at peace with France than with any other country. Charles' ambitions were set on Italy, and he equally wanted peace in the north. Henry was not to be tempted to take advantage of France's Italian involvement. His pacific policy towards France was not only directly beneficial to England, it also opened the way to a better understanding with France's ancient ally, the king of Scots.

By paying off his disbanded troops, Henry hoped to allay their frustrated hopes of honour and plunder in France. His captains had drawn up a reasoned statement to justify the abandonment of the campaign, and with this he also trusted to win approval for the treaty. It is apparent, then, that the king expected adverse criticism from his disappointed warriors and his no less bellicose taxpayers. With Edward IV's precedent in mind, however, he need not fear reproach from sometime followers of York. There was a risk of sedition springing from criticism, from those who compared the seventh Henry with the fifth. There was also the serious danger of apathy. Henry VII had done nothing to make him a popular hero and his subjects might show scant warmth in his defence should a new threat to his security appear.

Perkin Warbeck

The French war and peace both helped to set a new conspiracy into motion. A trio of obscure malcontents, still playing with the name of Warwick, had good cause to hope that King Charles would help to launch another 'Yorkist' claimant. At Étaples, he promised to expel all such plotters from his dominions, but Maximilian, aggrieved at his desertion, was ready to give them assistance; while his mother-in-law of Burgundy predictably continued to keep open house for Henry's enemies. Ferdinand and Isabella had no more immediate need for the English alliance after recovering Cerdagne and Roussillon in January 1493, and could not be trusted to adhere to the treaty of Medina del Campo and its clause against harbouring English conspirators. In Scotland, James IV was prepared only to make truces with England and was watching for an opportunity to win back Berwick. Then to complete the ring was Ireland, virtually an independent country since Henry's authority there was almost non-existent, and because of his French commitments he had been unable to impose it. A year after Simnel's rising, he sent Sir Richard Edgecombe there, but the sole fruits of his mission were oaths of loyalty. The earl of Kildare remained as lieutenant, blandly disregarding pressing invitations to visit the king in England.

It was in Ireland that the new trouble began. In the autumn of 1491 a Breton merchant put into Cork. One of his crew, a seventeen-year-old native of Tournai called Perkin Warbeck, so struck the citizens with his handsome bearing that they concluded that he must have been of royal descent. He denied the mayor's suggestion that he was the earl of Warwick, but was persuaded to impersonate Richard, the younger of Edward IV's murdered sons, 'and so', as he later confessed, 'they made me to learn English and taught me what I should do and say'. His promoters were men of humble origin, but they hopefully solicited aid from Kildare, and the kings of France and Scotland. Warbeck went to France to organise a descent on England in conjunction with a Yorkist rising, but the treaty of

Étaples compelled him to take refuge with Margaret of Burgundy, who received him as a nephew.

Although Henry professed scorn for 'this lad who calls himself a Plantagenet', his actions indicate his real alarm. He was for some time ignorant of Warbeck's true origin: after all, even if it was common belief that Richard III had killed his nephews, the bodies had not been found. Sovereigns abroad were taking Warbeck for a prince—might he not have been one? Henry's fickle subjects, he may have thought, might think likewise, or enough of them to instigate a rising, while the remainder might have left it to fate to decide the truth of Warbeck's claim. When Henry discovered where Warbeck was, he sent envoys to the Flemish court; when it refused to co-operate, he broke off trade relations, on 18 September 1493. This disruption of England's principal commerce is the measure of Henry's concern. More, he put the country's eastern defences on the alert.

Fortunately for Henry, Maximilian was too impoverished to win a throne for his protégé, but still more welcome to the English king was the distraction provided by Charles of France. His triumphal march through Italy to win the kingdom of Naples led to the formation at Venice on 30 March 1495 of a 'holy league' of the pope, Maximilian, Ferdinand, Venice and Milan. Charles escaped their net but manifested his intention to return. His operations gave Henry a two-fold advantage. In the first place, he was left free to deal with signs of revolt in England. In May 1493, a commission was appointed to investigate reports of conspiracies in fifteen northern and midland shires, and at the same time the county commissions of the peace were subjected to their most drastic purge since Bosworth and several members of the king's council were added to them.[3] In Ireland, only the earl of Desmond among the leading peers had emerged as an adherent of Warbeck, and when Henry sent Sir Edward Poynings there as lord-lieutenant in October 1494 he met little serious opposition.

Lord Stanley's treason

Henry's spies were active at home and abroad; they discovered Warbeck's origin and the names of some of his sympathisers. Sir Robert Clifford, who infiltrated the councils of Margaret of Burgundy, earned £500 for his disclosures. The suspects were arrested and brought to trial early in 1495. Sir Simon Mountford, a Warwickshire landowner and magistrate, and two more gentlemen were executed, while several others were hanged. The dean of St. Paul's, two friars and two priests were also convicted, but their lives were spared, as were those of some other laymen. The most notable victim of the tribunal was Sir William Stanley, brother of the earl of Derby and a major contributor to the victory at Bosworth. More serious still, Stanley was chamberlain of Henry's household, while another to be sentenced, Lord FitzWalter, had been its steward.[4] The actual extent of Stanley's treason, according to Polydore Vergil, was to have said that if Warbeck was indeed Edward IV's son, he would not fight against him. Had Stanley, perhaps, only been trying to insure against a Yorkist restoration? Henry is said to have decided that Stanley should be executed as an example, to give notice that he would spare no traitor, however eminent. This may be true, although he might not have acted with cool deliberation, but in a rush of alarm at realising how close to his person this canker of disaffection had taken root.

The conspiracy seemingly had wide ramifications, for high-powered judicial commissions were appointed to investigate and try suspects in twenty-six counties from the Welsh border to the south and east coasts. In the summer, the king made a progress by way of Worcester to Chester and Manchester with the obvious object of awing Stanley's tenants and retainers.[5]

When a parliament met on 14 October following, Stanley and the other convicted traitors were attainted. The same parliament, however, passed the celebrated *De facto* act which declared that service to an overthrown king was not treasonable, even if he had not rightly been king. Its object was to reassure former servants of Richard III that Henry did not harbour designs against them.* His lack of rancour was further publicised by the simultaneous annulment of acts of attainder against the earl of Kildare and the heirs of six adherents of Richard condemned in 1485. Henry was obviously most anxious to remove possible motives for revolt.

The treason had been discovered in good time. The Flemings were now becoming restive under the ruinous effects of the loss of their supply of English wool. Maximilian was stimulated to do something

* There could be another interpretation, *viz.* that the act would safeguard Henry's present supporters in the event of Warbeck's victory. This can be rejected because Henry's supplanter would not be bound by his statutes.

useful for his protégé and thus be rid of his presence. He was the more ready to act because, on 24 January 1495, Warbeck had made Maximilian and next his son, Philip, heirs to his rights in the kingdoms of England and France. In July, Maximilian was hoping that Warbeck would soon be king of England and join in a grand assault on France. But, of course, it was now too late. When Warbeck with the force provided by his host appeared off Deal on the 3rd of that month, the king was ready for him. There was no rising for the pretender. The two or three hundred of his men who landed were overwhelmed by the Kentish levies and the four score survivors were led off to the gallows. Warbeck then made for Ireland. Here again, thanks to Poynings' vigilance, he was forced to withdraw. This time he went to Scotland, where James IV received him with the honours due to his pretended rank and provided him with a cousin for wife.

Henry and the Holy League

Henry's second gain from Charles VIII's Italian ambitions was that the continental powers again became interested in England as a potential ally. As the Holy League prepared to face a second French invasion of Italy, its members hoped that Henry would join them, to complete the ring of enemies round France. Maximilian disagreed with his partners: he professed distrust in Henry, and preferred to await the outcome of Warbeck's efforts which, if successful, would make England a reliable ally. Other members were afraid that Henry would be enticed into an alliance with France. Their fears of this prospect were raised by cordial overtures from Charles to Henry, including offers of practical assistance against the pretender. Ferdinand now resurrected his interest in the marriage alliance originally arranged at Medina del Campo. He tried to persuade Maximilian to abandon Warbeck. Maximilian's son Philip had done this, with the result that trade between Flanders and England was resumed by a treaty concluded on 24 February 1496 (Bacon's 'Intercursus Magnus'). Maximilian, however, remained opposed to Henry, whom he suspected of exploiting his desirability as an ally for the sole purpose of ruining Warbeck. Despite his objections, an English delegate was received at a meeting of the League in Augsburg and on 18 July England was admitted as a member without being bound to wage war on France. Ferdinand's argument—that Henry's neutrality was preferable to his alliance with France—had prevailed. On 1 October

8 Bust of Henry VII

9 Chamber Receipts, August 1492, with Henry's old and new sign-manuals

10 Canterbury Cathedral

11 Morton's Tower, Lambeth Palace

following, the Spanish sovereigns concluded a new agreement with Henry for the marriage of Katherine and Arthur, this time with elaborate provisions to ensure that it would take place.

Ferdinand's championship of Henry did not end here. He also intervened with James IV to persuade him to give up Warbeck. His interest in doing this was clear enough, for Henry's envoy at Augsburg had blamed the Scottish danger for Henry's inability to fight in France. James had undertaken to assist Warbeck in return for a promise to cede Berwick and pay £50,000. Charles of France also endeavoured to detach James from Warbeck lest Henry should feel compelled to join the League for his own protection. Charles also tried to purchase Warbeck, who would have been a valuable hostage, but James honourably rejected all these overtures. When the invasion was mounted in September 1496, however, it petered out as another border raid. Warbeck failed to attract any English support. Henry retaliated by a declaration of war and on 16 January 1497 held a parliament which voted a heavy tax so that the king could punish this breach of the peace by his Scottish vassal; this renewal of the claim to suzerainty gave warning that Henry proposed to subjugate the Scots. The collection of the taxes, however, provoked a massive insurrection in Cornwall and Henry had to concentrate all his military resources against the rebels. They were overwhelmed in a pitched battle at Blackheath on 17 June; only the three leaders were executed, the remainder were fined, pardoned and sent home.

This dangerous revolt obliged the king to give up his plans against Scotland. Ambassadors were sent to propose a treaty of peace. James, in contrast, decided that Henry's position was crumbling. He planned a second invasion while Warbeck went by sea to raise a new Cornish rebellion. Henry easily repelled the Scottish attack, in August. Warbeck, meanwhile, had wasted time in a fruitless effort to enlist Irish support, and when he reached Cornwall on 7 September the king was able to bring some of his forces from the Scottish border. This was enough to disperse the few thousands who had rallied to the pretender. He took refuge in Beaulieu Abbey, in Hampshire, surrendered on promise of a pardon, publicly confessed his imposture, and was comfortably lodged in the king's household; as a foreigner, he could not be accused of treason. The miserable collapse of his schemes now inclined King James to put an end to his profitless war. Prompted by the Spanish representative, he took up

D

Henry's offer of friendly relations, and on 30 September a treaty of truce for seven years was sealed.

The conclusion of Warbeck's travels thus saw England in a much more assured place in the European community. Six years ago she had been isolated, now she had meaningful alliances with Spain and Flanders. The alliance between Spain and Flanders, whereby Philip was married to Joanna, the eventual heiress of Ferdinand and Isabella, and the economic interdependence of Flanders and England, gave this triple entente a fair prospect of continuity. Despite these connections, Henry kept relations with France on an amicable basis; there was a trading agreement in 1497, the death of Charles VIII in 1498 was marked, in London, with appropriate solemnity, and the treaty of Étaples was renewed with his successor, Louis XII. There are varying reports of Henry's demeanour in these critical years: Polydore credits him with complete self-control, the more contemporary testimony of foreign diplomats tell of his alarm. He had undoubtedly been favoured by fortune, by the incompetence of his adversaries, by the coincidence of French aggression in Italy. But he needed this dispensation, for his own throne was scarcely set on a rock, and he certainly made good use of his opportunities, exploiting European divisions to buttress his position. It is probable that but for Warbeck Henry would have preferred a less strenuous foreign policy; his own kingdom required his full attention. He had, however, shaped a pattern for his diplomatic policy and he intended to preserve it.

Marriages and deaths

With the capture of Perkin Warbeck, the reign of Henry VII took on a smoother course. To the end of his life, he continued to be beset by real or imagined threats from traitors of Yorkist provenance; but he never again was required to raise an army to repulse invasion or rebellion. Another self-styled earl of Warwick disturbed him early in 1499, but the impostor, Ralph Wilford, was given short shrift. The incident seemingly had a serious effect on Henry—he is reported to have aged twenty years in two weeks—and may well have prompted him to consider eliminating the genuine earl. Warbeck, who had been put in the Tower following an attempt to escape, was eager to entertain fresh plans for freedom. A scheme was put in hand on 2 August, and there are some grounds for suspecting that Henry knew all about it from the beginning, for it was discovered as soon as it had gone far enough, and one of the most active plotters, Robert Claymond, was pardoned; he may have been an *agent-provocateur*. Warbeck was hanged, and Warwick, who had been implicated, was beheaded on 28 November. He had been a prisoner since 1485, when he was ten, and his guilt of any design against Henry is more than questionable; his real offence was to be the only direct male representative of York as the son of the duke of Clarence. Henry's slight hold on popular affection was not enhanced by this judicial murder of an innocent youth.

It must be recalled, however, that hitherto Henry had shown marked reluctance to impose capital sentences on his defeated adversaries. His departure from this moderate record is partially explicable by the cumulative effect of the series of alarms he had suffered from conspirators, so that now, on account of advancing years and declining health, he lacked the resilience to take a balanced view of these dangers. He was also under some pressure to remove Warwick, for the Spanish ambassador quite pertinently argued that Katherine's parents would feel more assured of her future as an English queen if not 'a drop of doubtful royal blood' remained in England. The arrangements for her marriage were still being discussed, but the new alliance between England and Spain was defined by a treaty made in London on 10 July 1499. With Louis of France getting ready to occupy the duchy of Milan, and Henry no longer hamstrung with internal dangers, Ferdinand was prepared to accept him on equal terms. Neither ally fully trusted the other, and progress towards the marriage was marked by fresh guarantees and secret probings by envoys to discover each king's real intentions. Eventually Katherine arrived in England on 2 October 1501 and she was married to Arthur on 14 November following. Behind the splendour of the attendant pageanty, critics saw the ghost of young Warwick.

The marriage of a second of Henry's children was arranged in the following year. This was Margaret, promised to James IV of Scotland, with a modest dowry, when he and Henry concluded a treaty of peace on 24 January 1502. This wedding took place in Edinburgh on 8 August 1503. Although it led to the union of the English and Scottish crowns exactly a century later, this marriage alliance was no more enduring on the political side than the union with Spain. The personal relations of Henry VII and his Scottish son-in-law were generally good, but the ancient enmity of the two nations was not extinguished and the persistence of border 'incidents' put a severe strain on the goodwill between the monarchs. The Scots still clung to their French alliance; for England, peace with France remained her best guarantee of peace with Scotland. Henry's unique policy towards Scotland was successful because he avoided trouble with France, but James' English wife could not prevent his march to Flodden when her brother Henry VIII invaded France in 1513.

Henry VII's later relations with the continental powers were unhinged by mortality. His most grievous blow was the death of Arthur on 2 April 1502. With only one remaining son, the eleven-year-old Henry, his own house appeared in danger of extinction, and the execution of Sir James Tyrell and the arrest of two nephews of Edward IV in the following months suggests that others appreciated the fresh opportunities offered by Henry's domestic disaster; another nephew of Edward's, the earl of Suffolk, Lincoln's brother, had already fled to Maximilian; and it appears that even in the king's household men were weighing their chances against a fresh dynastic upheaval. Abroad, France and Spain were enjoying a robbers' honeymoon after their partition of Naples in 1500. Henry wished to renew the Spanish connection by marrying the younger Henry to the widowed Katherine. Ferdinand was complaisant but thought he could now exact better terms from England. Henry held out until France and Spain quarrelled in 1503, and a French rapprochement with Maximilian and Philip threatened Ferdinand with isolation. Thus when the young pair were betrothed on 25 June, it was on Henry's terms and Ferdinand had to fight France alone. Then, after expelling the French from Italy, the Spanish king made another complete volte-face and in October 1504 entered a close alliance with Louis XII.

The reason for this turnabout was the death of Isabella of Castile; in consequence, the sovereignty of her kingdom passed to her daughter Joanna, the wife of Philip of Burgundy. Ferdinand had espoused a French wife to gain Louis' support in excluding Philip and Joanna from her inheritance. Henry's reaction to the Franco-Aragonese compact was to turn to Maximilian and Philip for continental friends; his alliance was the more welcome because he was able to advance huge sums of money to finance Philip's expedition to Castile. The unfortunate Katherine received shabby treatment as a result of her father's diplomatic vagaries: Henry kept her on short commons, and although a dispensation was received from the pope for her re-marriage, the younger Henry registered a protest against the match in June 1505, while his father openly considered French and Burgundian brides for him. King Henry had himself entered the matrimonial market after Elizabeth of York died in 1502. As Ferdinand had illustrated, a king was never too old for a new wife. With only one male heir, a second wife might have appeared a necessity for Henry VII, but as he showed no real urgency in finding one it is clear that he was only using his marriageability as a diplomatic pawn. He contemplated the duchess of Savoy when he warmed to Maximilian and Philip, the widowed queen of Naples on veering towards Ferdinand, and even his Spanish daughter-in-law. There is to us something grotesque about Henry's matrimonial schemes, but to him and his contemporaries they were normal measures of foreign policy.

In these last years, moreover, Henry felt the need to make use of all the assets he could muster, so rapidly did the kaleidoscope of European relations revolve. He achieved a diplomatic triumph when Philip, en route for Spain, was driven by storm into a Dorset port in January 1506. Overwhelmed by the warmth of Henry's hospitality, he entered into a treaty of alliance at Windsor on 9 February, arranged for Henry's marriage to Margaret of Savoy, and, before leaving, empowered his agents to conclude a trade agreement. The last (Bacon's 'Intercursus Magnus') was signed on 30 April, but as it was never ratified, it brought no advantage to English merchants in the Netherlands. Philip was also persuaded, reluctantly, to surrender the earl of Suffolk, who was imprisoned in the Tower until his execution in 1513. The treaty of Windsor promised Henry the assurance of a strong continental ally, especially after Philip and Joanna had successfully established themselves in Castile, but this prospect was shattered by Philip's death in the following September. Ferdinand resumed control of Castile as guardian of the unbalanced Joanna, and Flanders once more passed into the unpopular charge of Maximilian. Fearful lest France should exploit this occasion to penetrate the Low Countries, Henry and Maximilian drew together and planned a marriage between Mary Tudor and Philip's heir, Charles. Henry expressed himself to be willing to marry Joanna himself, and renewed his proposal for a French wife for his son. These schemes were all designed to isolate Ferdinand of Aragon. They came to nothing, for Ferdinand, still the genius of the diplomatic scene, countered with a plan for a great coalition for the purpose of dismembering the republic of Venice. Blessed by the pope, Louis, Ferdinand and Maximilian formed their league at Cambrai in December 1508. It was Henry who was left outside. No doubt he considered the setback only a temporary one. He would justifiably not have given the league a good expectation of life, but he died twelve months too soon to witness its collapse.

Henry's diplomatic achievement

The lavish expenditure on the festivities at the wedding of Arthur and Katherine in 1502 signalled Henry's satisfaction at the fulfilment of hopes entertained since his accession to the throne. A Spanish bride for his heir proclaimed the respectability of the Tudors, both to Europe at large and to English subjects. The marriage was designed, of course, as the keystone of a political alliance, but to Henry it was a triumph in itself; for he knew Ferdinand of Aragon too well to rely on the observation of the treaty. Diplomatically, the value of the marriage was transient; although Ferdinand assented to Katherine's marriage to the future Henry VIII, and she remained in England, Henry VII did not allow it to take place in his lifetime. It is obviously untrue, though it has often been written, that Henry made marriage alliances with foreign powers in order to ensure his dynasty's tenure of the English throne. Much of his diplomatic activity was concerned with making Europe unsafe for English pretenders, and in this he had some success. But the only sure defences he had against rebellion were those at his immediate command, in England. His own experience, as both claimant and defendant, had shown that an armed struggle for the crown was settled much too quickly for foreign allies to be of any use.

The main objective of Henry's foreign policy was to prevent England from being drawn into war.* He lacked the resources to make any military impression on his continental neighbours; the effort was more likely to stir up unrest at home. After the treaty of Étaples, therefore, he sedulously avoided giving offence to the king of France, even when nominally allied against him. These other alliances were Henry's insurance policy against France. It was not his programme to keep a balance of power in Europe; the very idea

* The promotion of English trade is considered in Chapter 7.

is an anachronism. What he did was to follow the mutations of other powers and take steps to prevent his own isolation. Ferdinand of Aragon was the guiding spirit in this fluctuating diplomatic scene, of whom it was said that he was indignant when accused of once deceiving France: he wanted credit for a two-fold deception. The feverish activity of Henry's last years reveals his awareness of having achieved nothing durable. The deaths of princes accelerated the twists of European diplomacy. In this fluid situation Henry did his utmost to keep abreast. Possibly his fears were groundless; there is a parallel between his diplomacy and his conduct of government in England, which reveals how little he trusted in the loyalty of any subject. In both fields, his experiences justified suspicion.

5

Central Government

HENRY'S accession made him the master of a governmental system created and modified by the requirements of his predecessors in the previous four centuries. As in all earlier dynastic upheavals, the civil service remained in its posts, every member ready to serve the new king in the well-established functions of his office. All that was necessary for the bureaucratic departments of Chancery, Exchequer and Privy Seal Office, and the no less formalised offices of household and great and privy wardrobes, was the stimulus of royal initiative. If these ancient institutions merited reform, they escaped it, and their internal history in Henry's reign shows unbroken continuity. The Exchequer was the exception, but what it suffered was not reform but neglect and curtailment of its functions. These various offices, however, were only the instruments of royal government, impersonal in themselves, but directed by the personal inspiration of the king. The use he made of this machinery depended on his own qualities of character and intellect, the capacity of those who gave him counsel, the extent of his resources, and the eventualities he had to meet.

The council of Henry VII

In his sermon to parliament in 1484, Richard III's chancellor described the king and his council as 'the womb of this great body politic of England', 'this womb of busy thought, care and pensiveness'. It was essential for every king to have a group of advisers, a body which would not only provide him with information on any topic but could relieve him of much of the routine of day-to-day administration. To a new king, ignorant of English affairs and the organisation of English government, the formation of a council was of necessity the first act of the reign. Henry VII could certainly not have waited six months, as Polydore Vergil stated, before establishing a council. In fact, Henry already had a council before he left Brittany, and to this he added others who had served the Yorkist kings, accepted Henry as their new monarch, and possessed qualities and experience which he could not afford to ignore. The new council was no narrowly partisan body: to have made it so would have been dangerous politically and disastrous from a practical point of view. The council had to start work at once on the business of carrying on government in the name of the new king. Its first known act, significantly, was the reappointment of the chief justices on 20 September 1485.

Our knowledge of the council of Henry VII is restricted by a scarcity of relevant information. Most of the sources still available relate to its judicial work.* There are no files of minutes and warrants by the council like those surviving from the Lancastrian period, nor are registers of its proceedings extant; although the *Liber Intrationum*, a series of extracts made early in the seventeenth century, indicates that its business was recorded in registers. We know also that a clerk of the council was regularly employed, at the same fee as was paid to his predecessors early in the fifteenth century. The office, therefore, was an established one and so presumably were its duties. It had survived through the Yorkist period, for which the material concerning the king's council is scantier than it is for Henry's reign. No doubt Master Thomas Kent, Edward's first clerk of the council, had kept a register as he had done in Henry VI's reign, but if so it has disappeared without trace together with his files and memoranda. This serious gap in our sources makes it impossible to decide whether or not the organisation and functions of Henry VII's council were radically different from those of its immediate predecessors.

In one respect there was remarkable similarity, namely the number of men who were described as councillors. Before 1461, the title would rarely have been applied to more than a score at one time. From Edward's reign, a total of 124 named councillors has been traced; in the years after his recovery of the throne in 1471, when his control was more sure, 101 men were thus named. The better documented reign of Henry VII has a known tally of 227. Notices are also available, however, of the numbers attending 63 meetings

* See Chapter 6.

of Henry's council: at only three did the total exceed forty, and in 35 cases the number attending was not above twenty; an average of seven was present at half the known meetings. Clearly, then, every person called a councillor was not required to attend the council regularly: it would have been a very inefficient body if they had done. Some of Henry's councillors, indeed, are not known to have been present at a single meeting. Nineteen of Edward's councillors were so styled only in their letters of credence as ambassadors; this may have been done solely to emphasise their importance to a foreign court, but they probably took the usual councillor's oath to keep the king's secrets. Similarly some of Henry's councillors were given the description once only, on the receipt of royal grants or in other correspondence. They were, presumably, household or civil servants of some seniority, but it cannot be presumed that they had been sworn as councillors. It is known that others were sworn although they had previously attended the council, as if they had not taken the oath on their first appearance in it. If there was a rule that councillors should be sworn, clearly it was not persistently observed.

Composition of the council

When the lists of Edward's and Henry's councillors are compared, other similarities appear. In each there were the same proportions of nobles, prelates, other clerks and laymen. Neither king made a point of excluding lords from his council: in both reigns, a quarter of the named councillors were peers. It has often been said of Henry VII that he broke the lords' domination of royal councils and preferred the services of men of humbler origin, whom he could more easily curb. Actually occasions when the peerage monopolised the councils of medieval kings were exceptional, mostly occurring when kings were minors or otherwise incapable of ruling. The king normally pleased himself in choosing ministers and members of his council. No doubt his choice often included some peers, because he enjoyed their company, but they sat in his council by invitation, not by their right or might. Edward and Henry were following a well-established custom in appointing peers to their councils. It was only prudent that they should do so. While neither had any intention of submitting to baronial influence, they could not ignore the social consequence and resources at the lords' command, and wished to enlist them to assist the work of government and national defence. Again like their royal predecessors, the two kings took as councillors peers with ties of blood or service to themselves. Thus the earls of Arundel, Derby, Ormond and Oxford, and Lords Abergavenny and Wells, often sat in the council of Henry VII, but altogether 43 peers were admitted at various meetings.

The proportion of bishops and abbots also stood at about a quarter of the total number of councillors in the period 1471–1509. Prelates were lords, of course, and as such had a recognised political station, being called to parliament to sit with the temporal peers. The bishops, however, owed their sees to royal favour; once he had been installed, a bishop could hardly be removed easily, but as a rule the episcopate was strongly inclined to uphold royal authority and could be relied upon not to oppose the king in parliament or council. The leading prelates, moreover, the two archbishops and the best endowed bishops, were or had been holders of the senior offices in the king's administration; their loyalty to the king was assured, and their brethren were likely to follow their lead. Nor would the king have been likely to encounter serious independence of mind among the remainder of his councillors. The other half of their number in both Edward's and Henry's reign comprised clerks, knights and other laymen.

These men cannot satisfactorily be divided into categories: the clerks—a minority—and the laymen were mostly officials in the king's household or in the departments of state; judges, serjeants-at-law and other common lawyers appeared in both councils, while some of the clerks, who were doctors of canon and civil laws, had also presumably been employed for legal work. The employment by Henry of middle-class councillors was thus not an innovation, nor was it really a new practice in Edward's reign. Although total numbers of councillors in earlier reigns had been much lower, the proportion of secular lords had rarely been any higher; they had usually been outnumbered by ecclesiastics and knights, and medieval bishops were generally of middle-class origin. The new departure at the close of the fifteenth century was that so many royal officials and councillors were laymen, not clerks. This secularisation of public office was already well advanced in other West European governments: in France, for instance, the council of Philip IV (1285–1314) had been dominated by lawyers who were laymen. With the advent of the educated layman in England, the clerical monopoly of government office was broken. This is the real explanation for the secular middle class contingent in Henry's council. It had nothing to do with the king's attitude to the baronage; it was the result of a social revolution just beginning to transform English public life.

The working council

The rank of councillor, we might say, had been devalued through inflation. The prestige and influence given by a place in the king's council were obviously less substantial when two hundred rather than twenty were styled councillors. The king's personal authority, moreover, was seemingly enhanced in consequence; his will alone would have been paramount. Since Henry was at liberty to appoint which and as many councillors as he pleased, he could ensure that no individual or sectional interest would become dominant. As we have already noticed, however, the number of councillors actually present at meetings was rarely above forty and more often averaged seven. In the *Liber Intrationum*, those meetings when the attendance exceeded a dozen were concerned with judicial proceedings; we have no indication of the nature of the business dealt with in another set of lists of councillors which records various sessions with a small attendance. The editor of the *Liber Intrationum* was clearly selective in his choice from the now lost council registers; his interest was in litigation and not in the council's administrative work. He did, however, make note of a meeting on 10 July 1506 which appointed a date for the assay of the mint, when only the chancellor, keeper of the privy seal, treasurer and chief justice were present; the king, who regularly presided at the other sessions recorded in the *Liber*, is not shown to have been at this meeting. This is a significant although unfortunately isolated notice. It points to the existence of a small core of councillors with special responsibility for routine administrative matters.

Now the notion that there was an 'inner ring' of councillors has been largely accepted by historians of the reign: this was a small group drawn from the great number of councillors because Henry particularly valued their capacity to give him useful information and sage advice. The Spanish ambassador in 1507 wrote of Henry speaking in private to 'some of his secret council'. The term 'secret council' is not corroborated by English records and no doubt the Spaniard used it because it would be understood by his sovereign; but it does support the probability that there was an inner cabinet. There is also evidence of an 'inner ring' in Edward IV's reign, for Louis XI hoped to secure the goodwill of five of the English king's most regular councillors by giving them pensions; the largest went to Lord Hastings, equal amounts to Lord Howard and Sir Thomas Montgomery, and smaller annuities to the chancellor, Bishop Rotherham, and Dr. John Morton. This measure of the relative influence of these men with Edward is supported by other evidence. There was, without doubt, a small proportion of Edward's named councillors who formed a working committee, engaged from day to day in the arrangement of administrative details. But a body of this size and purpose had existed in previous reigns. This was the king's council. The small group of Henry's councillors most assiduous in their attendance corresponded to this informal but necessarily permanent institution of medieval government. The large meetings we know of as witnessing judicial proceedings were probably specially called for this purpose, for the interests of justice demanded attendance on a considerable scale; justice, if it was to seen to be done, could not be dispensed by a handful of councillors.

The small working council would normally sit at Westminster. Its membership would not be constant; some had duties in other parts of the administration, others might have military duties or be sent on embassy. The king did not regularly attend sessions of the council when its business was of a routine nature: Henry is not shown as present at fourteen known meetings in 1495 and 1496 when the average number of councillors was seven. He was, in fact, on progress in the west midlands at the time of some of the recorded meetings in 1495. Some members of the council would have been in attendance. When he was at his hunting lodge at Woodstock in September 1500, the bishops of Durham, Salisbury and Lincoln, and the earls of Northumberland, Derby and Surrey were with him, as well as officers of his household[1]. This detachment was not a novel practice: not only Edward IV, but also Henry IV, are known to have had councillors attending them on their travels while the working council continued its daily business in the capital. In Henry VII's case, however, there were also in attendance other councillors with special duties, the doctors of laws required to deal with poor men's requests. In addition, he had other separate councils for particular duties: the most interesting innovation in conciliar organisation in the reign was a practice of forming committees to deal with specialised or regional affairs, a practice which also appeared in the government of Ferdinand and Isabella in Spain. Thus small groups of councillors were charged in 1494 to prepare legislation against crime, and in 1504 to examine treaties with foreign powers. Other bodies were established to deal with various legal or financial matters, such as the council learned in the law, the surveyors of land revenues, the committee set up under the so-called Star Chamber Act of 1487, and dependent councils for northern England and Wales.

The president of the council

In the working council, the chancellor and treasurer were the most regular members; the third great officer of state, the keeper of the privy seal, was less constant as he regularly attended the king. The chancellor is known to have twice sat alone in Henry's council; like Henry V's chancellor in 1420,[2] he could make orders in the name of the king's council. For more than half the reign, the office of chancellor was held by John Morton, who took over from Bishop Alcock in March 1486 and remained in office until his death on 15 September 1500. According to Sir Thomas More, who was educated in his household, 'the king put much trust in his counsel, the weal public also in a manner leaned unto him'. Morton appears to have been the only councillor whom Henry considered indispensable. In 1489, when an embassy from the emperor reached Henry, at Hertford, he sent for Morton to have his advice.[3] Henry's esteem was evidenced by Morton's elevation to the archbishopric of Canterbury and the king's solicitation of the pope for a cardinalate, which Morton received in 1493. Morton's zeal for the administration of justice is revealed by the additional responsibilities laid upon him by statutes enacted during his period of office, and by the declining standard of the council's judicial morality after his death.

The great seal was next held by a temporary custodian in Henry Dean, a former chancellor of Ireland, who was promoted from the see of Salisbury to Canterbury in 1501. On his death in 1504, William Warham became both chancellor and archbishop of Canterbury. Like Morton and Alcock, he had begun his active career as an ecclesiastical lawyer, and then passed into royal service as a diplomat. Hitherto, the chancellor had traditionally presided over the council in the king's absence, but in 1506 the formal title of president of the

council was held by Edmund Dudley.* This new departure points
to the ending, after five centuries, of the primacy of chancellors
in the king's council; although in the next reign, Warham's
successor, Cardinal Wolsey, was to exalt the authority and prestige
of the chancellorship to a peak never surpassed in its medieval
history.

The king's part

The small continual council and the various conciliar committees all
presumably exercised some initiative in their different spheres of
activity. What matters were referred to them, however, and which of
their proposed measures were put into effect, rested, as always, on the
final decision of the king. As both the keeper of the privy seal and
the king's secretary appear to have regularly attended Henry, he
retained direct control of the secretarial machinery of his government. The most personal of the seals, the signet, was the central
instrument for the direction of the organs of government; its letters
not only directly or indirectly, through the privy seal, transmitted
royal commands to Chancery, the Exchequer and other offices, but
served also as the means of communication for the organisation
created in the king's chamber for the management of his estates and
other sources of revenue. The presence of Henry's sign-manual
('H.R.') on these signet warrants is still visible proof of his regular
participation in administrative work at all levels. He also took the
first place in the direction of foreign policy. In 1498, Spanish ambassadors were received in audience by Henry, Morton, and 'an old
gentleman whom they call the treasurer'. Then many other councillors
were called in to hear the ambassadors, but Henry then took them
aside to give a reply, and in further discussions Morton was the
only councillor present and only the king and he ever spoke on the
English side. Again in 1507, although Henry had recently been ill,
he had long private conversations with another embassy and only a
few councillors were admitted. The Spaniards concluded that Henry
had no confidential advisers:[4] he was his own prime minister and
foreign secretary.

* References to the title of president date from 1495, but apparently connected with
the embryonic court of requests. Dudley is the first president not known to have had any
association with requests.

Royal finance

Henry VII's inexperience in the ways of English government at the time of his accession is nowhere more clearly betrayed than in his ignorance of financial organisation. Under Edward IV, the exploitation of the crown's extensive territorial resources was managed under the direct supervision of the king himself. Instead of leaving it to the Exchequer to collect revenues from land by its time-honoured and time-consuming methods, royal property was administered by the same practices as were used by other great landowners, by receivers and other officials whose duty it was to extract the utmost profit from estates; these receipts were brought into the private coffers of the king's chamber, and here the king and his council audited the receivers' accounts. The Exchequer was allowed no part in these transactions. Edward's chamber system survived through the minority of his heir and was continued by Richard III, who made plans for its extension; there was no breakdown as a result of the crown twice changing hands. Thus the Yorkist kings had direct control over their land revenues, which gave them a ready supply of cash or could be put to immediate use by the receivers whenever the king gave instructions. By these means Edward and Richard became the first solvent English kings for many decades and enjoyed the assurance of having funds in their hands ready for use in any emergency.

In contrast, Henry's earliest financial arrangements showed a return to pre-Yorkist practice. While Edward and Richard had financed their households from the chamber, Henry permitted his first parliament to appropriate crown revenues from the Exchequer for this purpose; this was a device favoured by the parliaments of Henry VI, and, as then, it was by no means successful. By a further act of 1485, Henry received a grant for his lifetime of all receipts from customs, tunnage and poundage, a concession first made in 1453 and renewed at the accessions of Edward and Richard. Another measure popular with the Lancastrian commons proposed by Henry's parliament of 1485 was an act of resumption, to recover for the crown all lands, offices and revenues alienated since 1455. Henry accepted this proposal, but then destroyed its value by exempting a total of 461 royal grants made in the previous thirty years. Crown lands were secured for Henry by acts attainting

Richard III and his followers at Bosworth and giving possession of the duchies of Lancaster and Cornwall and the counties of Richmond and Kendal. As with the act of resumption, the king was unable to derive full benefit from these measures because he was obliged to make restitution of their lands to his mother, the earl of Oxford and others whose attainders by Edward and Richard were annulled.

If Henry's estates were less extensive than his immediate predecessors', the margin of difference was widened by incompetent administration. In 1487, the king declared in his preamble to a second act of resumption that he had been so preoccupied with his own preservation and the defence of the realm since his accession that he had not found time to appoint officials to manage his estates, with the result that they 'be greatly fallen into decay'. This lament is amply confirmed. In the first year of his reign, he received only £11,700 from his lands, less than half the £25,000 Richard is estimated to have gathered in a year. The Yorkist financial system had collapsed. Whereas these revenues of Richard had been paid into his chamber, Henry's officers were bringing their receipts into the Exchequer because, through his neglect, there was no longer any organisation in the chamber to control crown lands. Henry kept the office in being, but Sir Thomas Lovel, his first treasurer of the chamber, had been an exile with his master and was often employed on other business outside London. The Exchequer's recovery of land revenues resulted in the king being without a ready supply of cash. When he arranged for the feast of St. George to be celebrated at Windsor in 1487, the Exchequer failed to provide money for the expenses, with the result that certain noble knights of the Garter ungraciously departed.[5] In his early years, Henry was frequently obliged to raise loans, for the expenses of his coronation and marriage, for the costs of his progresses to suppress rebellion in the north.

The revival of the king's chamber

The lack of ready finance was obviously a serious handicap to Henry's government. If the heir of Lancaster was to avoid its reputation for bankruptcy, he would have to adopt the methods of York. That he had not so far adopted them is the more remarkable when we recall the considerable number of old Yorkist officials in his service, not only as receivers of crown estates but also in his council and household. The failure only emphasises how personal was the responsibility of the monarch for administrative efficiency. As Henry admitted in the act of resumption of 1487, when he had awakened to his danger, it was because he had been unable to attend to administrative details that his land revenues had diminished. His excuse that he had been preoccupied by the defence of his throne is only partially convincing: he had not been under constant threat of insurrection in the past two years, and had time enough for hunting. He had not, apparently, so far realised the need for application similar to that exercised by Edward and Richard. They had made the chamber system of royal finance work because they had given constant attention to its supervision. As Henry learned this lesson, he showed no less application and capacity than they had done. His task was eased, however, by the fact that many of his servants had been trained in the Yorkist school of royal finance.

The revival of chamber administration[6] was a gradual process. In 1487–9, annual receipts in the chamber averaged £17,000, in 1492–5 £27,000, and in 1502–5 £105,000. Revenues from crown lands formed the largest single item, at averages of £3,000, £11,000 and £40,000 respectively. The king's receivers in his various groups of estates were one by one diverted from the Exchequer and excused from making accounts there. Instead, they were required to pay their revenues into the chamber and make declared statements of their receipts and issues in the presence of the king, who charged two or three trusted officers to examine these accounts in detail. These were cast in a simpler form than was customary at the Exchequer, and the whole process of audit was more straightforward and speedy. The accounts of the treasurer of the chamber were also drawn up in a clear manner, easily read and understood. This was for the benefit of the king, who himself examined them and wrote his monograph against every entry of a receipt. Until 27 August 1492, this sign-manual was a complex gridiron, requiring several strokes; afterwards it was an elaborate flourish, written with one continuous movement.* From 15 April 1503, Henry initialled only once on a page; the receipts were now very much more numerous, with sometimes several coming on a single day.[7] Both changes suggest that Henry was altering his practice in order to keep up with the growing volume of business. The whole network of receivers, auditors and surveyors operated under his constant, personal supervision; he

* See plate 9.

appointed these officers and watched to ensure that they deserved his confidence. He directly handled some of the transactions in the chamber, recording them in his own hand, and showed, by his ability to calculate rates of exchange, that he clearly possessed a flair for finance. A Spanish envoy reported of Henry in 1498 that he spent all his time when not in public or in council 'writing the accounts of his expenses with his own hand'.[8] This was, of course, an exaggeration, for, as we have already noticed, Henry gave much time to religious devotions and ordinary pastimes.

This intensely personal system of financial administration was the very reverse of bureaucracy. Despite this, Henry naturally required the assistance of others even at the centre of his organisation, although in choosing and continuing to employ those officers his private judgment of their efficiency and integrity was freely exercised. The chief personage in the national financial system, the treasurer of England, was now purely a figurehead, with the office being given as a kind of retainer to a noble councillor. For almost a century, the working head of the Exchequer was the under-treasurer who, since Edward IV's time, had been appointed by the king and was a regular member of his council. Henry gave this office to two under-treasurers in 1485, to Alfred Cornborough, a former Yorkist official, and Sir Reginald Bray. Bray was Henry's principal financial minister. He had been receiver of Lady Margaret Beaufort's estates and was in 1483 entrusted by Bishop Morton with the delicate and dangerous task of weaving the Buckingham–Woodville–Tudor alliance against Richard III. After its failure, he joined Henry in Brittany; his fidelity, discretion and industry gave him a high place in Henry's favour, and from the beginning of the reign Bray emerged as one of the most influential men in the king's council; although, like his master, he was a newcomer to central government. He received numerous royal grants and offices, some simply as rewards, others as a means of uniting important revenue offices in his single hands; he was constantly appointed to formal commissions to survey sources of crown revenue, detect concealed issues and increase yields, and he frequently attended the king, giving counsel, providing information, auditing accounts, and executing numerous other tasks on the king's spoken command. Bray was named by the Cornish rebels together with Morton as responsible for the king's financial exactions. In contrast, Polydore Vergil hailed him as the 'very father of his country', restraining the king's natural avariciousness. It is impossible to say whether he was completely honest or not by modern standards: the records do not permit a final judgment. Certainly he made a fortune: he deserved to, but in addition to his well-earned rewards from the king, he had ample opportunities as a principal channel for royal favour to exact tributes for his good offices. At least Henry was well satisfied with Bray's services and employed them to the limit until his death in 1503.

The treasurer of the chamber obviously held a key position in Henry's financial administration. Sir Thomas Lovel, the first holder of the office in the reign, was given the more honorific but circum-scribed position of treasurer of the household in 1492. He was succeeded in the chamber by his hard-worked deputy, Sir John Heron, who was to hold the office until 1521. Like Bray, Heron was given other appointments, was frequently a commissioner, took part in all the king's important business transactions, and was regularly called into the council because of his special financial knowledge. As the chamber fastened its tentacles on to most of the agencies of royal revenue, Heron became, by 1506, appropriately known as the 'general receiver to our sovereign lord the king'.

Sources of revenue

The chamber was the king's private treasury, but in the later years of Henry's reign it was the principal financial agency in the country. It received not only revenues from lands which he could regard as his personal property, but the receipts from taxes, loans, customs, mines, feudal dues, fines, and the profits of Chancery, the mint, the staple at Calais and the chamberlain of Berwick-upon-Tweed. The Exchequer was now receiving only a small proportion of national revenues, the principal being the ancient county issues raised by the sheriffs, and most of its revenues were passed on to the chamber. While in 1505–6 the Exchequer paid out only £12,600 to other recipients, the chamber had disposed of an average total of £105,000 in the previous three years, that is, approximately ninety per cent of Henry's total revenues. When we recall that in the first years of the reign, the king's annual income was about £50,000, it is clear that the chamber system had done more than divert revenues from the Exchequer; it had acted as the key instrument in a complete overhaul of government finances. In some respects, improved yields had been due to fortuitous causes. Henry had more lands in his last years because of the deaths of his queen, her grandmother the duchess of York, his eldest son, and the duke of Bedford. The attainders of Sir William Stanley, Lords Suffolk, Audley and FitzWalter and many others had led to the seizures of their estates; the highest number of attainders in any of Henry's parliaments was 51 in 1504, and in view of his greater security then this looks like an attempt to derive the utmost profit from this source. The revenues from customs increased from £32,000 to £42,000 during the reign, largely on account of the growing volume of overseas trade. But the yields to the crown from both lands and customs would have been less without the vigilance of Henry and his ministers, who strove hard to ensure that the king received the last penny due to him, by making constant enquiries about crown estates and keeping regular watch for smuggling.

Crown lands and customs produced about three-quarters of Henry's gross annual revenue. In addition he was entitled to various other sources of revenue as appurtenances of his crown. The two regular, traditional regalian sources with the highest potential value were the profits of justice and feudal incidents. Although the *raison d'être* of feudalism—the provision of an army without cost to the king—had been discarded as impracticable for almost two centuries, it was increasingly realised in Henry's reign that the position of the king as feudal suzerain offered considerable scope as a means of raising revenue. Two serjeants-at-law, Robert Constable and Thomas Frowick, made this the subject of their readings on *Prerogativa regis* in 1495. On the death of every subject who held land direct of the king, that is without an intermediate lord, the crown was entitled to possession of his lands until the dead man's heir was given livery by the king; it did not matter how small the tenant's holding had been, and if he had also held other lands from different lords, these too fell under the king's control. If heirs were under the age of 21, they became the king's wards, and he had the use of their property until they were old enough to receive livery; and if they were unmarried, the king could dispose of their marriages, which were marketable commodities, attractive investments to parents anxious to set up their children with landed husbands or wives. Through the carelessness or connivance of escheators, the shire officers responsible for guarding the king's feudal interests, heirs of crown tenants were sometimes able to take immediate possession, and the estates and marriages of minors were 'concealed' from the king.

All kings made attempts to discover such concealments by spasmodically appointing commissions of enquiry. In Henry's reign, such enquiries were made with persistent regularity, and the official reports of escheators were stringently examined in the search for evasion of royal dues. Bray, Heron and other councillors kept open eyes for all efforts to cheat their master, and kept memoranda of cases where they thought he was entitled to feudal incidents. The king was able to ensure that no heir could take possession without suing for livery. The customary payment to him of a relief was then made. The revenue from reliefs was not great,* averaging £437 in 1505–9, but by insisting that heirs could only enter by royal licence, the crown's interest in their estates was acknowledged, recorded, and thus safeguarded against the next change of tenant. Wardship was the most lucrative feudal incident. The usual practice was to sell the custody of a ward, with his lands, and his marriage, or to grant them as a reward. In the past, the price for a sale had been arranged and paid in the Exchequer. Bray generally arranged the sale of Henry's wards, and got the best price he could; he sometimes had offers from more than one would-be guardian and aspiring father-in-law. Bray's memoranda about wards discloses the extent of his information and operations; he kept notes about prospective wards, so that they should not be overlooked when their fathers died. The revenue from sales of wardships, paid into the chamber, rose steeply after 1491. Then they were £343, but rose to £1,588 in 1494, and doubled in the next ten years. Bray's responsibility is attested by the fact that, four months after his death, the king created the office of master of wards for Sir John Hussey. Hussey appears to have had a free hand in the supervision and disposal of wardships, and organised a network of local officers in every county; these deputies managed and exploited the estates of wardships which were not sold. Under Hussey's management, the chamber's revenue from wards was doubled again, to £6,163 in 1507.

Archbishops, bishops and a number of abbots were tenants-in-chief of the crown. When they died, their lands also passed into royal custody until their successors were installed. The crown's opportunities to profit from this kind of wardship were limited, because in some dioceses the revenue due to the king in a vacancy was regulated

* The sizes of reliefs had been defined in Magna Carta.

by agreements between cathedral chapters and former kings. In Henry's reign, vacancies tended to last for at least twelve months, and with a relatively high mortality among prelates in his last years, the chamber's receipts from this source came to exceed £6,000 *per annum*. It can be shown, however, that for personal reasons Henry did not always exploit this source as fully as he might have done.*

Feudal custom as regulated by Magna Carta permitted the king to raise an aid on three occasions, to pay his ransom when captured, at the knighting of his eldest son and on the marriage of his eldest daughter. Although these aids had not been demanded in the fifteenth century, Henry demanded the second and third in the parliament of 1504 and received a grant of £30,000. Another ancient feudal practice given a new lease of life was distraint of knighthood. The Lancastrian kings had occasionally ordered all men with lands worth £40 *per annum* to receive knighthood or pay fines, but Henry VII made it his regular policy to do this. Men given the expensive honour of knighthood in the order of the Bath were fined for not appearing at the ceremonial dubbing; in one year these fines added £1,125 to chamber revenues.

Taxation

Taxation, apart from the regular customs duties on overseas trade, was an exceptional measure, only resorted to in times of war when it was manifest that the king had to incur great expenses in defending national interests. Parliamentary consent was required before taxes could be raised and it was politic to give an explanation on these lines when asking for them. The first tax voted to Henry followed the battle of Stoke, enabling him to repay the loans needed to raise his army. Parliament granted him two fifteenths and tenths. This antiquated form of subsidy was raised by assessment on movable goods; each fifteenth (in the countryside) and tenth (in the towns) was expected to yield £30,000. This was an unsatisfactory basis for taxation, and inequitable in that it did not touch all sources of wealth. When Henry next asked for money in 1489, to finance his operations in Brittany, he wanted £100,000. Parliament reluctantly agreed that the laity should pay three-quarters of this, the clergy finding the remainder. This time the money was to be raised from the laity by a graduated income tax on land and other revenues, a method tried several times between 1404 and 1474 without particular success.

* See p. 186.

Henry was no more fortunate: only £27,000 of the £75,000 was paid. The next parliament, in substituting a fifteenth and a tenth for the balance, showed its preference for the traditional type of subsidy. The clergy were taxed by grants of tenths (on the assessed values of benefices) voted by the convocations of Canterbury and York, which were called for this purpose at about the same times as parliaments.

In 1473, when Edward IV was preparing his expedition to France, a new method of raising money was employed. This was the benevolence, as it was nicknamed. Commissioners were appointed in every county to receive from subjects sums proportionate to their estimated wealth. They were called upon to make this contribution to the king's expenses in token of their goodwill to him and as they desired his. The benevolence was thus a form of general tax, tapping sources of wealth exempt from the traditional tenth and fifteenth, and imposed without the preliminary consent of parliament. It was not, however, an arbitrary royal exaction. The reason for Edward's demand was the imminence of war, and it was a long recognised obligation of every subject to put himself and his property at the king's disposal in time of national emergency. As in the past two centuries when loans were widely raised under official pressure, the benevolence was approved of by the great council on the grounds of public safety, the members made personal contributions, and the circumstances of its imposition were announced by the commissioners to the designated contributors. Edward's benevolence presumably roused resentment, for Richard III found it expedient to enact a statute declaring benevolences illegal. Henry had conveniently deemed all Richard's statutes to be void, and when, in 1491, he proposed to invade France, he followed Edward's example of raising an army by the profits of a benevolence. The same procedure was followed. Subjects were not allowed to evade their obligation to do war-service or pay. One good lady who offered only a quarter of the £20 she was thought able to afford was threatened with a summons before the king's council.[9] The wealthy citizens of London were reluctant to pay, and on account of the stringent measures employed in its collection, 'it was named after, for benevolence, malevolence'.* Resistance was finally overcome when the parliament of

* '*Morton's Fork*'
Cardinal Morton incurred odium in the city by his severity, extracting up to £60 a head whereas Bishop Fox was content with 40 marks (£26 13s. 4d.). In contrast, Eras-

1495 required payment of all outstanding balances of assessed contributions to the benevolence. By these means nearly £50,000 was raised, 'with less grudge of the commons, for to this charge paid none but men of good substance'.[11]

In the event, this sum alone covered the costs of Henry's brief French campaign. The parliament of 1491 had granted two tenths and fifteenths for the cost of the war, and the clergy had also contributed their tenths. The receipts from these taxes gave Henry an unearned increment, and in addition he gained the French pension of £5,000 *per annum*. He did even better with the Scottish war of 1496–7. A forced loan was raised for immediate expenses, and parliament and the convocations granted a total of £160,000 in subsidies. Thanks to the early success of his diplomacy, Henry had to spend only £45,700 on military and naval expenses. It cost him a further £13,155 to deal with the Cornish revolt and Perkin Warbeck, but this outlay was more than recovered by the £14,700 paid in fines by the rebels. Though these wars were to Henry 'as a mine of treasure', as Bacon put it, this was the result of good fortune rather than deliberate design. The risks of war were too great to be hazarded merely with an eye to financial profit at the expense of Henry's subjects.

Bonds

The customary method of collecting debts due to the king was by process in the Exchequer which, as a court of common law, had long-established procedures whereby debtors could be constrained to pay the sums which it adjudged to be owing. Like other aspects of the Exchequer's work, these processes were slow, inefficient, and consequently uneconomic. As the chamber had become Henry's principal treasury, it was obviously undesirable that it should be dependent on the Exchequer for the enforcement of payments by obstinate debtors. The object of diverting revenues from the Exchequer to the chamber was to give the king more rapid possession of funds, and it followed that means had to be devised to provide for

---

mus on the testimony of Thomas More said that Fox, as chief commissioner to take a benevolence from the clergy, invented the argument that the manifestly rich could obviously afford to pay, while the apparently poor must have laid up savings. Holinshed also attributes this method of broaching clerical coffers to Fox. It was Bacon who transferred its authorship to Morton.[10]

the prompt payment of money assigned to its coffers. The answer to this problem was found in the extensive use of bonds. These were written undertakings to pay stated sums at fixed dates. In the event of non-fulfilment, the defaulter would be liable to legal prosecution, and eventually to suffer confiscation and outlawry if he failed to give satisfaction. In order to ensure punctual payment, however, and so avoid resort to legal action, Henry's debtors were constrained to seal obligations to pay larger sums than those actually due, on the understanding that the bond would be cancelled on payment of the original debt on the stipulated date. In the case of large sums, debtors made a number of obligations in respect of successive part-payments at annual or half-yearly intervals.

The yearly total of receipts by the chamber of sums due under bonds rose from nearly £3,000 in 1493-4 to £35,000 in 1504-5. These debts to the king were incurred through a wide variety of causes. A large proportion arose from the exercise of the king's feudal prerogative. When a man bought a wardship or received livery of his lands, or when a newly created bishop was delivered his temporalities, he was not required to give cash down in full—often an impossibility—but to seal obligations for deferred payment of the amount determined by the king or his officers. Business transactions by the king, such as the hire of his ships, his sales or leases of lands or minerals, or his loans, involved the sealing of obligations to ensure payment. Merchants made bonds in respect of customs dues. Men who purchased offices from the king, then an accepted arrangement, likewise sealed bonds. So did these who bought the king's licence to give land to the Church or received his dispensation from other statutory restrictions. For all kinds of transactions requiring royal permission or pardon after the event, monetary payments had to be made. There was no novelty in having to pay for the king's favour, but what was a new departure was this systematic direction of its recipients to make bonds to deliver the price into the chamber at precise dates.

These obligations were usually made payable to a group of royal officers for the king's use: Fox, Bray, Lovel, Heron and a few of the lawyers in the king's council were frequently named as the immediate recipients, and thus any legal proceedings against defaulters would be prosecuted with them, not the king, as plaintiffs. The treasurer of the chamber kept a record of these bonds due in a special section of his volume for receipts, and entered payments when they were made. Henry took close interest in these transactions: he sometimes determined the sum to be paid for a particular piece of business and himself made a note of the bond, he initialled the records of receipts and the warrants sent to Chancery under his signet to order the cancellation of paid bonds which had been enrolled there at the time they were made.[12]

The enforcement of payments of obligations by dilatory debtors was at first left to individual members of the king's financial staff. When the council learned came into being, it was given responsibility for this work. Two of its members, Empson and Dudley, have achieved particular notoriety for their diligence as collectors of Henry's debts. Dudley's book of accounts, dating from his entry into royal service on 9 September 1504, records the obligations and sums he received on the king's behalf; once again, Henry's direct concern is revealed by the presence of his monogram against the receipts for every day. Dudley's recruitment to the council learned coincided with a considerable increase in its activity: its records are nearly three times more numerous after 1504 than they were before, and it appears that both Empson and Dudley were keeping notes of its proceedings, most of which concerned the enforcement of bonds. As a committee of the king's council, manned by common lawyers, the council learned was a formidable instrument for collecting the king's debts, certainly a great improvement on the leisurely processes of the Exchequer. Whether those subjected to its pressure shared this opinion is another question. Had the bonds enforced by Dudley and his colleagues been contracted only in the course of feudal or business arrangements there would be little justification in the charges of extortion later made against them. The debts had been incurred in return for specific benefits received, and even if the price of royal consent was high, or the means to collect it rigorous, the debtors concerned were not the innocent victims of arbitrary oppression.

Profits of justice

After Henry's death, allegations were made that justice had been perverted for his profit. He did undoubtedly owe a useful contribution to his revenue to fines and forfeitures, but it cannot be agreed that these exactions were all improperly made. The fines imposed by the king, although sometimes high, were penalties for serious misdemeanors.* The case of Lord Abergavenny, at least, shows that the maximum pecuniary advantage was not always extracted; his fine of £5,000 was stiff enough, but according to statute he was liable to pay over £70,000 for his offence of unlawful retaining. The visitation of Cornwall to impose fines on the rebels there was a profitable undertaking. These men were, however, guilty of high treason for which the penalties were death and complete confiscation. Henry was following merciful precedents in preferring cash payments to mass executions. Henry IV, for instance, had punished humble followers in the Yorkshire rebellion of 1405 in the same way.[13] Treason was a crime against the king, and he had both right and conscience on his side when he sold his pardons to those who had committed it. It is more doubtful if he had equal justification in the cases of murderers and other felons. With the police organisation so inadequate, however, it was not difficult for criminals to escape justice, and by admitting them to his grace, at a price, the king imposed the modified punishment of a fine and gave them the opportunity to return to law-abiding lives. But the considerable receipts Henry VII derived from sales of pardons for murder and other felonies suggests that financial gain was his principal motive in this connection: profits from this source totalled £3,846 in 1504–5.

The yield from pardons thereafter increased annually. Then, on 19 August 1508, the office of surveyor of the king's prerogative was created and granted to Edward Belknap, who had already been prominent as a chamber official. What was understood by the prerogative in this connection is indicated by Belknap's commission. He was empowered to seize the lands and property of all people whom he discovered to have been convicted or outlawed for felonies, or had violated the king's prerogative (presumably here meaning feudal) rights, particularly widows of tenants-in-chief or themselves crown tenants who had married again without the king's licence. Belknap was instructed to administer or sell these lands and goods, and to impose and levy fines. Under his direction, deputy surveyors were soon appointed in eighteen counties. Neither they nor Belknap received salaries, but they were allowed proportions of the profits of the office for their fees, a strong inducement for zeal. Within seven months they collected nearly £3,000 and a great deal of ill-will. By searching out and fining outlaws, however, they had given greater

* See p. 127.

effectiveness to the law. Outlawry was common enough, being imposed on all those who refused to answer summonses to a court of law in civil as well as criminal litigation. Despite this deprivation of legal rights and nominal confiscation of their property, many outlaws were able to survive in complete immunity. Belknap's operations made outlawry the sanction it was meant to be.

The later charges against Empson and Dudley state that they resurrected old statutes with penal clauses and searched out men who had broken them in order that they should be mulcted. Profits from penal statutes figure in Dudley's book of receipts. He took an average of £1,000 a year for escapes of prisoners. These fines were imposed in accordance with the statute of 1504, which aimed to make keepers of gaols more vigilant in their detention of suspects. Before Dudley entered royal service, fines for this negligence had been made into the chamber after being assessed by the king or council. So had fines for breaches of the statutes concerning customs, that is, for smuggling. The only innovation in practice, in fact, had been to delegate the enforcement of penal legislation to the council learned. According to the accusations, however, this body's methods in obtaining convictions included perjured evidence, flagrant intimidation of the accused, and the packing of juries. Complaints of this kind were the common resort of defeated litigants, but the council learned, as both judge and prosecutor, was scarcely an impartial champion of the king's interests. The particular statutes it was said to have enforced do not appear to have been over twenty years old. This pursuit of those who thought that the passage of time had cast their offences into oblivion was unpopular because it was unusual, but it was also accompanied by practices of doubtful legality in actions promoted for the benefit of either the king or of individual members of his council learned. The growing volume of receipts 'for purchase of the king's favour' has a sinister ring: they averaged nearly £3,000 between 1505 and 1508. On balance, it would probably prove that the law fully warranted the great majority of exactions by Dudley and his fellows, but their concern was less with justice itself than with profits to their no less exacting master.

Chamber expenses

The king's chamber was not only the principal treasury of receipt in the kingdom, it was also the chief paying office. The Exchequer, from its curtailed revenues, paid only annuities and wages; most of its balance went to the chamber. This still retained its function as the king's privy purse. Many of its issues were small and personal: 10s. 'to the Scottish boy with a beard', 3s. 4d. 'to him that watches the crows', other rewards to those who earned the king's pleasure, moved his compassion, prompted his piety. The chamber also paid for the king's purchases of clothing, furnishings, plate, books, musical instruments, hawks, for small and great building works; its records give a fascinating picture of his interests and needs. The wages of chamber officials were likewise paid from its coffers. But the treasurer spent only a small proportion of his revenues on the customarily ordinary charges of the chamber. He paid over at least £1,000 a month to the cofferer of the household for the wages, food and other charges of the royal court. The wages of troops employed against Scotland and in Ireland, maintenance of the king's ships, ordnance and fortifications, the wages of English envoys and the entertainment of foreign embassies, necessary expenses of government such as these were likewise paid from the chamber. In 1505, £138,000 was lent to Philip of Burgundy to finance his voyage to Spain. Other loans were made to English merchants; for these the king had adequate security, and his accounts show that he got repayment. The money lent to Philip, however, and to the Emperor Maximilian, was presumably lost for ever, spent in fact to buy continental allies and make Flanders unsafe for traitors in exile.

Henry's ability to give subsidies on this scale, and the splendour of his court, naturally enhanced his reputation. Milanese envoys told their duke in 1497 that Henry had amassed a treasure of £1,350,000. The duke of Saxony was told that Henry was the 'richest lord that is now known in the world', in 1509. Venetian and Spanish ambassadors believed that he left a great treasure in gold at his death, and Bacon founded the tradition that he left £1,800,000 in his coffers. The figure is absurd: it is doubtful if the total receipts for the reign greatly exceeded this sum, and chamber records rarely show much of a balance in hand at the end of any year. Its disbursements kept pace with its receipts. Only £9,100 was left unspent when Henry died, only enough to pay for his funeral. He had bought plate and jewels on a large scale, but over the whole reign only about £140,000 can be accounted for as being spent in this way, and many pieces had doubtless been given away as the customary presents to foreign rulers and their ambassadors. Typically for his age, Henry's greatest single investment was made for the benefit of his soul, in his magnificent chapel in Westminster Abbey with its lavish endowments.

The revenues of the crown had without doubt been greatly augmented, enabling the king to maintain his estate with splendour and free his government of the crippling dangers of poverty. His credit balance, however, was never very great, and he could not feel able to relax the stringency of his financial policy; he had to keep up the drudgery of his own book-keeping, and keep alive the vigilance of his ministers. The machinery of financial administration increased its efficiency year after year; after Bray's death freed Henry of dependence on one general factotum, the creation of specialised departments for audit, enforcement of bonds, and exploitation of wardships and prerogative rights led to greater profits and set the pattern for bureaucratic development in the reign of Henry VIII.

Parliament

Parliament was the highest organ of government in that there was no higher authority for the business of the kingdom. It was being called 'the high court of parliament' at this time, paradoxically since its function as a law court was rarely now in evidence. Its supremacy over the regular courts of law was, however, accepted as an established fact: the legislation it enacted was applied by the king's justices whether it was by way of amendment or addition to the existing body of customary and statute law. The statutes of parliament touched all aspects of national activity, social and economic as well as legal, and could be employed either to enlarge or diminish the privileges of individuals and corporate bodies; even the Church, most entrenched of all immunities, had already been subjected to some regulation by statute.

Despite its great authority, parliament had no life of its own. A parliament was held only when it was summoned by the king, it met in his presence, and its acts required his assent to become law. But although the king was not under any constitutional bond to hold parliaments, regularly or otherwise, political and financial exigencies often obliged him to do so. Parliament was the forum of national opinion: it could both inform the king and receive royal declarations for further dissemination. Official policies requiring new legislation and public comprehension demanded assemblies of parliament, as did additions to the king's revenues by means of taxation. In the period of the Wars of the Roses, it had become a regular item in the parliamentary agenda to pass bills of attainder against enemies of the king for the time being, and since these became statutes, they could only be annulled by other parliaments. The parliaments of this period did not confer royal titles; the mere fact that they met, in response to royal summonses, was recognition that new kings were already accepted.

Parliament was an institution of royal government, but the king was restricted by custom and statute with regard to its composition. The division of parliament into two houses dated from the fourteenth century. The composition of the upper house was determined by custom but susceptible to modification in individual cases. Both archbishops and all nineteen English and Welsh bishops were called except when sees were vacant, and with them about thirty abbots and priors. The temporal members of the upper house were called because they were the heirs of men summoned in the past; although the initial summons to an ancestor was made on the king's initiative, the custom of calling his heirs had hardened in the fourteenth century. The king was at liberty to add to this list, but new peerages, as we now call them, were conferred only on men with the means thought to be adequate for this dignity. Reductions in the number of secular lords came about through the natural extinction of families or through their legal extinction by acts of attainder. The small number of lay peers called to Henry's first parliament, twenty nine, was due to attainders and the minority of some heirs. The total later rose to about forty, with the reversal of attainders, other lords reaching full age, and new creations; there were only five of the latter, but it cannot be said that Henry was any more sparing in conferring titles than most previous kings had been.

The house of commons

Long usage had also determined the composition of the lower house. Every English county except the palatinates of Durham and Chester was represented by two elected members. A large proportion of these seventy-four shire knights were not actually knights, but they had to meet the statutory qualification of possessing lands worth £40 *per annum*, and they were chosen by the votes of freeholders holding land worth at least forty shillings a year. London was represented by four

12 The Justices of King's Bench

13 Henry VII's first Act of Parliament in Thomas Pigot's Book of Statutes

members and 109 boroughs each by two burgesses, generally chosen by the limited governing bodies of their towns. Although the minority in a house of 296 members, the shire knights took precedence and the leading part in its business; they sat while the humbler burgesses stood. The social distinction between the two types of commoner was, however, becoming blurred as landed gentry unable to secure county election were, in the later fifteenth century, being elected to represent boroughs; thus in 1491 two knights were returned for Cricklade in Wiltshire. This development underlines what had long been apparent in the shires, namely the desirability to the more affluent gentry of a place in parliament. Some shire knights sat in as many as ten parliaments in the fourteenth and fifteenth centuries, few in only one.

The reign of Henry VII is one of the dimmer periods of parliamentary history. The official records are rarely supplemented by private reports and the picture which emerges is of quiescent meetings expeditiously fulfilling the king's wishes. Most important legislation was introduced by official bills drafted by judges and other councillors; their passage through the commons was directed by its speakers who, as servants of the king, would have made his interests their first consideration. The complaisance of Henry's parliaments has been explained, in the case of the lords, by the habitual loyalty of the spiritual peers and the destruction of baronial ambitions in the bitter experience of civil war, and by the repressive measures of the king; while the commons, of course, represent those new men of the rising middle class, ever ready to identify royal policies with their own best interests. Unfortunately, a full list of members survives for only one of Henry's parliaments, that of 1491,[14] and the returns of the Yorkish period are incomplete. What information we have shows that sixteen of the seventy four shire knights in 1491 had sat in parliaments of Edward IV's reign. The best record was that of Nicholas Gainford, who had attended five and possibly ten parliaments since 1453, the longest that of Sir Edmund Mountford who had first been elected in 1447. Besides this, the fathers of eighteen other shire knights in 1491 had been M.P.s, and most had inherited estates in the counties they represented. Only about a dozen of the newcomers lacked a record of public service, generally as justices of the peace, dating from Edward's reign. The record of borough representation in parliament shows still stronger continuity: most burgesses sat

E

three times, while John Ashwell was representing Cambridge for the seventh or eighth time in 1491. There is little evidence here for the legend of the new middle class emerging for Henry's benefit.

The quiescence of Henry VII's houses of commons was not due to their members being newcomers to parliament. The history of parliament in Edward IV's reign is very similar to what it was in Henry's. Legislation then was more often than not initiated by official bills, and bills from the commons of any significance rarely received the royal assent. The commons had been the chief begetter of legislation in the early fifteenth century, but from the parliament of 1453–4 their bills were often rejected and officially inspired statutes became more numerous. The loss of the initiative by the commons thus antedated the outbreak of civil war and was not its consequence. Nor was there anything novel in the commons of Henry VII's reign electing speakers who were royal ministers, such as Thomas Lovel in 1485 or Edmund Dudley in 1504. A high proportion of the shire-knights elected as speakers since the office first appeared in 1376 had been men in the king's service. As the commons' mouthpiece to the king and lords, it was desirable that the speaker should be personally acceptable in the highest quarters, and his administrative or legal experience was an asset to the house in the organisation of its business. The speaker was, however, the servant of the house while he held the office, his statements to the king and lords were framed by the commons, and they could disown him if he did not act in accordance with their corporate decisions. Even the most stubborn and critical of medieval commons, that of 1406, had a king's knight as its speaker. There remained a possibility that the responsibility of the speaker for organising the commons' business might be converted to one of managing the commons on behalf of the king. This development appears to have come about in Edward IV's reign, as he regularly paid speakers a reward of £100 or £200 for their good services, a practice which Henry VII was only continuing. If brevity of sessions is a guide to the efficiency of parliamentary management, Edward was as successful as Henry. In his twenty-three years, Edward held six parliaments, which sat for a total of seventy-seven weeks; some had more than one session, none of which lasted more than two months. These figures closely resemble those for Henry's reign, when in twenty-four years there were seven parliaments sitting for a total of fifty-nine weeks.

Infrequence of parliaments

There is another common feature in the parliamentary statistics of the two reigns. As both progressed, parliaments were less frequently held: three years intervened between the last session of Edward's fourth parliament in 1475 and the assembly of his fifth, for six weeks, in 1478, another five before the last met in 1483 for five weeks; while Henry, after his sixth parliament in 1497 (eight weeks), held only one other in the last twelve years of his reign, in 1504, for nine weeks. The decreasing frequency of parliaments was due to the same reason in both reigns: they reflect the success of Edward and Henry in avoiding war and realising adequate incomes from ordinary sources. In 1467 Edward himself told the commons, 'I purpose to live upon my own and not to charge my subjects but in great and urgent causes.' This promise he was able to keep through his exploitation of crown lands under the then new chamber system. When he so swiftly made peace with France in 1475, he remitted the subsidy still due, behaviour which contrasts favourably with that of Henry VII. Edward did not require a tax of the 1478 parliament—its purpose was to attaint the duke of Clarence—and in 1483 he needed subsidies for war with Scotland. Henry's wars with France and Scotland account for his later parliaments, save that of 1504, when he sought the two feudal aids. It would appear, then, that parliaments were not called primarily in order to legislate; statutes were introduced in parliaments whenever some were sitting, but they were not assembled for this purpose.

The fact that neither Edward nor Henry made heavy and constant demands for subsidies, and did so only for purposes of national defence, goes far to explain the tractability of their commons. Henry's parliaments must not be considered in the light of our knowledge of parliaments a century later, but rather in relation to their predecessors. Medieval houses of commons did not normally criticise the king's government or oppose his policies. 'The great business of the king and kingdom' were not their province; the commons were required merely to give their consent to what was determined by the deliberations of kings and lords, nor did they consider themselves competent to interfere in these high matters. The commons' attention, as shown by their petitions, was given to the enforcement of public order, the efficiency and equity of judicial procedures, the improvement and regulation of trade, industry and agriculture. They only concerned themselves with the organisation of government when they believed it to be inefficient, and in their eyes the test of efficiency was whether the king could 'live of his own'. The interest taken by the commons in Henry IV's council, and the proposals by Henry VI's commons to recover royal revenues, arose from their anxiety to prevent or reduce taxation; but while they tried to restrict royal patronage in order to defend the king's income, the commons left the enforcement of their proposals to the king and the councillors of his choice.

The improved financial position of the crown under Edward and Henry removed the principal occasion for criticism of government by the commons. There is no evidence to indicate that Henry prevented opposition by securing the election only of hand-picked shire knights and burgesses. Members of his council like Bray and Lovel were elected, but there were many precedents for counties choosing royal servants, while the majority of members remained independent of court connection. Although no king had formally granted the commons the right to speak freely, in practice such freedom had long been enjoyed: how otherwise would the commons, from the fourteenth century onwards, have from time to time devised measures contrary to royal wishes? Henry overbore protests against an act of attainder in 1485, but the point to be noted is that 'there was many gentlemen against it' and they were not afraid to say so. Although Henry initiated most legislation, the commons did not abandon their tradition of law-making: most of their bills were of limited significance, or called for the renewal of existing statutes, but they did initiate some important measures, such as the navigation act of 1489, the act of 1491 reforming weights and measures, and a statute in 1495 which strengthened the powers of justices of the peace to deal with riots.

Even after Henry had been king for nineteen years, his last parliament delivered a serious rebuff, although Dudley was its speaker. Henry asked for two feudals aids but the commons had no desire to allow royal officers this excuse to investigate feudal tenures in order to find who were liable to pay, and instead of acceding to the king's demand for three subsidies (£90,000), offered a grant of £40,000. Henry showed good sense in remitting £10,000 of this sum, doubtless hoping that by this gracious concession he would soothe the commons.

He knew how far he could go with them. Foreign observers thought that Henry would have preferred to govern in a more authoritarian manner, like the French king; but as one wrote, 'if the king should propose to change any old established rule, it would seem to every Englishman as if his life were taken for him'.[15]

The great council

The emergence of the commons as the dominant house in parliament lay very much in the future. In Henry VII's reign, as throughout the previous history of parliament, their position was the humble one of petitioners, called upon only to give their consent. In contrast, the lords in their writs of summons were called to counsel the king, and he presided in their chamber. The higher political stature of the lords is emphasised by the fact that they alone were called to other assemblies, again for the purpose of advising the king. They met in these great councils almost as frequently as they did in parliaments; in other words, the king called meetings of the lords spiritual and temporal about twice as often as he summoned representatives of the commons. The great council was an ancient institution, the successor, by a slow course of evolution, of the traditional feudal assembly of great tenants-in-chief.* In outline, the composition of the great council was the same as that of the house of lords in parliament, but the king exercised his discretion to call additional members such as judges, councillors who were not peers, and sometimes particular knights and squires from the shires, or burgesses to represent their towns. He could also exclude peers whose presence was objectionable to him.

Very little is known about great councils in the Yorkist and early Tudor periods, but it is important to remember that they were still being held, if only to see parliament, particularly its elected element, in proper perspective. Since the time of Edward III, kings had not attempted to make permanent modifications to the law by ordinances in the great council, nor could it authorise general taxation. Its assent was desirable, however, when the king planned to make a general call on his subjects for loans; since this would be made on a plea of national necessity, the great council as representative of the

* In the mid-thirteenth century, these meetings were often called parliaments; only by the mid-fourteenth century was the name *parliamentum* only given to assemblies including elected representatives of the commons. The term great council then comes to be applied only to meetings without elected commoners.

feudal order was the proper assembly to recognise the existence of a situation when subjects were obliged to put their property at the king's disposal. Great councils were held to discuss high matters of state because the king required the agreement and support of his most important subjects before embarking on policies of national importance. In Edward IV's reign, great councils discussed foreign affairs and authorised declarations of war, the despatch of embassies, the revocation of a treaty, and a marriage alliance; and with regard to internal matters, it considered measures against rebels and the reform of the currency.[16]

Henry held an assembly of councillors and other prominent subjects in September 1485, which was presumably a great council; here he announced his intention to marry Elizabeth of York, and no doubt other arrangements to regularise Henry's position were made, such as the decision to call a parliament and the appointment of officers of state. A great council was held at Richmond in February 1487 to devise means to counter the rebellion being planned by the Irish lords who had rallied to Lambert Simnel. The lords advised Henry to issue a general pardon and show the earl of Warwick to the public, authorised him to seize the estates of the queen mother, and passed other unspecified ordinances to reform the administration. The three other known great councils of the reign were all called to hear reports of deteriorating foreign relations and to assent to financial levies for military purposes: in November 1488 it authorised the king to anticipate a parliamentary subsidy to pay for an expedition to Brittany; in June 1491, the lords agreed to the opening of hostilities with France and to the benevolence required for this purpose; and in October 1496, they licensed the raising of a loan on account of a threat of invasion from Scotland. From this time there is apparently no further record of great councils in Henry's reign.[17] As with parliaments, Henry's need for them disappeared when he made peace with England's neighbours.

6

Law and Order

FOR every medieval king of England the most imperative and also the most intractable of problems was the preservation of public order. It was the constant theme of constitutional commentators that the king's first duty, indeed his *raison d'être*, was to dispense justice to his people so that they would live in harmony. The obligation was clear enough, but it was reinforced by necessity. The corruption of the legal system in Henry VI's reign through partiality in the king's council and unrestrained intimidation and perversion in the shires had produced conditions of social disorder which culminated in civil war. The responsibility for this state of affairs cannot be laid upon the 'overmighty subject' alone. Not only were less potent subjects culpable of malpractices, but the venality of a royal court where the king was a helpless simpleton was a principal cause in the evolution of a party bent upon its destruction and of the popular indifference to its downfall. The public easily reconciled itself to Henry VI's removal, hoping that their new king would restore law and order.

Edward IV did make considerable efforts to fulfil this promise: he signalised his concern by sitting in King's Bench for three days in 1462 and, more directly, by spending much of his first fifteen years as king on the road, travelling to scenes of disturbances, seeing that justice was done, and receiving complaints as he went. Although his council was employed in some judicial work, he generally left the enforcement of the law to the common law machinery. His legislative record is thin, but this may only be a reflection of his robust, practical approach: his preference was for direct action, to enforce statutes already existing, and to manifest his determination to discharge his primary obligation. Richard III likewise exhibited zeal in the same cause, by his legislation, in making enlarged provision for humble suitors for redress, and most notably in his arrangements for northern England. Both kings, however, were hampered by political considerations. While they were merciless against rebels, they were chary of keeping too tight a rein on magnates of assured loyalty, such as the dukes of Norfolk and Suffolk, even though these peers adopted high-handed methods in their pursuit of local aggrandisement.

Henry VII was in a stronger position than his immediate predecessors had been. The English aristocracy had certainly not killed itself off in the Wars of the Roses, but it was a less formidable body than it had been in 1460, or even in 1484. There was no duke of York in 1485; the great estates of this duchy, including the earldom of March, had become royal property when Edward seized the crown, and Henry was now their owner. The earldom of Warwick had disappeared, for the 'Kingmaker' had fathered only two daughters who added their inheritance to the lands of York. The heir of the duke of Buckingham executed by Richard III had been restored the title in 1485, but as he was a child his estates remained in Henry's keeping. Another powerful magnate, the duke of Norfolk, had been killed at Bosworth, his heir the earl of Surrey was kept in prison for four years, and his lands were confiscated. No doubt Henry's humbler subjects wished him well in so far as his security would preserve them from turbulence. From his own point of view, however, the basis of his strength, the effective foundation of his authority, was his highly advantageous position in relation to the nobility. The balance of real power had swung markedly in favour of the crown.

In the preamble to a statute in 1489,[1] Henry declared that 'to him there is nothing more joyous than to know his subjects live peaceably under his laws'. He made a point in other statutes of making public his personal concern for justice and order. His record in this respect is very different from that of Edward IV. Henry strove to prevent illegal practices and strengthen the machinery for their punishment by legislation. Bacon's encomium on Henry as the best royal lawgiver since Edward I was justified, for most of the remedial legislation in the intervening period had been initiated by the parliamentary commons. Henry's use of his initiative in making statutes revealed no less awareness than they had done of current abuses and some of his remedies followed similar lines. In further contrast with Edward, Henry was not so ready to visit the scene of every disorder. When he did take the road, and it was often enough in his early years, it was to oppose open rebellion or recover obedience in disaffected regions: his motive, in fact, was political. Nor is he known to have attended the proceedings of any court of common law. He preferred to leave the enforcement of law in the countryside to the local authorities, and through various channels keep these agents under regular supervision. Where Henry did take a direct part in the administration of justice was in his council: not only did he preside at its judicial sessions, he also took sole charge in some cases, examining parties and imposing fines.

The king's council as a court

The authority of the king's council as a court of law was derived from the inherent and inalienable status of the king as justiciar to his people. For this reason it was the oldest court in the kingdom, for it was in the presence and with the assent of those called to attend that the Anglo-Norman kings dispensed justice. Although they later delegated judicial powers to judges under whom permanent common law courts were established, kings continued personally to exercise judicial authority in their councils. The occasions on which they did so were now infrequent and the causes exceptional, generally arising from the failure or inability of the regular courts to provide remedies: these were cases where subjects could not proceed at common law because their problems were not catered for in its procedures, others when the influence or violence of one party threatened to pervert the ordinary course of justice, and litigation involving foreign persons or powers. From the late fourteenth century, Chancery developed a court which relieved the council of much of this business, but the latter continued to exercise judicial functions. The quarrels of lords and other influential persons and corporate bodies were the council's particular concern, because these disputes endangered the peace and the parties involved might scorn to accept the judgment of any lower court.

Although the medieval king's council was not given a formal code of regulations, it established a pattern for its judicial procedure. Acting on information received from crown officers or by the petitions of complainants, it summoned parties before it by writs of privy seal, examined them under oath—a practice unknown to common law—and then gave sentence; by these means serious cases could be resolved in a fraction of the time usual in actions at common law. Thus in 1439, only four weeks after the justices of the peace for Bedfordshire complained of a riot caused at their sessions by Lord Fanhope, all the principals involved were examined before the king's council in Star Chamber,* and a fine of a thousand marks (£666 13s. 4d.) was imposed on Fanhope.[2] Beside inflicting monetary penalties, the council had men detained in prison for indefinite periods and required others to seal bonds making them liable to financial loss in the event of non-compliance with its decrees; but it did not inflict the death penalty. The council also investigated reports of rebellion, treasonable conspiracy and seditious speech, and examined the accused, but then sent them for trial by jury in the appropriate court of common law.[3] Under Edward IV, the council used torture in its investigation of treasons.[4]

The activity of Henry VII's council as a court of law used to be greatly exaggerated and misunderstood. It was thought that he used his council as the principal instrument in a direct attack on the powerful influences and illegal practices which stultified the work of the courts of common law, with offenders being prosecuted before the council; here violent and corrupt methods would not rescue them from condign punishment. The records of Henry's council show that it rarely passed sentences in cases of this kind. Although these records are incomplete, they give information about 194 actions before the council. Very few of these were introduced as official prosecutions. Most, indeed, were the result of petitions by subjects against their private adversaries. In half the cases, the cause of dispute was over the right to possess land, another score were civil suits in other matters, and eleven were disputes concerning the rights of municipal and trading bodies. Although many of the petitions about land included allegations of riotous behaviour, these were made almost as a matter of course, and in only about a score of bills was violence itself the subject of complaints. In a dozen other petitions the charges were of a criminal nature. Only the small remaining number of cases concerned maintenance and other abuses of the legal system.

* This room in the palace of Westminster was the regular place for meetings of the council since it was rebuilt in 1349. Its name derived from the decoration of its walls or ceilings with gilded stars.

This evidence nearly all comes from the bills which began suits; how these ended is rarely known. Of the few decrees which have been traced, all concern suits between parties, none relate to criminal matters. The council did inflict fines, particularly for riots, although the sums were rarely large: few above £10 have been traced. Sometimes the fines were heavy when the means of the offenders and the gravity of their misdeeds warranted it, like 400 marks (£233 6s. 8d.) on the Vernon family for abducting an heiress. A fine of £10,000 was imposed on the earl of Northumberland for a similar breach of the king's rights of wardship in the court of Common Pleas;[5] it was not only the council which inflicted heavy penalties. On the whole there is little reason to believe that Henry's council was a harsh tribunal. Its judicial activity was largely stimulated at the behest of subjects as a convenient means of redress. Nor did it supplant the common law courts as an instrument for punishing crime and other illegalities. Even cases initiated by the government, against rioters and corrupt juries, were sent to the ordinary courts for trial. The records of these courts provide the only evidence there is during the reign for trial on charges of maintenance, perjury and the like. They remained, in fact, the customary tribunals for prosecutions for breaches of law and statute.

On the other hand, the council endeavoured to assist the common law courts to function effectively, and kept watch over their proceedings, as was evidenced by the official prosecution of jurors whose verdicts defied the evidence put before them. By initiating prosecutions for retaining, riots and other malpractices, the crown ensured that the courts took action in such cases, avoiding the possibility that grand juries—the usual source of charges for all offences—might fail to present bills of indictment. The attorney-general, Sir James Hobart, was one of the king's most active servants; he was responsible for these crown prosecutions, a member of the council and of the council learned, a justice of the peace in several counties, often an itinerant justice of gaol delivery, and in practice general overseer of all the courts of law.

Conciliar committees

Henry's council had a number of subordinate bodies of a judicial character. The eleven lawyers who formed the council learned[6] were mostly members of the full council, which they assisted by examining evidence and giving counsel in cases heard in the latter. The council learned also acted as a court by itself, sometimes in suits initiated by plaintiffs, but more often in government prosecutions; the latter generally concerned breaches of penal statutes, when the council learned cited defendants without stating the cause of summons and acted as both prosecutor and judge. Another conciliar committee with powers of jurisdiction was established by statute in 1487 to enforce the laws against maintenance, retaining, corrupt practices in the formation and conduct of juries, and riots. Some cases have been traced of proceedings before this body, eight against jurors for corrupt verdicts, one for misconduct by a sheriff, and one for a riot at a fair. It would appear that this tribunal was no longer functioning by the end of the reign, and the reason for this, again, seems to have been the council's preference to leave common law work to the ordinary courts; by an act of 1495, justices of the peace were authorised to proceed to judgment in a similar range of offences without a jury. This act of 1487, of course, achieved notoriety as the supposed foundation charter for the court of Star Chamber. The title *pro camera stellata* was written against it on the statute roll in the later sixteenth century and that is its only connection with the court of Elizabeth I and the earlier Stuarts. It is evident enough that neither the committee set up in 1487 nor Henry VII's full council resembled the later court of Star Chamber either in its range of jurisdiction or in its methods of trial and punishment.

The reign of Henry VII was a period of experiment in conciliar organisation, with small offshoots being established for special purposes. Another statute of 1487 set up a court in the household to try any of its servants accused of conspiracy against the king, and a third gave the chancellor jurisdiction in cases of usury. A further small tribunal was established by a statute of 1495 against corrupt jurors; only four possible instances of prosecution before this body have been traced, the statute was allowed to lapse in 1504, and the common law courts remained the principal channel for prosecuting perverse juries. These experimental judicial committees may have been designed only as reserves, to be employed when the resources of the ordinary courts had been exhausted, and presumably jurors aware that the council had these powers available were thus deterred from giving questionable verdicts. Two other subordinate councils with judicial responsibilities in northern England and the marches of Wales were based on York and Ludlow.

There was yet another new judicial tribunal attached to the king's household and accompanying him wherever he went. This was the embryonic court of requests,[7] which sat under the keeper of the privy seal and a number of ecclesiastical lawyers who were called councillors, although they mostly did not belong to the full council. Keepers of the privy seal had long had much to do with petitions addressed to the king, though earlier most of these were requests for specific favours, calling on the king to exercise his bounty or mercy. By the time of Richard III, so many of these bills were praying for redress in difficulties at law that a clerk was designated for the special task of taking charge of these 'poor men's requests'. The petitions under this head which came to Henry VII rarely originated from people who could be described as poor. Rather were they litigants of the same class, and with the same kinds of grievance, as those who sued before the king's council. For the really poor, Henry made a concession in a statute of 1495 that they should be exempted from paying fees for writs, and the chancellor was empowered to assign them counsel and attornies free of charge. Once again, the king showed that he preferred full use to be made of the common law courts.

The central courts

There was therefore no attempt to deprive the courts of common law of their customary functions. The tradition of the central judiciary to apply statutes in their strictest sense was its best guarantee of immunity from royal interference. Judges were given appointment during the king's pleasure, but in practice their tenure was almost invariably for life; dismissal was as rare as voluntary retirement. The independence of the judges was amply recognised from the beginning of the reign, when all the three justices of King's Bench and their five brethren in Common Pleas were reappointed. They had served under Richard III without incurring suspicion of being his minions; five of the eight had in fact first been appointed by Edward IV, and the intervening replacements were due to deaths. The judiciary had kept itself free of political entanglements and prudently denied itself any authority to pronounce on great constitutional issues. That they considered the person of the king to be outside their jurisdiction was again emphasised in 1485 when they declared that, as Henry had become king, he was no longer attainted. On the other hand, Chief Justice Hussey* successfully maintained that judges should not be consulted in cases which the crown was preparing to bring before them, a practice which would obviously have reduced the accused's prospect of a fair trial.

The procedures of common law were notoriously slow, particularly for the private litigant: two years would normally pass between the day he bought his original writ from Chancery and received judgment in Common Pleas. The courts, moreover, refused to provide remedies in many cases, and those aggrieved turned in large numbers, perhaps five hundred a year, to Chancery and now also to the king's council or his court for 'poor men's requests'. In the case of a contract, for instance, a common law court might award damages for non-performance, but Chancery would order the undertaking to be kept. A popular method of trying to win release from prison was to make a complaint of wrongful detention to Chancery, which by its writ of *corpus cum causa* ordered local authorities to supply reasons for these suitors' imprisonment.[8] This procedure invaded the jurisdiction of the higher common law courts. Chancery also trespassed in the sphere of ecclesiastical courts when, at the behest of plaintiffs, it entertained pleas concerning the performance of wills and testaments. The kind of litigation which formed the largest category of Chancery business arose from grants of land under certain conditions. The common law courts would not remove a man from possession of land because he failed to keep the conditions of his grant, and he enjoyed an unwarranted degree of immunity from legal responsibility. The latter anomaly was largely removed by a statute of Henry's first parliament which allowed actions against occupants of this kind (tenants to uses). This act, in adopting the principle that the user should be treated as the owner, was a major legal reform which strengthened the authority of the courts of common law.[9]

Legislation

This measure had in fact been anticipated in one of Richard III's statutes. These were considered void, of no force as Richard was not a lawful king. Another of his statutes was re-enacted in 1489, that which required that records of transfers of land by fictitious actions

* He may be the central figure in the drawing on the plea roll for Hilary term, 1487 (plate 12).

in Common Pleas (final concords) should be published in open court in order to prevent fraud. Bacon singled out this statute of Henry VII to illustrate the king's great qualities as a legislator. We might wonder if he would have said as much for Richard had he known the real author of this useful reform. Another statute, in 1491, was directed against the practice of granting lands to trustees. One of the results— and intentions—of this practice was to deprive lords of their feudal rights of wardship. The statute again decreed that the user should be regarded as the tenant and the feudal incidents of relief and wardship would be due to the overlord on the user's death. The crown, as the supreme tenant-in-chief, stood to gain most by this act, and it helps to explain how Henry gained so much revenue from wardships. The statute, however, was designed for the benefit of all lords, and must therefore be taken into account with regard to Henry's attitude to the baronage: it indicates his intention to preserve their feudal rights as well as his own.

Only a handful of Henry's other statutes dealt with anomalies in the laws of property and they were not of great moment. It cannot be said of him, in this connection, that he was a great law-reformer. The principal aim of his legislation was to enable the common law machinery to function effectively, particularly against crime and riot. Every parliament of the reign enacted some measures to prevent the corruption of juries. They were the most sensitive point in the legal system. The issue of every trial at common law, whether it was a private action over land or a prosecution for felony, was determined by their verdicts. Juries were notoriously exposed to all kinds of pressures, and their impartiality was often open to doubt. Some suspects, moreover, might not be brought to trial at all if grand juries refused to endorse indictments as true bills. The selection of jurors, and numerous other stages in the business of the courts, were the responsibilities of the sheriffs. These officers were also prone to misuse their powers, and a number of Henry's statutes aimed to bring them to order. Another local officer of the law to receive his attention was the coroner. The negligence of coroners in initiating prosecutions for murders was assailed in a statute of 1487; among the measures it made to ensure their diligence was the agreeable one of allowing them a fee of 13s. 4d. for every post mortem. The main emphasis in Henry's legislation against disorder was on the role of justice of the peace.

Justices of the peace

While the principal business of the professional judges sitting at Westminster was to ensure that disputes between subjects were settled according to the precepts of law and statute, responsibility for the protection of public order throughout the country was largely delegated to between two and three hundred amateur justices. The judges of the central courts did undoubtedly take part in proceedings against people accused of crime, on their circuits of gaol delivery and when charges were called into King's Bench for trial. The continuing task of suppressing lawlessness in the towns and countryside, however, had of necessity to be left to the charge of residents whose private means enabled them to act as the unpaid agents of royal justice among their neighbours. Since 1361, the crown had been appointing a number of 'the most sufficient and discreet' men of every county to exercise judicial powers within its boundaries. What 'sufficient' meant was later defined, in a statute of 1439, which decreed that these justices of the peace should hold land worth £20 a year.

Since 1430, from when the formula for the commission of the peace remained unchanged for many decades, the first charge laid on the justices was the execution of the statutes of Winchester (1285), Northampton (1328) and Westminster (1361) for the keeping of the peace, and those of Cambridge (1388) for the regulation of wages, Westminster (1399 and 1401) against the giving of liveries by unauthorised persons, Leicester (1414) against Lollards, and Westminster (1416) against the forgery of money. Then they were required in general terms to see that all statutes for the defence of public order were observed. Next the commission gave the justices authority to make enquiries by juries into all kinds of felonies and trespasses, naming in particular conspiracies to disturb the peace, riots, ambushes to commit violent assault, unlawful trading by the purchase of commodities for resale at high prices, and disregard by innkeepers and others of the approved standards of weights and measures. On receiving these indictments at their sessions, the justices were next to proceed to conduct the trials of those accused and pass appropriate sentences on those found guilty by the verdict of a jury; in cases of felonies like murder or theft, common law prescribed the death penalty, while certain statutes enjoined monetary penalties for their breach. The only capital offence excluded from the justices' competence was treason. They were also responsible for the execution of other statutes not mentioned in the commission; various enactments of a social or economic nature required their attention, such as acts concerning the resale of wool (1390), the apprenticeship of children (1406), the pursuit of fugitive labourers (1414), the regulation of gilds (1437) and the inspection of Norfolk worsteds (1445). The justices might be required to take action at any time throughout the year, although their main judicial work was done in the quarter-sessions. A justice, for instance, might have to intervene in a riot and bind over the participants to behave in an orderly manner, or he might be called to the scene of a violent seizure of property to require the transgressor to abandon his spoil.[10]

The number of justices of the peace commissioned in any one county varied according to its size in both population and acreage, and was probably also in part determined by other local considerations, such as the incidence of lawlessness among its inhabitants. The average number of members in a commission of the later fifteenth century was between seventeen and eighteen. It was customary for the local bishop to head the list of those appointed, with magnates and other peers with territorial interests in the county following in order of precedence. Then would come the names of two or three professional judges or serjeants-at-law, presumably selected because they also had estates in the county or regularly served on the commissions of gaol delivery which visited it. The remaining half of the membership consisted of knights and squires resident in the county. They were the working members of the commission, constantly on duty: lords spiritual and temporal rarely, if ever, took part in the work of the commission, while the presence of professional lawyers in the county was very infrequent. The terms of a commission empowered a minimum of any two of the members to exercise judicial authority, of whom ('*quorum*') one was to be a member specially named in a shorter list; this quorum consisted of between three and six of the knights and squires already named in the full list. It followed, then, that the lords had no authority to hold a session of the peace if none of the humbler members of the quorum was present.

Justices of the peace took an oath on entering office to discharge their duties faithfully. In some counties, at least, it is known that justices acquired volumes of statutes and copies of earlier judicial proceedings to give them guidance in so doing. While some members of the quorum might have received legal training as students at the inns of court, their clerk was probably always qualified to give legal advice. This official—the clerk of the peace—was generally appointed by the justices to make and keep their records, but he also acted as the king's attorney in legal proceedings and was occasionally appointed by the king. He also was a man of some substance in the county, who might perform other offices, like those of under-sheriff or coroner. Like the justices, he was paid only for his attendance at quarter sessions, but he also received fees from litigants.[11]

As an instrument for defending public order, the commission of the peace was well conceived and has, basically, stood the test of time down to the present day. It became glaringly obvious in the fifteenth century, however, that the system lacked the inherent strength to fulfil its purpose in conditions of serious political and social tension. Without effective support from the central government, county magistrates lacked the means to disperse riotous gatherings or bring dangerous offenders to account. Nominally the sheriff should have placed the county's manpower at their disposal, but he was often neither able or willing to do so. Faced with the peril of encountering baronial retinues, the gentry justices naturally considered their safety as individuals and tended themselves to become the retainers of magnates. Either through fear or favour, therefore, their impartiality was suspect. Sessions of the peace were frequently threatened by armed bands, individual justices were subjected to threats and were sometimes the victims of violence, and the juries, without whose verdicts they could not proceed to judgment, were exposed to the same dangers. Cases are also known of county justices quarrelling among themselves. Thus in 1439 and later the Bedfordshire bench was divided between the retainers of Lords Grey and Fanhope, and the dispute between these factions prevented sessions from being held.[12]

Late fifteenth-century reforms

Henry VII has been credited with revitalising the office of justice of the peace. Before we consider his policy in this respect, we should consider what is known of the record of the Yorkist kings. They did so much to repair the authority of government that we may assume that they endeavoured to make the county commissions more effective. Unfortunately this is not a subject on which we yet have adequate information. As we have already noticed, Edward IV did take a personal interest in the suppression of local disorders, and it is arguable that the greater might of the crown and the destruction of a number of baronial families did create a climate which enabled justices of the peace to perform their duties without fear of incurring vengeance, at least in some parts of the country. The legislation of Edward's parliaments in the field of law and order is not impressive, but it did include a number of statutes which increased the responsibilities of justices of the peace. The most important of these was an act of 1461, promoted by a petition from the commons, which transferred the allegedly misused criminal jurisdiction of the sheriff to the justices of the peace. By other statutes of the reign they were required to supervise such diverse matters as the conduct of escheators, the granting of liveries, and the manufacture of cloth and tiles, and to ensure that no subject presumed to wear clothing unsuited to his rank in society. In Richard III's only parliament, the justices were empowered to release on bail any person of good repute arrested by the sheriff. Beyond these indications that the Yorkist kings appreciated the utility of the county justices, the frequency with which they issued commissions of the peace suggests that they paid close attention to the suitability of their nominees to hold office. Although the case is not proven, we have pointers that, as in other aspects of government, Henry VII's policy had been anticipated by his immediate predecessors.

Various statements have been made about Henry VII and the justices of the peace which are no longer acceptable. One relates to the whole character of his monarchy. It has been said of Henry that he made the middle-class his ally in the work of government, and that this alliance was exemplified in the commissions of the peace; non-baronial landowners and professional men shared Henry's desire to make England peaceful and rich, and so they accepted his authoritarian government and readily and freely served it by acting as county magistrates. As we have already seen, however, the responsibility for combating lawlessness in the shires had been carried by this same class of gentry since the fourteenth century; indeed, the development of a centralised legal system for the kingdom had rested on the services of their ancestors since the twelfth century. There was no change in the social composition of Henry VII's commissions of the peace: they were still headed by the local grandees. Nor, in fact, did he make a clean sweep of individual justices in 1485.

Richard III had obviously attempted to purge his commissions of all 'security risks' and reinforced them by adding his closest associates, like the duke of Norfolk, in every county, and Lords Northumberland, Lovel and Zouche, and Catesby and Ratcliffe, each in eight or more counties. Their names, inevitably, did not appear in Henry's first commissions. Yet from the hand-picked lists of Richard's last nominees, he reappointed half the members, and they formed the majority in his smaller commissions of 1485[13]—a striking illustration of the continuity of public life after Bosworth.

Another misconception is the claim that Henry extended the scope of the justices' work, setting them on the road to becoming the 'Tudor maids of all work', with wide responsibilities for the social and economic regulation of the country added to their peace-keeping duties. Enough has been said above about the pre-1485 justice of the peace to show that he had already been introduced to these spheres of activity and that kings and parliamentary commons regarded him as a suitable agent for the enforcement of all kinds of statutory regulations. The commissions of Henry's reign were drawn up in the same form as had been employed since 1430. His legislation undoubtedly added to the justices' work, but did not diversify it at an accelerated rate. They were required in 1485 to arrest and examine persons suspected of poaching at night or in disguise, in 1487 to enquire whether the king had been defrauded by dishonest jurors and which suspected murders had escaped arrest, in 1495 to regulate beggars and ale-houses, in 1504 to compel civic officials to accept legal coin at face value and supervise inspection of the quality of pewter and brass. Other enactments in 1495 for the enforcement of wages and weights and measures touched matters with which the justices had long been concerned.

The parliament of this year also strengthened their powers in the judicial field. The tendency of many juries to give untrue verdicts, it was said, enabled men who had taken part in riots, giving liveries, and breaches of other statutes, to escape trial and punishment. As a remedy, the justices were empowered to try and punish these offenders without a jury. This action could be taken on receipt of information, and the justices were allowed to reward their informants. This summary procedure was not to be followed in cases of murder and other felonies. This was an important addition to the powers of the justices of the peace, although it was not a complete novelty; the use of summary procedure was authorised in Edward IV's statute against retaining. The act of 1495 was repealed by Henry VIII's first parliament, no doubt because it was regarded as a serious breach in the traditional liberties of the English subject, but authority to use summary procedure in the trial of various cases has become one of the established features in the work of modern justices of the peace. Another act of 1495 allowed the justices to convict the promoters of riots in their absence if they ignored summonses to quarter sessions, and a third authorised them to remove and replace suspect members of juries summoned to indict or try men accused of lawless conduct.

Supervision of the justices

Although the king made these notable reinforcements to the justices' powers, he showed himself less than confident in their discretion and zeal. If the commission of the peace was to be effective as the principal guardian of public order in the shires, it was necessary not only that the justices should be able to exercise the powers entrusted to them, but also to ensure that they did use them on all requisite occasions and in the prescribed manner; watch had to be kept lest favour, negligence or ignorance did not deflect their operations, and that their own behaviour as individuals did not bring their office into contempt and provide a bad example to others. High claims have been made for Henry VII's policy of supervising the justices of the peace. He is reputed to have reviewed every county commission once a year, and struck out the names of all whose conduct had earned his disapproval; since the justices esteemed the consequence their office gave them among their neighbours, their knowledge that this was the king's practice kept them on their best behaviour. This myth is far from true. In the first place, it was not the king, but the chancellor, who supervised the county justices: commissions were issued by his authority, without royal warrant, and he is known to have made several appointments from his private residences when the king was elsewhere. What is more, the Chancery records of issues of commissions show emphatically that they were not issued annually: in some counties, the commissions stayed unchanged for four or five years.

A very large number of commissions of the peace were, nevertheless, issued in the course of Henry's reign,[14] every one of course replacing its predecessor. There were forty county areas in which the crown appointed commissions, and the average annual total issued was thirty eight. Yet there was much variation in their frequency with regard both to time and place. Thus 106 commissions were issued in the first two years of the reign, but only 84 in the next five years (1487–93). As for geographical distribution, Bedfordshire had but eight commissions in the whole reign, while at the other end of the scale Gloucestershire had thirty—nine in the first four years of the reign and twelve between 1500 and 1505. In most cases the issue of commissions can be explained by the succession of new prelates or lords on the deaths of their predecessors, the addition of members of the king's council, or the removal of men implicated in treasonable conspiracies. There does remain, however, some evidence of central supervision of the ordinary working justices, as we can trace instances of individuals being dropped from their commissions and later restored. Thus Sir John Cottesmore, an Oxfordshire justice appointed in 1502, was dismissed in 1504; he had been in trouble, for he received a royal pardon in 1506 and three years later, having presumably established that he was a reformed character, was again put on the Oxfordshire list. Again, Ralph Chamberlain's name was on the commission for Cambridgeshire in 1505, the last of the reign, but in 1509 he was described as a former justice of the peace when he likewise was given a pardon.[15] We might note that both these men could be described as members of that middle-class supposed to have been devoted agents of royal government.

There were various means whereby the central authorities could obtain information about the public and private conduct of county justices. There were official channels. The professional judges in their circuits of gaol delivery would learn of shortcomings and report them to the king and council. There were two or three members of the council on the commissions of most counties. Their official duties would keep them elsewhere for most of the year, but they might visit their estates in the summer. Sir James Hobart, the attorney-general, was a justice and landowner in East Anglia, and he sat on the Suffolk bench in July 1496 and brought one of its records into King's Bench in the autumn of 1508.[16] A colleague of his standing would have kept the resident justices on their toes. The professionals undoubtedly took a close interest in the work of their amateur brethren. Thomas Marrow, a serjeant-at-law, lectured on their execution of the Westminster statute of 1275 at Lincoln's Inn in 1503. This 'reading', *De pace terre*—from the statute's opening words—was multiplied for circulation and used as a basis for sixteenth century manuals for justices of the peace. An anonymous *Boke of Justyces of Peas* was first printed in 1506.

A new method of supervision was provided for in 1489 by a remarkable statute. This required the justices to publish a proclamation at every meeting of quarter sessions. The reading of it cannot have given them any pleasure. It declared that the prevalence of crime and disorder of all kinds was the result of their own negligence; there were sufficient laws, but the justices were failing to enforce them. The proclamation invited all subjects to see to it that the justices performed their duties, and if any justice refused to act on a request for legal redress, the complainant should go to a neighbouring justice; if he got no satisfaction there, he should take his grievance to the justices of gaol delivery, but in the last resort he could go on to the king or chancellor. If it was then established that the first justice had been negligent, he would be dismissed from office and punished according to his offence. By the quarterly publication of this proclamation, no one could fail to know that even the king was ready to listen to complaints against the justices. Even in the more remote parts of the kingdom, this threat was a constant spur to diligence.* Yet the two instances already cited, and they could be supplemented, show that the problem of making the county justices irreproachable pillars of public order was never completely solved. On the other hand, there is good reason to believe that in some counties the justices were exercising their powers to an extent they had not dared earlier in the fifteenth century, notably in their enforcement of the statutes against livery and maintenance.

Sheriffs

The sheriff was the chief executive agent for the administration of justice in his shire or shires.† It was his task to deliver or obey the numerous writs whereby legal actions were begun, prosecuted and concluded; he summoned defendants to whatever court the plaintiff had chosen, and carried out decrees seizing property and pronouncing outlawry on those who did not appear to answer; he selected jurors

---

* Henry made a number of appointments of clerks of the peace,[17] but not, apparently, with the object of making them watchdogs over the justices. The terms of the grants suggest that these were rewards to servants who could take the profits and leave the work to deputies.

† Several counties had long been paired under one sheriff (*e.g.* Norfolk and Suffolk).

in both civil and criminal suits; he enforced the verdicts of the courts. The sheriff had charge of all local police arrangements, with authority to require the service of all able-bodied men in his bailiwick, to pursue and capture miscreants or suppress disorder. He arrested accused persons and was responsible for their detention in the county gaol until the time of trial. Until 1461, he held a court—the sheriff's tourn—where suspects were charged and arrested. Numerous orders came to him from other agencies of the central government. He was its mouthpiece in the shire, publishing its proclamations. He was required to arrange for the election of knights and burgesses for parliament. The crown's ancient sources of revenue in the county, including the profits of justice, were collected by the sheriff. He had to account for these at the Exchequer, although he might have had to spend some on the king's behalf. He was, in fact, the crown's general factotum in the shire.

Needless to say, in the disorderly years of the fifteenth century, a sheriff found ample opportunities to turn his office to improper purposes. His duties in legal administration offered considerable scope for abuse. He was not paid by the crown, but numerous pickings could be made here. In return for certain considerations, he might fail to serve writs or he would select jurors whose verdict could be guaranteed; his authority to arrest suspects could be employed in a corrupt manner, against enemies of his clients, or he might hold innocent men until they paid to be released. Like justices of the peace, the sheriff was often a baronial retainer, and he would exercise his authority to the local advantage of his 'good lord' and other members of the retinue, impeding attempts to bring them to justice and harrying their opponents with the machinery of the law.

Another reform in local government claimed for Henry VII was the reduction of the sheriff's importance: the office had 'decayed', it had fallen into the control of the nobility, and Henry's remedy was to place sheriffs under the supervision of the reliable justices of the peace. This view requires modification in all points. Admittedly, individual sheriffs had as retainers come under the direction of magnates, but the office itself was conferred by the king in all but three counties.* According to fourteenth century statutes, sheriffs were appointed annually by the crown: it was forbidden for a sheriff to retain his office for more than one year. As there was no salary,

* Durham, Westmorland and Worcester.

sheriffs were generally chosen from the same social class, the more prosperous gentry, which provided the counties with parliamentary knights and justices of the peace. In view of the importance of the office, the king naturally preferred men whose loyalty to him was beyond doubt; this was a more weighty consideration than their behaviour in other aspects of their work. From the middle of the fifteenth century, there was a growing tendency for the crown to appoint sheriffs attached to the king's household; they would, probably, also be landowners in their shires. Of course, when the authority of the king was weak, baronial interests would effect his choice of sheriffs; magnates with influence in his council would press for their retainers to be appointed.

It cannot however be said that the baronage usurped the king's prerogative in the making of sheriffs. When the king was master, he could dispose of shrievalties at will. The resurgence of royal authority under Edward IV proves this. Nor can it be said that the sheriff's office had declined in importance. It was deprived of its judicial functions in 1461, but Edward appreciated its value sufficiently to introduce the practice of giving his sheriffs 'tallies of reward', that is, authorising them to draw payments from the royal revenues they collected; there was a sliding scale, running down from York, the largest shrievalty, with £340, to £13 6s. 8d. to the sheriff of Rutland.[18] The reason for this innovation was the large expenses annually incurred, which were sometimes cited as an excuse by men unwilling to accept appointment. This payment may have inclined sheriffs to eschew dubious ways of making profits, but Edward's aim was presumably to improve the efficiency of their police work, particularly against rebels.

It is obvious, therefore, that in the years immediately preceding Henry VII's accession the sheriff was not a baronial agent; he was a paid servant of the Yorkish king. There was no need for Henry to devise any measures to bring the office under royal control. He made annual appointments of sheriffs, as his predecessors had done, and he chose them from the same class of men. His sheriffs of Kent, for instance, were all gentry holding land in the county, several of them the descendants of past sheriffs there; of these, perhaps a quarter had positions in his household—a proportion similar to that in past reigns—and, we might note, three at least had actively served the Yorkist kings.[19] Nor did Henry place less value on the services of his sheriffs, for he continued the practice of giving 'tallies of reward' at the same rates as Edward had done.[20] There is yet more telling evidence of his conservatism about the shrievalty. If he had wished to secure complete control of all the shrievalties in England, he could have done so in 1485. In the palatine counties of Lancaster and Chester, he appointed sheriffs, not in his capacity as king, but as their territorial lord. He gave the Lancashire office to the earl of Derby's son, for life, and in Cheshire the office was held for long terms by a succession of royal nominees. The only two ancient hereditary shrievalties were in his hands by forfeiture: Westmorland was restored to Lord Clifford and Worcester granted to Sir John Savage and his son for their lives. Henry also restored the shrievalty of Northumberland to its earl, to whom it had been given for life by Edward IV. In all these cases, the shrievalty had been treated as a sort of property which could be given to reward good service, and thus Henry had lost a unique opportunity to keep these shires under the same measure of control as he exercised elsewhere.

Control of sheriffs

The king's ability to choose sheriffs, however, was a secondary consideration when set against the problem of how to ensure their good behaviour in office; it would not have mattered which men became sheriffs if in the performance of their duties they exhibited unswerving devotion to the service of the king and to the administration of impartial justice to his subjects. As in the case of justices of the peace, the crux of the matter was the degree of respect which royal authority could command. The corrupt practices of sheriffs in selecting jurors and handling writs was one of the matters specifically mentioned in the so-called 'Star Chamber Act' of 1487, and four cases are known of sheriffs being summoned before the king's councillors to answer complaints about their misconduct. In 1495 another statute said that 'great extortion is yearly used and had within diverse counties' by sheriffs and their officers; they defrauded plaintiffs by failing to summon and arrest defendants who had given bribes, they concocted fictitious suits and fined people for not appearing in court although no summonses had been served, and they falsified their accounts to have excuses to extort money from 'the poor commons'. To prevent these abuses, justices of the peace were charged to hear complaints and also to audit the sheriffs' records of fines, and to proceed against offenders at quarter sessions, inflicting monetary penalties on the guilty.

Although this statute attacked abuses in only one sector of the sheriff's work, it has been hailed as an important departure in royal policy, whereby Henry subordinated the sheriff to the justice of the peace. Now, complaints about the behaviour of sheriffs had been made by the commons in parliaments long before 1495. There were allegations which resulted in the statutes of 1340 and 1368 requiring the king to appoint new sheriffs every year. They were accused in 1404 of embezzling revenues belonging to the king, in 1425 of not executing writs to produce juries, for corrupt reasons, in 1439 of taking bribes to empanel jurors who would favour particular litigants. Statutes were made in the attempt to provide remedies; in the last case, complaints were to be made to the justices before whom the juries were to appear, and these could have been justices of the peace. In 1445, the justices of the peace were empowered to enquire whether sheriffs exacted higher fees than they were allowed by statute, or embezzled money raised to pay the wages of shire knights in parliament. The commons sought in 1455 to restrain the sheriff's power to arrest and imprison people by authorising justices to release detainees of good repute on bail; this parliamentary petition was rejected then, but Richard III granted a statute to this effect. The statute of 1461 transferring the sheriff's judicial authority to the justices likewise originated as a petition from the commons. Seen against this record of legislation, Henry VII's statute of 1495 cannot be regarded as revolutionary. It was but one more step in a process begun fifty years earlier, and the credit for devising the subjection of the sheriff to the county justices must be given to the commons in Henry VI's parliaments.

It was natural that these shire knights should have had an exaggerated respect for the capacity of justices of the peace as agents of reform, for they were mostly justices themselves. It is hard to share their confidence. Obviously, the statute of 1439 against packing juries had little effect since the matter was again legislated for in 1487. The cancer of bastard feudalism accounts to a large extent for the futility of legislation in the Lancastrian period. Kings who could curb this evil gave new life to all the laws in the statute book. But there is a further reason for doubting if justices of the peace were ideally suited to be watchdogs over the shrievalty. This is that both offices were filled by members of the same social class, by men not only of similar means and interests, but also often closely connected by personal relationships. Sheriffs were frequently men who served on the commission of the peace, and *vice versa*. Returning to Henry VII's sheriffs of Kent, we find that ten were justices at the time of their appointment, and ten others became justices after they had been sheriffs. When Lewis Clifford, who had been sheriff of Kent in 1497–8, made arrangements for the performance of his last will and testament in 1506, six of the trustees he appointed were also ex-sheriffs and most were justices.[21] Although a justice left the bench for the time he was sheriff, we may well imagine that his former colleagues took a charitable view of his shortcomings in office, either because they were his friends and kinsmen, or because they could one day expect him to be in a position to sit in judgment on them. A number of cases have been traced of Henry VII's sheriffs being prosecuted for taking bribes, but none of the evidence shows that justices of the peace were responsible for initiating these proceedings. It was unfortunate, from the king's point of view, that he had no alternative but to trust county gentry to look after county affairs; it required the constant vigilance of his council to ensure that they honoured this trust.

Distant provinces

The outlying parts of his kingdom provided Henry with most cause for alarm in the early years of his reign. In Ireland particularly, it seemed, any declared opponent of the Tudor was assured of a base for an invasion of England. His resources, however, were entirely inadequate to keep the island in subjection; indeed, since Henry II had made himself lord of Ireland four centuries earlier, no English king had been able to establish his mastery over the country. It was only possible to maintain a semblance of order in the immediate vicinity of Dublin, the Pale, but even here the great Anglo-Norman houses were dominant. In more remote and inaccessible parts, chieftains of ancient lineage commanded the loyalties of a primitive society. Although Henry appointed nominal lieutenants of Ireland, the office was exercised by the resident lord deputy, and despite a Yorkist past and adherence to Lambert Simnel, this post was held by Gerald FitzGerald, earl of Kildare, until 1492. Fortunately for the English king, the FitzGeralds of Kildare and Desmond, and the Butlers of Ormond, were bitterly divided by feuds of long standing.

Henry was thus able to intervene, replacing Kildare with a Butler as lord deputy. Then in 1494 he sent over his well-proved councillor, Sir Edward Poynings, with a necessarily small retinue. As deputy for the new lieutenant, Prince Henry, Poynings held a parliament at Drogheda. By its most celebrated act, the so-called Poynings' Law, this parliament conceded that no future Irish parliament could be held unless the king of England and his council approved of the legislation to be laid before it. A second act agreed that statutes made in England would apply to Ireland as well, and further measures aimed to provide for the orderly administration of the Pale.

Although the Irish parliament was thus hamstrung for three centuries to come, the success of the other arrangements appears to have been transient. Poynings' measures ensured the failure of Perkin Warbeck's landing in 1496. Later that year, Kildare returned from England as deputy; Henry is said to have observed that as Ireland could not rule Kildare, Kildare should rule Ireland. It was a realistic arrangement. The crisis had been happily passed, and Henry had no money to hold Ireland by force. Kildare might use his authority for personal aggrandisement, but he no more troubled Henry with treasonable designs, and he could be relied upon to restrain his rivals. Henry had cut his losses: all he wanted from Ireland was its neutrality.

The lands north of Trent and west of Severn posed similar problems to a king ruling from Westminster. Distance was the most obvious, and the terrain itself was in many places wild and inhospitable. The economic development of these districts was naturally less advanced than in central and southern England, while hills and moors gave cover to the lawless. Both areas had been frontier zones when England came under the rule of Norman kings. Their practice in dealing with such outlying territories had been to make fiefs with lords enjoying greater autonomy than vassals in the more settled parts of the kingdom were allowed. These franchises did not all survive until the fifteenth century, but there remained considerable tracts of the northern counties where 'the king's writ did not run', in other words, where the administration of justice lay, in varying degrees, in the hands of the territorial lord, with royal officers being excluded from his domains; the lord of Westmorland was its hereditary sheriff, in Cumberland the king's officers were excluded from the honour of Cockermouth, and in Northumberland from Tynedale, Redesdale and Hexhamshire. On its border with Scotland, Norhamshire belonged to the bishop of Durham, who had in his county palatine almost complete independence of the crown in the administration of justice to his subjects. Lancashire also was a county palatine, with equally extensive 'liberties', although it was under royal control because its lord was the king of England.

The Welsh marches

Cheshire was another palatinate similarly united to the crown. It owed its creation to the former independence of the princes of Wales. The eastern half of modern Wales had been conquered by Anglo-Norman marcher lords, and in these 'marches of Wales' royal authority had no jurisdiction. With the exception of Pembroke, the western part of the country formed the principality of Wales, a royal possession. During the fifteenth century, many of the marcher lordships had fallen into the king's hands. Some were part of the duchy of Lancaster. The earldom of March, embracing lands in central Wales, Shropshire and Herefordshire, became royal estates when their ruler took the crown as Edward IV. The confiscation of the earldom of Warwick increased royal possessions in the modern county of Glamorgan. Whether these lands belonged to the king or not, however, the structure of local government was varied and confusing. There still existed numerous lordships, each with its own hierarchy of officers, its own system of courts, its own body of legal customs. In this situation it was impossible to provide a uniform and efficient system of preserving law and order. Opportunities for abuse and evasion abounded. It was the same in northern England, with its complexity of franchises. Distance from Westminster not only impeded control, it deterred inhabitants from litigation there and encouraged them instead to take their suits to the courts of their local overlord. The personal authority of the northern baronage was thereby strengthened, and their command of local loyalties added to the problems of a king anxious to secure complete mastery of his kingdom. Lawlessness easily engendered rebellion, and the provision of adequate judicial machinery was an essential step in the establishment of royal authority.

The Yorkist kings developed a policy of giving regional government to Wales and the north. When Edward's son was granted the principality of Wales in 1471, a council was set up to manage his domains.

There was nothing unusual in this, because it was the customary practice of lords to form councils of administrators, lawyers and other advisers to manage their estates. Two years later, however, the prince's council was charged to put down crime and disorder in the shires of Hereford and Salop. Then, formally established at Ludlow and organised under the presidency of Bishop Alcock, it began to acquire large judicial powers throughout Wales and the English border counties. It acted not only to punish crime, but also to organise legal administration in the various royal and private lordships; it is known to have intervened at Shrewsbury to regulate its civic arrangements for keeping the peace. This council seemingly lapsed in 1483 and Henry VII's earliest attempt to keep order in Wales was to empower his uncle Jasper, duke of Bedford, to appoint justices with full powers to try treasons and all other crimes in the same area, that is, all Wales and the shires of Hereford, Gloucester, Salop and Worcester. This may have been a temporary arrangement connected with the rising of the Staffords, but in 1493 Arthur was given similar powers after his creation as prince of Wales. As he was also granted numerous lands in the same area, it may be said that Arthur was now filling the place once held by Edward IV's son. Like the younger Edward, Arthur kept his household at Ludlow, with a council under the presidency of a bishop (William Smith). After the prince's death in 1501, the council was kept in being to exercise the same powers for the enforcement of law and order.

The council in the north

In northern England, a second princely council was converted into a regional authority. Richard III, when duke of Gloucester, had become the greatest northern landowner by his wife's inheritance and royal grants. His private council remained in Yorkshire with his heir after 1483, and in 1484 it was empowered and given instructions to administer justice. It was required both to keep order by suppressing riots and the like, and by punishing offenders, and to receive complaints and pleas for redress at quarterly sessions to be held in York. It had, in fact, civil as well as criminal jurisdiction, the first being of an equitable nature. This was a great amenity to the inhabitants of the district, particularly to poorer people unable to resort to the courts at Westminster, and this consideration for their difficulties does much to explain Richard's popularity in northern England. This council in the north was the king's, and subordinate to his royal council in the capital. The functions and even some features of the organisation of this council of 1484 were identical with those of the council of the north established in 1537 and employed until its abolition in 1641. Richard effected another reform in the north. Before 1483, he had been warden of Carlisle and the west march, but thereafter retained the office and engaged a lieutenant at a modest salary; he thus abolished an office which was both expensive to the crown and dangerous in its opportunities for private aggrandisement.[22]

In 1485, Richard's northern council disappeared with its creator. Henry did not revive the wardenship of the west march, but he soon restored the earl of Northumberland to the wardenship of the east march and gave him charge of northern affairs, here acting, no doubt, in the same spirit as when he sent Kildare back to Ireland in 1496. The earl proved his new loyalty against Henry's enemies and showed some initiative in settling local disputes. Then in 1489, despite his warnings, Henry insisted on the collection of a tax in Yorkshire and the earl was murdered in the ensuing riot. To fill the breach, the king appointed his son Arthur as warden-general, with the newly released earl of Surrey as his lieutenant. These arrangements again suggest that Henry regarded the north in the same light as he did Ireland.

Surrey established his headquarters in Yorkshire, with a council under the presidency of William Senhouse, abbot of St. Mary's, York, and subsequently bishop first of Carlisle and next of Durham. There were lawyers on this council, but it apparently lacked full judicial powers like those of the council of 1484. From time to time it was commissioned to deal with particular matters, and north country pleas to the king's council in Westminster were referred to its attention. Archbishop Savage of York became the king's lieutenant in the north after Surrey's departure, and he is known to have summoned defeated litigants who opposed a verdict to explain their behaviour, and to have ordered a jury to indict William Plumpton and his servants; and he also made enquiries into the relations of two knights whose feud was disturbing the peace. There is little other positive evidence of the work of Henry VII's northern council, but the position held by Savage resembles that of later lord presidents of the council of the north. Unlike Surrey, he was better qualified as a judge than a soldier, being a doctor of laws and former member of the king's committee for requests. The council was allowed to lapse on Henry VII's death, presumably in deference to protests against the extent to which some of its lawyers had exceeded their commissions to levy royal debts and simultaneously enriched themselves.

The meagre evidence of the work of Henry VII's council in the north indicates that its activities were confined to Yorkshire. Several of its members were commissioned as justices of the peace there, which gave them criminal jurisdiction in the county, and ensured that the other justices were attentive to their duties. The commissions of the peace for Northumberland from 1485 show that at first the earl, through his dependents, and as sheriff, was left in complete control until his death. Then an entirely new commission under Prince Arthur and the earl of Surrey was appointed. Towards the end of the reign, when Savage was lieutenant, two of his clerical lawyers, Thomas Dalby and Thomas Magnus, were appointed to the Northumbrian as well as to the Yorkshire commission. We may presume, then, that the council did take an interest in Northumberland. There is no similar reason to believe that it concerned itself with Cumberland and Westmorland. Indeed, only five commissions of the peace were issued for each county in the course of Henry's reign, which is scarcely evidence of much interest by the central government in their affairs. This was not because their inhabitants were distinguished for good behaviour. By 1522 their condition was appalling: as their bishop wrote, 'there is more theft, more extortion by English thieves than there is by all the Scots of Scotland'. Murders were followed by feuds or arbitration and monetary compensation. One reason for this state of affairs was that there were so few justices of the peace and thus quarter sessions were not held. The government's neglect of the west march dates from Henry VII's reign. When Richard III was its warden, he would not have tolerated these conditions; but, presumably, to Henry, Cumberland and Westmorland, like Ireland, could generally be left alone: they were safely isolated by their fells.

Franchises

As we have noticed in the cases of hereditary shrievalties, Henry's attitude to franchises was conservative. It is true that he had the 'liberties' of Tynedale abolished by statute in 1495, because of its notorious lawlessness. On the other hand, he extended the privileges

F

of the lord of another Northumbrian franchise, Redesdale, in 1509, by allowing him to appoint his own justices of the peace.[23] Hexhamshire was left alone, although thieves abounded there in 1522, as they had throughout the previous century. This liberty belonged to the archbishop of York, and as the crown controlled episcopal appointments, Henry had little cause to fear that the government of the shire would fall into politically undesirable hands.

This was also the case with the greatest of all franchises, the Bishopric of Durham. In 1485, the see was held by John Sherwood, a scholar and diplomat high in Richard III's esteem. The bishop, however, preferred Rome to Durham, and continued to spend most of his time at the Curia, in the service of the pope and as Henry's representative. After Sherwood's death in 1493, Richard Fox took his place, and when Fox left, he was succeeded by William Senhouse, the former president of the council at York. Henry's last appointment to Durham was another absentee, Christopher Bainbridge. Throughout the reign, therefore, Durham was either held by a trusted royal minister or its bishop was not at hand to defend its privileges against royal intervention, as, when after the battle of Stoke, Henry appointed commissioners to enquire about treasons in the Bishopric. Even during Sherwood's pontificate, however, the traditional episcopal policy of appointing royal judges to the Durham judiciary was continued.[24] There was no reason to doubt that the common law of England was applied by the ruler of the county palatine, and its franchises escaped radical challenge by the crown until Henry VIII's statute of 1536.

Clerical privilege and sanctuaries

While the king generally made no attempt to reduce the rights of territorial franchises, he effected a breach in the privileges of a growing proportion of the population. Since the twelfth century, English kings had allowed clergy convicted of felonies in the common law courts to be delivered to the custody of the local bishop instead of suffering the penalties which would have been inflicted on a layman. The proportion of men in clerical orders in England in the later middle ages was about one in twenty, but as the courts took it as proof of a man's 'clergy' that he could read, the number who could benefit was larger, and with increasing literacy among the laity, was rising to a very considerable proportion. The commons in the parlia-

ment of 1449 urged the restriction of this clerical privilege, alleging
that it encouraged crime; clerks committed to their bishop easily won
their freedom and then resumed their evil ways. This petition failed,
as did another in 1455. A more moderate measure was enacted in
1489. Henceforth criminals not in clerical orders would be allowed
to benefit only once by their ability to read; they were to be branded
on the thumb and treated as laymen if charged a second time.
Clergy proper were exempted from this treatment if they produced
their letters of ordination.

A second ecclesiastical privilege which protected wrongdoers was
the right of sanctuary. A criminal who escaped arrest and gained
shelter in any church was allowed to remain there for forty days, when
he would be banished from the country. A man who reached one of
the great sanctuaries like Westminster Abbey or Beverley could stay
there for ever. Kings had tended to disregard these immunities in the
case of traitors and so there were precedents for Henry's action in
removing Humphrey Stafford from Abingdon Abbey in 1487. The
king's right to do this was upheld by the judges, whose dislike of
ecclesiastical privileges is revealed in the reports of their discussions
in the *Year Books*. Certain abuses in the use of sanctuaries were
attacked. Debtors took to sanctuary to evade arrest and lived on the
income of their property entrusted to friends. An act initiated by the
commons in 1487 forbade assignments of property for this purpose.
Criminals who made sanctuaries bases for their operations were
threatened by an agreement between the king and the pope in the
same year. Henry was given papal authority to order the removal from
sanctuary of felons who returned to this shelter after committing
a second crime. These, again, were limited measures, discreetly
arranged, disclosing the king's desire not to offend the susceptibilities
of churchmen. His respect for traditional vested interests, secular
as well as ecclesiastical, explains his failure to attempt really radical
reforms.

Livery and maintenance

Of all the problems troubling medieval legislators, the most obdurate
was maintenance. From the close of the thirteenth century, statutes
were made banning the practice of intervention in legal causes by
improper means on behalf of one or other party. This kind of interference with the course of justice was not committed only by lords on

behalf of their retainers. Men of humbler station were equally prone to help their friends in the courts, to give assistance in return for payment. Juries in municipal courts could be subverted by gangs of townsmen no less easily than could the jurors in the shire courts by the armed retinues of noble lords; the officials of both kinds of court were equally exposed to pressure. Yet while parliaments thundered against maintenance and other corrupt practices, defined new offences and prescribed new penalties, their statutes could be rendered useless when juries would not present or convict transgressors.

Although baronial retinues [25] were not alone responsible for this state of affairs, their existence was a serious danger to the administration of the law, and for other reasons they were a cause of particular concern to the central government. These liveried companies were an organised and relatively permanent feature of English society, and gave their employers great weight in local affairs. Their power could not only manipulate judicial proceedings but could also disrupt the peace of the countryside. The lords were not always responsible for the illegal exploits of their followers: a retainer in trouble with the authorities, or at odds with a neighbour, might call upon his fellows for their armed support. There was always a possibility that a lord might lead his retinue in war against the king. The armies of Lancaster and York were formed by alliances of lords commanding the services of companies of gentry.

The crown's attitude to baronial companies, however, was also influenced by other considerations. In the first place, it was regarded as entirely proper that a noble should be attended by a company of men of respectable social status and sartorial appearance. A king who attempted to deprive the lords of this conventional support to their dignity would have incurred ill-feeling likely to jeopardise his own security. Moreover, it was to his advantage that these bodies should be available for military purposes; they could be considered as equivalent to the Territorial Army, already organised in units and easily assembled for service against a foreign invader or powerful rebel. In times of continuing unrest, as in the aftermath of civil war, the king could regard as relatively well-ordered those districts where the gentry had been retained by lords whose loyalty he did not doubt. It was undoubtedly the king's duty, nor did parliaments let him forget, to restrain lords from employing their retainers against the interests of justice; but how far he could go in this direction was measured by the strength of his own position. The lords had obligations to their followers: in the indentures of retainder, they undertook to be 'good lords' to their men. This was a second kind of maintenance, resting on notions of honour and prestige. It committed a lord to accepting responsibility to advance and protect the interests of his clients, and it need not have led to his perpetrating the other sort of maintenance condemned by statutes. All too frequently, however, nobles championed their retainers beyond the legitimate bounds of 'good lordship'.

Royal policy to baronial retaining had thus tended to be a combination of connivance and restraint. The practice was allowed while the lords were called upon to prevent breaches of the law by their followers. On occasion—as in 1433 and 1461—they were required to take oaths in parliament not to take evil-doers under their protection. The right to give liveries to men retained for life was confined to the peerage, and penalties were pronounced against those of lower rank who presumed to form liveried retinues. By confining this privilege to the lords, the king should then, in theory, have been able to control 'bastard feudalism' through his personal relations with them. Beyond this, no king tried to do more until Edward IV, in 1468, passed a statute which commanded that 'no person, of what[soever] degree or condition he be . . . give any livery or sign or retain any person other than his menial servant, officer or man learned in the law'. Offenders were to pay £5 for every month for every retainer outside these categories, and those retained would also forfeit £5 a month. This statute was to be enforced by all justices, including justices of the peace, on receipt of information, and they could convict after examining the accused, or proceed to a formal trial, 'as the case shall require, after the discretion of the judges'. Informers would be paid for their expenses and receive half the sums forfeited. Thus, it would appear, Edward had outlawed the entire practice, by lords as well as others, of engaging retainers and giving them liveries; for the only persons specifically given permanent exemption from this prohibition were the wardens of the marches, although others would have temporary exemption when engaged on military duties.

As far as the lords were concerned, however, this seemingly momentous statute was a dead-letter. Sixty-four indentures of retainder of knights and esquires to Lord Hastings survive from the years

1469–82. The statute had not provided for the king dispensing individuals from its observance, nor is there any evidence of royal
licences to this effect being granted to Hastings or anyone else. It is
arguable that the act left a loophole by a provision that it should not
prejudice grants of fees or property 'by the king or any other person
or persons to any person or persons for their counsel given or to be
given and their lawful service done or to be done and for any other
cause not unlawful'. We may doubt if this clause does prove that
Edward confirmed the lords' privilege to engage retainers provided
that they did so for lawful causes: the clause does not refer to lords,
but to 'any person or persons'. It is ridiculous to suppose that
Edward was giving all and sundry liberty to engage retainers. Nor
does the clause allow livery or badges to be given; they were still
included in the general prohibition. Moreover, if Edward's intention
had been to allow lords only to retain, what was the purpose of the
statute? The act of 1390 had already forbidden retaining by men of
lower rank. Our conclusion must be that Edward's statute was an
ambitious declaration of purpose. Events soon compelled him to
abandon it. He owed his recovery of the throne in 1470 to lords like
Hastings who had retinues available for military service. The statute
was not enforced against the lords because it would have been
against the king's interest to disband baronial retinues.

Henry VII and retaining

This was the legal position at Henry's accession. The judges, literal
interpreters of the law, believed that it was illegal for any person to
retain others apart from domestic servants. The king, however, was as
cautious as his Yorkist predecessors. He also was too aware that he
might need the services of the lords and their followers. He owed his
escape from ambush in Yorkshire in 1486 to the earl of Northumberland, and companies provided by lords helped to form the armies
which defeated other rebel forces. When he prepared for war against
France in 1492, the army was raised by indentures with lords who in
their turn enlisted companies. The law against retaining by men
below baronial rank was vigorously enforced in the common law
courts. The king's council and the special tribunal set up in 1487
do not appear to have been much involved in business of this kind,
but numerous indictments for retaining taken before justices of the
peace were sent into King's Bench; and as the county justices were

empowered to conclude proceedings in their own courts, there were presumably other prosecutions and convictions of which records have not survived. In none of the known cases of Henry's first twenty years, however, were charges made against a peer. So far as the lords were concerned, Henry kept to the customary royal policy of urging them to restrain their retainers from illegal conduct. An oath, similar to that of 1433, was taken in his first parliament by lords and commons alike that they would not protect known felons. By new legislation and by the activities of the conciliar and, more frequently, the common law courts, the crown waged war against illegal maintenance, intimidation of juries, and other malpractices; although these offences, as we have noted before, were not the monopoly of baronial retinues.

As Henry became more assured in his tenure of the throne, there came a gradual change in his attitude to retaining. In a statute of 1487, the retainder of tenants of royal estates was forbidden;* they might wear only the king's livery. Then the king, in an act of 1495, expressed the principle 'that every subject, by the duty of his allegiance, is bound to serve and assist his prince and sovereign lord at all seasons when need shall require'. The notion that loyalty to the king overrode all other obligations was of course generally understood—it was recognised even in indentures of retainder—but subjects were prone to overlook it when their immediate interests were at stake. Again, in a proclamation in 1502, Henry reminded the people of Kent and Sussex that their services belonged solely to him, and they were commanded not to be retained or take liveries from any man. This extension of the prohibition against accepting retainder to subjects who were not crown tenants marks the growth of Henry's confidence. He was, apparently, aiming to dissolve retinues by cutting off the supply of recruits. Then in 1504 came the celebrated statute against liveries. It was largely a repetition of the act of 1468, but the procedure for prosecution was changed: justices of the peace were to report breaches of the law to King's Bench for trial there or in the king's council, and the latter might also proceed against suspects on its own initiative. This change suggests that the king's complaint in the preamble to the statute, that liveries were still being given, arose from a suspicion that justices of the peace were unable or unwilling to enforce the law against all offenders. A further tightening of the law

* Richard III had made a similar claim on his tenants at Tutbury.

came with the omission of the 1468 clause in favour of grants for
'lawful causes', but a new opening was made by adding a provision
that the king could now license men to raise companies for his
service.

Even now, the king's exhortations and legislation were falling on
deaf ears. The only documented prosecution of a peer for retaining
was that of Lord Abergavenny,* a kinsman and councillor of the
king, who was indicted before justices of the peace in Kent in 1506
and stood trial in King's Bench in the following year. It was disclosed that from 1504, the year of the statute, Abergavenny had retained a total of 471 men, most described as yeomen, from four score
towns and villages in mid-Kent. Obviously the king's proclamation to
the people of this county in 1502 had made little impression. Abergavenny pleaded guilty and incurred a total penalty of £70,650.
There is further evidence from other parts of the country that retaining persisted despite the king's efforts. Nor is it clear that he really
desired the complete abolition of the practice. Abergavenny's prosecution does not prove that he did. In the previous year, Abergavenny had been arrested on suspicion of treasonable relations with
the earl of Suffolk, and although he cleared himself of the charge,
Henry probably decided to make him harmless by destroying his
local influence through these proceedings for retaining. The king at
least once licensed the recruitment of a retinue to be constantly available for military service, and other Tudor monarchs similarly
authorised select persons to enjoy the attendance of liveried companies.

The king and the lords

The social pre-eminence of the baronage was one of the facts of life
Henry VII had to live with. To make it a prop rather than a danger
to his throne demanded that he made sure of the lords' loyalty to himself. The final destruction of the political unity of the magnate class
in the Wars of the Roses was an obvious asset to the king, and
memories of fathers and brothers slain and executed may well have
inclined his noble subjects to quiescence. Their caution would have
been increased by Henry's employment of spies and his record of
promptitude in following up rumours of treason. There was, however,

* Bacon's famous story about the earl of Oxford still awaits substantiation by record
evidence.

also a lesson for the king in the affair of William Stanley: even after ten years in intimate and well-rewarded royal service, a lord's loyalty could still be fragile. Henry enjoyed noble companionship and the conventional pursuits of their class, but he had good cause to have reservations even about lords who attended his court. His abiding mistrust is revealed by his dealings with a number of important peers.

There was one group with whom he was understandably wary. These were the men attainted for supporting Richard III at Bosworth. The earl of Surrey was kept in the Tower for four years, until 1489, when Henry was sufficiently convinced of his loyalty not only to set him free but to give him command against rebels in Yorkshire. Surrey's attainder was reversed in 1489, but only gradually, in recognition of useful services in the north over several years, was he successively allowed to recover various parts of his father's estates, and he had to purchase those manors which the king had given to others; he did not retrieve the title of duke of Norfolk until Henry VIII thus rewarded his victory at Flodden. This was how Henry VII treated a man who served him well. Others of whom he had less expectation fared worse. Lord Zouche also had his attainder reversed in 1489, but was allowed possession of only a portion of his lands. Later he was permitted to recover other estates if he could persuade the king's grantees to part with them. More obscure men were forced to pay high prices for the reversals of their attainders. A total of 138 people were attainted during the reign, of which sentences 46 were reversed. The figures closely correspond with those under Edward IV, although he gave pardons in a more liberal spirit. With both kings, however, the power to reverse attainders appears as an instrument of policy designed to strengthen royal authority.[26]

Other men who incurred Henry's suspicions without committing treason were subjected to restraints of another kind. The most commonly used device here was a bond to the king, acknowledging a debt which would be cancelled if its maker remained loyal. Richard III had adopted this means of securing loyal service, but from no more than ten knights in his two years as king. Henry throughout his reign made a practice of taking bonds for loyalty from men of all classes, including clergy, with the sums involved ranging from £400 in respect of a barber to £10,000 from peers; while, as a clerical example, the bishop of Worcester was bound in £2,000 to be loyal and not leave the realm. In his later years Henry regularly required captains of royal castles, receivers of lands and other officers to make recognisances for their loyalty and satisfactory execution of their duties, the captain of Calais in £40,000, for instance, and the porter there in £200. These pledges were formidable weapons. It would, after all, have been the king who decided whether the subjects in question had been loyal. The sums involved were large enough in every case to permit him to sequestrate all the property of those who displeased him. In fact, Henry is not known to have enforced such bonds, but the legal stranglehold he thus established provided the most compelling inducements to meticulous fidelity.

A variety of circumstances gave the king opportunities to secure bonds from a number of peers. Henry's brother-in-law the marquess of Dorset, who was detained in 1487 on suspicion of treason, was in 1492 forced to grant all his lands to a group of the king's nominees; if he gave offence or failed to disclose the treasons of others, the king would enjoy the revenues of his lands, but if he behaved satisfactorily until his death, his heir would have the inheritance; the king was to have immediate custody of Dorset's heir. The earl of Kent, whose debts put him entirely at Henry's mercy, was bound in 1507 to 'be seen daily once in the day within the king's house'. Lord Dacre in 1506 made a bond to pay £2,000 which the king respited 'at his gracious pleasure', and Lord Willoughby de Broke undertook in 1508 to pay £2,000 on two months' notice. On 20 November 1507, the earl of Northumberland sealed a bond acknowledging that £5,000 was due to the king on that same day. Abergavenny made a recognisance of £5,000 for his allegiance in 1507 and a second that he would not enter Kent, Surrey, Sussex or Hampshire without the king's licence.[27] These lords had been guilty of offences which made them liable to pay enormous penalties, but while the king had reduced these fines to more realistic if still large amounts, the price of his generosity was conditions leaving them at his mercy. The legend that Henry pursued a policy of simultaneously enriching himself and depressing the nobility with crushing fines clearly requires modification.

This was the period when Henry's legal interests were being managed by the notorious Empson and Dudley, when they and their colleagues in the council learned were rigorously exacting all possible profits of justice and statute for the king. Henry's personal preference for noble companionship, and his political caution, would have deterred him from causing the complete destruction of these lords which full payment of their initial fines would have entailed. Common lawyers were less inclined to show solicitude to representatives of that order of 'overmighty subjects' which had been such a threat to the country's legal institutions, and doubtless welcomed these opportunities to extend the king's power.

7

The Nation at Work

THE face of England offered a pleasing prospect to a visitor from Venice in Henry VII's reign. It 'is all diversified by pleasant undulating hills and beautiful valleys, there being nothing to be seen but agreeable woods, extensive meadows or lands in cultivation, and the greatest plenty of water springing everywhere'. The climate was healthy: 'the cold in winter is much less severe than in Italy, and the heat proportionately less in summer owing to the rain, which falls almost every day during the months of June, July and August'. Such was the fertility of the soil that the people were able to produce an abundant quantity of all the necessities of life, with the exception of wine; but they made beer and ale, which 'are most agreeable to the palate'. The rivers yielded many kinds of fish, although sea-fish were more popular, and there was an equal abundance of wildfowl. The Venetian thought that if more land were put under the plough, grain could be exported to neighbouring countries, but this negligence was remedied by the enormous numbers of comestible animals —deer, pigs, oxen, and, above all, sheep. He was also impressed, however, by seeing so few people as he travelled from Dover to Oxford. 'The population of this island does not appear to me to bear any proportion to her fertility and riches.'

Population

In the last quarter of the fifteenth century, the level of population in western Europe was beginning to show a generally upward trend for the first time since the opening of the fourteenth century. By that time the pace of demographic expansion had already stimulated modifications in the classic feudal structure of rural society; the pattern of largely self-contained village communities tied to their places of birth and bound to provide their lords with free labour services was no longer common to all parts of the western kingdoms. The growth of towns with the development of trade and industry also made breaches in this feudal economy. The demand for more land led to the reclamation of marshes, the clearance of scrub and woodland, the farming of 'marginal' land, and, in eastern Germany, the establishment of colonies in virgin territories. With no significant development in farming technology, it is probable that the ever-pressing need for increased production of foodstuffs brought about a reduction in the fertility of the soil. Whether this was the cause, or a succession of wet summers, or both factors, there was in the second decade of the fourteenth century a run of disastrous harvests which caused widespread conditions of famine.

Many people died at this time, but a second consequence of these bad harvests, and presumably of others which followed periodically, was that the undernourished survivors were ill-prepared to withstand epidemic disease. Thus when the Black Death reached Europe in 1348, it found millions of victims, between a quarter and a half of the total population. Further visitations followed, the fourth serious English outbreak being in 1375, and there were more throughout the following century. Although the mortality in these later plague years did not reach the appalling figures of 1348–9, it was sufficient, in England at least, to keep the level of population fairly static, at about 2,250,000. In France and Germany, recovery was further retarded by the devastations of war. More settled conditions began to obtain in the second half of the fifteenth century: France expelled the English and suppressed the freebooting companies, the Hussite invasions of Germany came to an end, and authoritarian governments took control in France and the electoral states of Germany. Simultaneously, it would appear, plague was no longer able to check the growth of population.

A new epidemic, the sweating sickness, appeared in London as an ominous curtain-raiser for Henry VII's reign, but although this first outbreak seemingly caused many deaths, people learned how to treat its victims and future attacks consequently produced less fatalities. Some diseases which are still of common occurrence today were inevitably more serious at this time of primitive medicine. Thus at Christmas 1489, 'there were the measles so strong and in especial amongst the ladies and the gentlewomen that some died of that sickness'. The Black Death itself reappeared in England in 1490 and 1500 and many deaths were attributed to it. Although it continued to return throughout the sixteenth century,[1] the increase in population was sustained so that, by its last years, there were in England approximately the same number of people as there had been three centuries earlier (about 3,750,000).

This new trend in European population inevitably had important repercussions on England's economy. Her exports of woollen cloth to the continent increased from the last quarter of the fifteenth century, and obviously one factor to promote this trade was the expansion of the European market. At home, the result of the population growth was that labour became more plentiful and the demand for land was strengthened; it was also stimulated by the enlarged orders for wool. The effects of these developments on the peasant majority were slow in gathering momentum. The prices paid for land began to rise from about 1470, but the purchasing power of wages remained unchanged for another thirty years. There was, probably, what we might call a 'slack' in the economy which was gradually absorbed in this interval: alternative employment was still available for those evicted from their tenancies, on other estates, in the expanding cloth industry, and in the building trade which was operating on a greatly extended scale at this time. Thus although the reigns of Edward IV and Henry VII did not witness any drastic change in conditions for the working population, they saw the end of a period when circumstances had favoured the wage-earner and tenant farmer and depressed the fortunes of the landowner.

Agriculture

The shortage of labour in the later middle ages had accelerated the transformation of the rural economy. In the classic type of feudal manor, there had been two categories of land: the domain, farmed by the lord, and the common fields, shared among his unfree tenants. Depopulation obliged lords to abandon the domain and instead to lease it whole or in parts to tenants whose only regular charge was the payment of rents, and these remained low while there was a scarcity of potential farmers. The villein who performed labour services for his lord in return for his tenure of strips in the common fields and the right to share in the use of the village meadows and waste was now transformed into the customary tenant. Lords of manors renounced or tacitly gave up their claims to services lest their peasants should be tempted to leave in order to become tenants or wage labourers elsewhere. Villeinage was practically extinct in England by 1500 except on the estates of ultra-conservative ecclesiastical proprietors. The real line of distinction in rural communities became one of material means rather than legal status, between the well-to-do yeomen farming part of the domain and possibly also their ancestral strips, and the husbandmen working for their wages.

The level of wages remained high and even rose slightly in the fifteenth century. Attempts to curb it by legislation were unavailing. It was high, that is to say, because it more than kept pace with the prices of basic commodities. Only in the immediate aftermath of the Black Death of 1348–9 did the price of wheat and other foodstuffs rise sharply. Despite the labour shortage, the level of prices subsequently remained steady except in years of bad harvests. This suggests, clearly, that agricultural productivity per head had been increased. The countryside had in any case been overpopulated in relation to its producing capacity at the opening of the fourteenth century. Moreover, in the years after 1348 the less attractive arable land was abandoned, some never to be ploughed again until the 1940's. The more favoured land, more economically managed by peasant tenants, was able to produce enough corn both for their consumption and for the urban markets; indeed, contrary to the Venetian's observation, some grain was exported, as we know from orders by Henry VI and Henry VII (in 1491)[2] that it was not to be taken to the lands of their enemies.

Enclosures

The volume of abuse directed against the enclosure of land in the sixteenth century suggests that this was a new and unmitigated evil. The type of enclosure to be condemned, however, was of formerly arable land given over to sheep, so that only a shepherd was employed where many small peasant farmers and labourers had previously been engaged. The enclosure of land for cultivation had obvious advantages. In some places it was necessary to prevent deer and cattle eating crops. Where manors had been broken up among numbers of peasant proprietors or tenants, or in common fields where tenants had by agreement exchanged their strips to form consolidated holdings, the farmer might erect a fence round his land. It is possible that in Kent fields never had been held in common, and here and in Essex and Suffolk pastures for cattle and pigs were enclosed. In northern England there was probably little arable land still unenclosed by 1500.

The conversion of arable land into sheepruns was not a novelty of the Tudor period. Indeed, it is likely that most of the enclosures for this purpose were carried out before the end of the fifteenth century. Sometimes this could be done without any need to eject tenants, in the cases of settlements in marginal land abandoned after the Black Death. Other villages forcibly depopulated are known to have been declining long before their final elimination, and much of their land had already gone under grass. Thus at Wiverton (Notts.) there had been 47 taxpayers in 1377, but only five dwellings were standing when the fields were enclosed in 1510. These small communities, particularly if they were tenants-at-will, were unable to defend themselves. The most seriously affected counties were in the central midlands. The Warwickshire antiquary John Rous reported that 58 villages of his county were so destroyed in his lifetime. He died in 1491.

The first official measure against enclosures was Henry VII's statute in 1489. It aimed to prevent depopulation and the decay of husbandry by forbidding the destruction of houses attached to twenty or more acres of land; but its enforcement was misguidedly left to the initiative of landlords. Within five years the new owner of Stretton Baskerville (Leics.) turned out 80 people, let their houses tumble down, 'and turned the fields from cultivation to be a feeding place for brute animals'. More grievous still, he let the parish church fall into ruins and allowed animals to shelter in it. The preservation of church dues had been another aim of Henry's statute. When in 1517 commissions enquired into depopulations since 1488, they discovered that many thousands of acres had been enclosed in the midlands. The larger part had been enclosed before 1500 and thus it appears that, although Henry VII's statute had been ineffective, the pace of enclosure was slowing down. In two thirds of the cases reported in 1517, only one house had been destroyed. The largest depopulations had taken place before 1488: only a handful of the villages appearing in Rous's list are shown in the 1517 returns.

The driving force behind enclosures was economic gain. Once he had stocked his fields with sheep, the owner's annual expenditure

14 Country buildings

15 A countryman at work

16 Merchant ships

17 A wool merchant's house

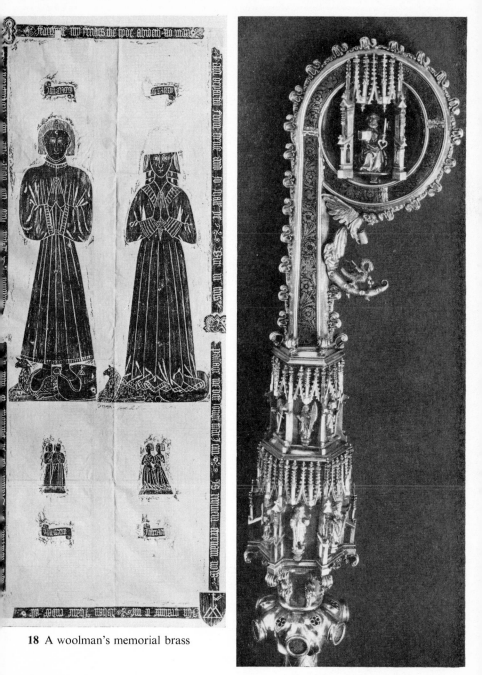

18 A woolman's memorial brass

19 Bishop Fox's crozier

20 Long Melford Church

21 Lavenham Church

was small compared with the running costs of arable land, and the profit from the sale of his crop of wool correspondingly greater. As an investment alone, and land still was and long remained the most favoured form of investment, the enclosing of it greatly added to its value; fenced fields are known to have changed hands for half as much again as did open fields. This commercial spirit of land exploitation seems to indicate the invasion of the countryside by capitalists with mercantile backgrounds, and indeed another statute against enclosing in 1515 specifically blames merchants who had newly bought lands for the wave of depopulations. The known evidence says otherwise; of 45 documented enclosures in Leicestershire before 1550, 37 were carried out by long established landed proprietors. The squirearchy were the principal depopulators, and religious houses were no more tender to their tenants.

The reviving fortunes of the proprietary classes is reflected in the buildings they were now able to erect. Even the abbeys, after the long depression of their finances and an absence of patronage by the laity, were able in the last 50 years of their history to put up commodious houses for their rulers and similar monuments to their affluence. The great tower of Fountains Abbey, completed about 1525, was doubtless paid for by the monks' four-legged flock. Although the tide had now turned in favour of the landowner, there was during Henry VII's reign little perceptible change for the worse in the condition of the great majority of the population living by agriculture. Depopulation must have caused some hardship, but the annual number of victims could not be numbered in more than hundreds. A statute of 1495 providing for oversight of vagabonds suggests that they were a growing problem, but the steadiness of average wage rates to about 1500 indicates that there was no sudden glut of labour and it may be presumed that most dispossessed villagers found other employment. Until its last decade, the fifteenth century remained, in the words of Thorold Rogers, 'the golden age of the English labourer'. Forty years were to pass before it became manifest that his wages were failing to keep pace with soaring prices, and then rioting countrymen blamed enclosures as the cause of their poverty.

Industries

In using the terms 'industry' and 'agriculture' in the context of this time, we must bear in mind that they refer only to different kinds of productive activity and not to mutually exclusive sections of the working population. With the exception of London, English towns were very small by modern standards, with open country pressing closely around their narrow confines; they had their common fields and pastures on which many of the inhabitants were part-time farmers. On the other hand, there were industries in the countryside operated by members of agricultural communities. These cottage industries flourished in most areas where agriculture tended to be mainly pastoral. In the north, farmers also worked in mines and quarries, in the uplands of Wessex and East Anglia they wove cloth. Only in districts specialising in crop production was agriculture a full-time occupation. Arable Norfolk was an exception to this pattern, for worsteds were manufactured here.

England had been famed for her mineral products in Roman times. The stannaries of Cornwall and Devon produced tin through-out the middle ages; despite the inevitable slump immediately after the Black Death of 1348–9, the industry speedily recovered and at the beginning of the sixteenth century its annual output was still increasing. There were silver-bearing leadmines in the Mendips, Derbyshire and eastern Cumberland. Fresh veins were discovered in the neighbourhood of Keswick and southern Northumberland in the reign of Edward IV, who leased them to five German miners in 1478. The Forest of Dean and the Weald of Kent and Sussex had iron industries which, from the fifteenth century, are known to have been using water-power to operate bellows for their charcoal furnaces. Coal was used in tin smelting but otherwise only for domestic heat-ing. Although most English coalfields had been broached, the most exploited fields were in County Durham and around Newcastle-upon-Tyne, England's busiest port for colliers which sailed not only to London but also to Germany and the Low Countries. An import-ant development in the industry was signalled in 1486 with the earliest known employment of a water-powered pump for a coal-mine at Finchale, near Durham; the working life of medieval pits had been short on account of their miners' inability to control flooding.

In the manufacturing industries, there was some specialisation in centres close to the sources of raw materials, as with nails in Coventry, cutlery in Sheffield and effigies and altars of Derbyshire alabaster in Nottingham. The goldsmiths and silversmiths of London had an international reputation for fine craftsmanship, and other metal-workers there cast bells and cannon. In most sizeable towns there were groups of tailors and hatmakers, glovers and other leather-workers producing for the local market. The principal manufacture of the kingdom was woollen cloth. It was made in many towns, although from the close of the fourteenth century the principal areas of growth in the industry were in the countryside, particularly in the valleys of the Cotswolds and Mendips, the East Anglian Heights, the Yorkshire Pennines and the Kendal district of Westmorland. Here there was water-power to work the fulling mills close to the supplies of raw wool. This dispersal of industry led to the growth of a class of wealthy middlemen, who bought and transported cloths from the manufacturing villages to markets and ports. While some cottagers weaved wool they had grown or bought, others were the employees of capitalist organisers like Thomas Spring of Lavenham.

Despite the spread of manufacturing activity to the countryside, there was still a marked increase of industry in the towns. One of the most marked developments in late medieval England was the advance in urban wealth. There were exceptions. Boston was disastrously hit by the loss of its overseas trade, Yarmouth was similarly impover-ished to a smaller extent, and York, Winchester, Lincoln and Oxford also lost business in the face of rural industry. Yet over the country as a whole towns were earning a larger share of the total national income. In 1334, the townships of Warwickshire accounted for only a tenth of the county's taxable income, but in 1524 they held over two-thirds. This was an exceptionally high rate of shift, doubtless to be partially explained by the high incidence of enclosures in this county, but in the same period the cloth and other industries of Coventry had expanded to multiply its wealth sixfold. In 1334, only in two cases did towns have incomes as high as fifteen per cent of their counties' total, but two centuries later there were fourteen counties where the towns fell into this category; indeed their share now averaged thirty per cent. English town populations, however, were still insignificant when measured against cities abroad. Only London, with perhaps 60,000 inhabitants, was in the same class as Paris, Rouen, Milan and Florence. There were dozens of European towns with populations around or above the 20,000 mark, but York, Bristol, Norwich, Coventry and Plymouth, England's largest centres after London, had 8,000 or less. London was the centre not only of government, but of all English commercial activity: her citizens paid a fifth of the £50,000 raised by the benevolence in 1491.

Overseas trade

There is evidence of an increase in internal trade during the reign of Henry VII in his grants of a score of licences for annual fairs and weekly markets, mostly in places south of the Thames.[3] As with the cloth industry, however, there is no satisfactory means of measuring the growth of domestic activity. Much of the cloth woven in England was presumably required for the home market, but the rate of growth in output can only be measured by the records of customs paid on exports.[4] Before the fifteenth century, raw wool was England's principal export. The number of sacks being exported in the second half of the century was about 10,000, only a third of the figure before 1360, but the yield in duties was still sufficient to pay the wages of the garrison of Calais. In 1466, Edward IV leased the customs to the company of the Staple, who undertook to maintain the fortress and its troops, sending any balance to the Exchequer; Henry continued this arrangement. The crown's income from cloth exports doubled during the fifteenth century. Before the trade depression of its middle years, the number of cloths sent abroad passed 60,000. Then for twenty years the figure hung around half this total. After 1470 there was a marked rise until the previous maximum was passed; in 1482 the total was 65,000. Henry's first years saw a slight recession, but as the century closed annual figures were on their way to a peak of 90,000 in 1506–8.

Cloth and sacks of wool accounted for at least nine-tenths of England's exports. Apart from isolated exceptions under royal licence, all the raw wool was exported by the merchants of the Staple of Calais, a convenient outlet for the Flemish manufacturers who bought the wool. There was no similar restriction on the trade in woollen cloth. It was taken wherever English merchants could find a market. In contrast with the staplers, whose market was assured, merchants who took the risk of loading a ship with cloth and possibly other commodities like pewter, lead, tin and leather, and sending it in search of customers, came to be known as 'merchant adventurers'. Like foreign merchants in England, English merchants abroad formed associations for mutual support and to sue for privileges from the rulers of the countries in which they were trading. Thus, around

1400, there were organised communities of English merchants in the Low Countries and at Danzig (now Gdansk). At home, these merchants belonged to different trade gilds. Then in Edward IV's reign, those members of the mercers', drapers', haberdashers', skinners' and other London companies who 'adventured' abroad came to assemble to discuss matters of common interest, as when the king wished to consult them on relations with Burgundy. These assemblies also had to arrange to raise funds to meet expenses for their general concern, like the despatch of an embassy. In 1486, these informal and occasional arrangements were regularised by an act in the common council of London, which established a general court of merchant adventurers, with power to make ordinances and punish members who broke them.

Although there were groups of merchant adventurers in other English ports, the London company became dominant; thanks to Henry's support, the London adventurers appointed a governor over all English merchants in the Low Countries, and London became the national headquarters. The merchants continued to trade individually, but the company's court chartered ships, organised them in fleets, and decided when they were to sail. The ascendancy of the London merchants is fully reflected in the figures for cloth exports: two-thirds of the total despatched by English merchants went from London. As the total volume of cloth exports rose, London's share increased at the expense of other ports, whose figures show an almost invariable picture of decline at the end of Henry's reign.

Only about half of the cloth exports were carried by English merchants, and their trade was largely with the Low Countries, with a growing volume going to Antwerp as it developed into Western Europe's greatest international market. English merchants had lost their foothold in the Baltic in the first half of the fifteenth century, and after the conclusion of a long feud with the Hanseatic League of Germany by the treaty of Utrecht in 1474 the latter were left an unchallenged monopoly in trade with northern and eastern Europe. The Hansards then returned to their London 'factory', the Steelyard, fully restored to their privileges. From London in particular, but also from Hull, Boston and Yarmouth, they carried cloths destined for Scandinavia, the Baltic countries, Poland, Hungary and even the Black Sea coast; while, returning, they brought herring, timber, pitch, tar, canvas, linen, furs and, in times of English scarcity, corn.

The Steelyard was the most substantial, royally favoured and popularly resented colony of foreign merchants in London. There were others, of merchants from Ragusa (now Dubrovnik), Venice and other Italian cities. The Italians were also firmly based at Southampton. When cloth exports from this port rose to a record total of 18,000 in 1505–6, nine tenths were taken by Italians. From them England received the costly manufactures of Venice, silk, velvet, cloth of gold, dried fruits, spices and sweet wines. This trade in the luxuries of the Mediterranean was jealously guarded and adventurous English interlopers were given short shrift.

Bristol, the largest town in the country after London and York, was able to develop its trade without competition from resident foreign colonies. She had for many years been the principal port for trade with Ireland. Like Southampton, Bristol's chief import used to be wine from Gascony, but after its final conquest by France in 1453, Bristol's merchants turned to friendly Portugal for supplies of wine. Claret was again being imported in considerable quantities after the treaty of Picquigny in 1475, and Bristol's trade returned to its early fifteenth-century levels. The treaty with France led to improved relations with Castile; Edward IV's negotiations to further Anglo-Spanish trade prepared the way for Henry VII's alliance with Ferdinand and Isabella. Laden with cloth from the looms of the Cotswolds, ships from Bristol went to the Basque ports for iron and woad, to Seville for almonds, figs, dates, raisins and oil for soap.

Many who visited Spain and Portugal in the winter months spent the spring and summer on the Iceland voyage. From Henry V's time, seamen from England's eastern ports had been fishing off Iceland, while ships from Bristol were almost universal providers to that barren land, returning with cargoes wholly of dried cod. This trade was declining during the 1460's before the hostility of the Danish king, Iceland's sovereign, and the competition of the Hanse. Henry VII, at his visit to Bristol in 1486, was told about the decay of the town's prosperity.[5] It recovered thereafter, but after a peak of 8,600 cloths exported in 1495–6, the number sank to 3,000 in 1508–9. The decline continued until the discovery of North America retrieved Bristol's fortunes, when she realised the truth of the claim by her seamen returning with Cabot from Newfoundland that 'they could bring hence so many fish that they would have no further need of Iceland'.

Shipping

Just as in the coal and iron industries the fifteenth century saw
technological progress with the use of water-power, so was this also
an important period in the development of shipping.[6] The profits
of trade—and piracy—prompted the application of a considerable
amount of capital to the purchase and building of ships. A share in
the ownership of a vessel was one of the most common forms of investment by prospering merchants; the risks of loss were great, but
the ship which escaped wreck and robbery could repay the cost on
its outlay within two or three years. Merchants were not the only
ones to put capital into shipping. Magnates and gentry did so. Warwick 'the Kingmaker' thus made a great haul by freebooting and
also found that sea-power was a political asset. Ships designed for
trade could be converted for warfare by the addition of timber
'castles' to provide platforms for archers. During the century there
appeared men like John Taverner of Hull and William Cannings of
Bristol who made it their sole business to form and run groups of
ships. This new class of shipowner made its living by hiring ships to
merchants and did not otherwise engage in trade. England's merchant
navy had a cosmopolitan flavour: ships were built in England, but
numbers were bought abroad, notably from Spain and Germany;
while some foreign ships were acquired by less lawful means.

Ships were larger now. The average size of cargo boats doubled in
the fifteenth century, so that at its close a ship of 200 tuns was not
unusual. Cannings, who died in 1474, had two ships twice this size,
and his *Mary and John* was reputed to carry 900 tuns. Altogether he
had ten ships, totalling about 3,000 tuns, and employed 800 men.
More significant than the growth in size was the development in rig.
Until the fourteenth century, as from classical times, it was normal
for a ship to carry only one large, square sail across the waist. Ships
now came to have two or three masts, with a triangular sail on the
hindmost.* These progenitors of the modern sailing ship were far
more manœuvrable than the single-masted vessel: properly handled,
they could tack and be sailed fairly close to the wind, and with their
higher prows they were better able to withstand gales. Captains of
the later fifteenth century had a further advantage with the introduction of the mariner's compass with a pivoted needle and compass

* See plate 16.

card. This aid to navigation had been employed by Italian seamen in the fourteenth century, but only became general in northern waters at the close of the fifteenth.

Exploration

English merchants had shown no want of enterprise in the fifteenth century, seeking—and finding—new markets in Iceland, and, without success, in the Mediterranean. Bristol men may well have heard about Greenland, perhaps even of 'Vineland the Good', when in Iceland, and at Lisbon they would have been told of the voyages of Portuguese navigators to the Azores and along the western coast of Africa. From the last quarter of the century, Bristol seafarers began to consider sailing beyond Ireland in search of the legendary isle of Brasil. The first recorded attempt took place in the summer of 1480, but within nine weeks of sailing rough sea had driven the little boat (80 tuns) back into an Irish port. Two more ships made an equally fruitless expedition in the following year, but the Bristol men were not disheartened and were seemingly still searching the North Atlantic ten years later. There are even some grounds for believing that some of these voyagers reached Newfoundland in the early 1490s, thinking that this was their 'island of Brasil'.

John Cabot, a citizen of Venice although Genoese by birth, was in Seville in 1493 when Christopher Columbus returned from his discovery of the 'Indies', actually the West Indian island of Hispaniola. To Cabot it was clear that Columbus had failed to discover the 'Cathay' described by Marco Polo, who had travelled overland to China in 1271–5. He determined to reach the Orient by the Atlantic route. Failing to obtain support in Spain, Cabot came to Bristol, doubtless inspired by the port's record for exploration and its seamen's discovery of 'Brasil'; this, he presumed, was the north-east cape of Asia. On 5 March 1496 he obtained from Henry VII a licence to search for unknown lands beyond 'the eastern, western and northern' seas; Henry had no intention of challenging the Spanish and Portuguese interests in the southern and central Atlantic. Cabot, his sons and heirs, were licensed to hold their discoveries as the king's vassals. To the merchants of Bristol who financed the expedition, the most attractive royal concession was that all merchandise from the discovered lands was to be brought to their port. Hoping that Cabot was going to open a new route to the Far East, they could envisage Bristol becoming the principal European market for the spices and other luxuries hitherto distributed, to their great profit, by the Italian merchants who controlled the western termini of the Asian caravan routes.

Cabot made a first attempt in 1496, but was soon forced to turn back. Next year in the *Matthew* of Bristol he did reach Newfoundland and spent a month exploring an unidentifiable portion of the North American seaboard, possibly Nova Scotia. On 10 August he was making a personal report to the king, claiming that he had found Asia. A third expedition of five ships went in 1498, Henry himself equipping one of them, with the purpose of seeking tropical shores. Whether or not they reached them is unknown: what is certain is that Cabot did not return, while the prize for discovering a sea passage to Asia was earned that same year by the Portuguese Vasco da Gama by turning the Cape of Good Hope.

In England the idea now seemingly came to be mooted that an approach to Asia might be found to the north of the western landfall, and between 1501 and 1505 there are annual notices of the king rewarding Bristol men who had returned from 'the new found land' (possibly Greenland), bringing him a falcon and three natives dressed in beasts' skins. This quest for a north-west passage was taken up by Cabot's son Sebastian with the backing of the new Bristol company of 'adventurers into the new found lands'. What he did discover in his voyage of 1508–9 is, again, shrouded in obscurity, but one authority has concluded that he discovered Hudson Strait and part of Hudson's Bay. Sebastian returned to England after Henry VII's death, which concluded the first period of English exploration. Several years were to pass before the new king took an interest in this cause.

Mercantile diplomacy

Henry VII was evidently sympathetic and prepared to make some contribution to the search for a passage to China. His motive, no doubt, was economic; he hoped for new markets and sources for English trade. A similar aim appeared in his relations with foreign powers, although it would be mistaken to claim that the expansion of English commerce was a constant element in his foreign policy. He was, in fact, prepared to sacrifice trade to political considerations, as in 1494 and 1504 when he put embargoes on traffic with Flanders in retaliation for its ruler's hospitality to 'Yorkist' pretenders. Henry's constructive commercial measures were more often the by-products of political agreements than the outcome of purely mercantile initiatives. Thus economic clauses were included in the treaties of Medina del Campo and Étaples, and in the two treaties with Philip of Burgundy. The first two did open new fields for English merchants in Spain and France, while the latter enabled the merchant adventurers to hold their own with the government of the Netherlands.

The king's revenue from customs provided him with a strong stimulus to advance English overseas trade. As in past reigns, however, the king did not lack interested advice in this connection. The plea to revive Bristol's fortunes which Henry received in 1486 doubtless had some part in his decision to negotiate with the king of Denmark; of the four envoys he sent, two were merchants of King's Lynn. The result was a treaty in 1490 whereby English merchants were allowed to trade in Iceland and reopen their old depot in Bergen. Although Henry renewed the privileges of the Hanseatic League, it refused to yield reciprocal concessions to English traders. An opportunity to break its Baltic monopoly came in 1499, when Riga asserted its independence and was persuaded to favour English merchants there in return for parallel concessions to Rigan traders in London. This treaty bore little fruit for Riga's breach with the Hanse was soon healed.

English attempts to penetrate the Mediterranean were more successful. A treaty with Florence in 1490 established Pisa as the Italian staple for English wool. One of the two English ambassadors in these negotiations was an alderman of London and the city's interest is evident.[7] A further indication that Henry was influenced by a pressure group appears in the parliamentary records of 1491. Then a petition from the commons resulted in a statute making additional charges on Venetian imports of wine in retaliation for the republic's impositions on English merchants sailing to Crete for Malmsey. By the end of the reign, a small though lucrative trade had been established with Pisa and Chios. Henry himself engaged in this Mediterranean trade: in 1496, he spent £8,000 on wool to be exported to Pisa.[8]

The navy

A further reason for the king's encouragement of trade was that its increase would foster English shipping. The king of England could no more afford to keep a navy[9] than a standing army; just as men were raised for war by enlisting baronial retinues and issuing commissions of array, so when he required a fleet did the king commandeer his subjects' ships for naval service. It was highly desirable, therefore, that the merchant fleet should be large and fit for possible contingencies. Here again, however, there is good reason to believe that Henry was prompted to show concern for English shipping. The parliamentary commons had a long record of interested championship in many aspects of the country's economic activity. In 1439, for instance, a petition resulting in a statute opened with the words, 'Whereas many people of the commons aforesaid, owners of ships and vessels of this realm'.

There obviously was a similar 'shipping lobby' in Henry VII's parliaments, and this group, not the king, was responsible for the two navigation acts held to his credit. The first, in 1485, forbidding the import of Gascon wine in foreign ships, was initiated by a private petition to the commons. That of 1489 extended the ban to Toulouse woad and also required native, though not alien, exporters to employ English ships whenever these were available. This statute began as a commons' bill. The measure in 1491 against Venetian importers had a similar origin. On all three occasions the reason for legislation put forward was that English shipping required protection and encouragement, but we may suspect that the promoters of these bills had private profits in view. Henry, however, possibly in direct imitation of Spanish practice, did encourage the construction or purchase of large ships by the payment of bounties in the form of remittances of customs due on the first voyage; the first known instance when he did so was in 1488, for a new ship of 140 tuns.

The king had some ships of his own which he regarded as private possessions: like other shipowners, Henry hired ships for use in trade. These royal ships would, in time of war, be the nucleus of a navy. They could also be employed against pirates. Henry clearly saw little point in the conditions of his reign to incur heavy naval expenditure. Previous kings had only built up fleets in times of war. Edward IV had done this from 1480 onwards as relations with Scotland deteriorated, having previously found six or seven ships sufficient for his needs. Richard III is known to have possessed ten vessels. Both kings employed their ships to 'convoy the wool ships' between 1480 and 1485.[10] The merchant adventurers found Henry less prepared to escort their fleet to Flanders in 1491. Possibly he saw less need. He had in fact run down the size of his flotilla to five vessels, and although he had four built, the total remained unchanged at his death. Two of Henry's ships, both completed in 1490, were the most powerful warships hitherto built in England. The *Regent* of 700 tuns, modelled on a French ship,[11] had four masts, and the *Sovereign* three, and they respectively carried 225 and 141 cannon and heavier serpentines; some of this artillery was placed below decks, behind portholes, a deadly innovation permitting double broadsides to strike the hulls as well as the decks and rigging of their targets. Henry also had a dry dock built at Portsmouth in 1495–6, the first of its kind known in England, and a new 'haven' at Sandwich.[12]

The crown and the economy

The growth of overseas trade, with its stimulus to English industry and agriculture, made the reign of Henry VII a period of economic advance and well-being. How much the king contributed to this upward trend is a very open question. The absence of serious domestic disorder was obviously a factor of importance, yet in fact the expansion of trade had begun a dozen years before 1485 and it is beyond dispute that the spasmodic strife of the nobility had done little direct damage to industrial activity. A more serious effect of the Wars of the Roses had been the repercussions on international commerce due to the needs of conflicting factions for foreign support; it has already been noticed, however, that Henry also interrupted trade for political reasons. On the other hand, when such considerations were not pressing, he gave the full support of his diplomacy to English merchants searching for new markets or seeking to recover old ones.

The legislation of the reign has often been called in evidence to demonstrate that Henry followed certain principles to foster English trade and industry. It has just been shown that, in the case of shipping, the protective measures were not initiated by the crown. The house of commons, with over 200 burgesses, had a long record of promoting statutes to safeguard the country's economic interests against foreign competition. It did not relax its concern in Henry's reign. There had been a statute in 1478 forbidding foreign merchants to export their profits in the form of gold, plate and jewels, thus compelling them to buy cloth and other native products. In 1491 the commons complained that since this act expired in 1485 the country's reserves had been drained, and they obtained its renewal for twenty years. The Venetian ambassador considered that this ban on the export of bullion largely explained the great quantities of gold and silver he saw in the country, not only in churches but even on the tables of modest hostelries. Another restriction on foreign merchants was that they were not permitted to export woollen yarn and unfulled cloth. This prohibition for the benefit of English fullers had been enacted on the motion of the commons in 1467–8 and was renewed in 1487.

The commons were equally attentive to the practices of English traders and manufacturers. They successfully petitioned for the abolition of an ordinance of the city of London which forbade its freemen to sell their wares at fairs in the country, thus causing customers to go to London to buy necessities. They obtained a statute forbidding cobblers and tanners to engage in each other's business, another limiting the prices of caps and hats. The commons also gave their support to private bills. The embroiderers complained that Italian gold thread was underweight, the pewterers about the shoddy workmanship of roving tinkers, the upholsterers that dishonest persons were making featherbeds 'of corrupt stuffs' and filling quilts and cushions with such adulterated materials that 'by the heat of man's body the savour and taste is so abominable and contagious that many of the king's subjects [have] thereby been destroyed'. Legislation was consequently enacted against these mischiefs. Likewise the merchant adventurers of London were ordered to cut to one third the fee of £20 which they charged their provincial associates for trading in the Low Countries.

The number of statutes of social and economic significance introduced by royal bills did not exceed that initiated from the commons, although the topics concerned were generally of wider public interest. Such was an act for the regulation of wages in 1495, and a second for its repeal in the next parliament. Usury by the subterfuge of taking bonds for sums higher than those lent was condemned in 1487. An act of 1495 required vagabonds to be sent home, not imprisoned as prescribed by a statute of 1383–4. Here royal law-making was turning to social problems with a bearing on public order. Some of the official bills with an economic flavour were concerned with matters affecting the defence of the realm, like the depopulation of the Isle of Wight, the export of horses and the price of bowstaves. Others touched the crown's financial interests, aiming to prevent the loss of revenue by evasion of customs or forgery of coins.

Industry rarely came within the direct range of government legislation. The statute of 1489 restricting the sale of wool grown south of the Trent to English manufacturers was a protective measure which Edward IV had refused to concede to his commons. Henry also took up the cause of reforming weights and measures after the statutes initiated by his commons failed to achieve their purpose. He maintained the standards of the currency and introduced two new coins, the gold sovereign in 1489 and the silver shilling in 1504, further testimony to the growing commerce and wealth of the country. In fine, there are no grounds for supposing that Henry had an economic policy beyond a general desire that the nation should prosper; he cannot be regarded as the architect of national prosperity. On the other hand, he was prepared to assist schemes to promote commercial enterprise, although it is probable that he seldom furthered the ambitions of individual or groups of subjects without some immediate or anticipated benefit for himself.

8

The Church

In England and Wales, as elsewhere in Western Europe, the late medieval church was a part of two great establishments. It was a full member of the Catholic Church under the supremacy of the pope. The Roman court was the highest ecclesiastical tribunal in Christendom, able to set aside sentences in any other church court, whether it was that of archbishop, bishop or archdeacon; litigants defeated in these courts were continually appealing to Rome, and English kings and prelates regularly provided for the care of their interests there by the employment of resident agents. Clergy were frequently soliciting papal favour to grant privileges or dispense them from restrictions enjoined by the law of the Church, and laymen likewise turned to the pope as the only authority which could licence marriage to a cousin, for instance, or possession of a portable altar. To the clergy, moreover, the pope was the universal patron, able by the exercise of his long exercised powers of provision to appoint to bishoprics, canonries and all other kinds of benefices.

The Church was also an inseparable element in the public life of every kingdom and principality and an ever-present influence in the lives of all their subjects. England was divided into some 9,000 parishes and in every one the inhabitants were required to be present at services on Sundays and on the numerous feast-days of the medieval calendar; they were obliged to keep the nave of their parish church in good repair, the chancel being the incumbent's responsibility, and to pay tithes for his support and other occasional charges, such as mortuaries. The Church had oversight of their religious beliefs and practices, as also of their morals, and its officials investigated and its courts punished lapses in faith and private conduct ranging in gravity from adultery to scandalmongering, from usury to short-measure in paying tithes, and they also exercised jurisdiction over wills, granting probate and disposing of the goods of intestates. In the eyes of many laymen, bishops and archdeacons must have seemed to be judges rather than pastors, indeed the clergy as a whole might have appeared to have been more anxious to enforce obligations and receive payments than to confer benefits.

The church establishment in England was rich, possibly owning as much as one quarter of the land. Twelve of the seventeen English archbishops and bishops were among the forty wealthiest prelates in Christendom. No less well-endowed were the greatest abbeys, like Christchurch at Canterbury, St. Albans, Bury St. Edmunds and Glastonbury; altogether there were at least 825 religious houses including nunneries and friaries, although many were small and poor: the total number of their inmates did not greatly exceed 9,000. These houses provided memorials in every county of the piety of previous ages, for the fifteenth century witnessed no new monastic foundation after Henry V's convent at Sion. The greatest foundations of the later middle ages were colleges—for scholars at Oxford and Cambridge, for communities of priests in a number of towns and villages, such as Leicester and Fotheringhay. In addition to the members of these monastic and secular communities, the chapters of cathedrals and their colleges of vicars-choral, and the beneficed clergy in the parishes, there was a great number of others in orders, priests serving as curates, chaplains engaged to say masses on a permanent or temporary basis, and others in lower grades acting as scribes in offices of royal government, episcopal and baronial administrative organisations, and elsewhere. Altogether they numbered between forty and fifty thousand, perhaps one in fifty of the whole population. They all enjoyed a special status in society, the protection of their cloth, exemption from many obligations falling on laymen, and the privilege of immunity from punishment by secular courts.

Despite this, the association of Church and state was so close as to make the dividing line almost invisible. Nothing illustrates this point more strongly than the problem of heresy. In England, an heretic was not only an outcast from the communion of the faithful, he was also regarded as a traitor against the king; he was a source of contamination to the whole established order. After condemnation in the ecclesiastical court, therefore, he was delivered to secular officers for

22 Much Wenlock Priory

23 Kirkoswald Castle

AFter that I had accomplysshed and fynysshed dyuers hystoryes as wel of contemplacyon as of other hysto ryal and worldly actes of grete conquerours & pryn ces / And also certeyn bookes of ensaumples and doctryne / Many noble and dyuers gentylmen of thys royame of Eng lond camen and demaunded me many and oftymes / wherfore that I haue not do made & enprynte the noble hystorye of the saynt greal / and of the moost renomed crysten kyng / Fyrst and chyef of the thre best crysten and worthy / kyng Arthur / whyche ought moost to be remembryd emonge vs englysshe men tofore al other crysten kynges / For it is notoyrly knowen thorugh the vnyuersal world / that there been ix worthy & the best that euer were / That is to wete thre paynyms / thre Jewes and thre crysten men / As for the paynyms they were tofore the Incarnacyon of Cryst / whiche were named / the fyrst Hector of Troye / of whome thystorye is comen bothe in balade and in prose / The second Alysaunder the grete / & the thyrd Julyus Cezar Emperour of Rome of whome thystoryes ben wel kno and bad / And as for the thre Jewes whyche also were tofore thyncarnacyon of our lord / of whome the fyrst was Duc Jo sue whyche brought the chyldren of Israhel in to the londe of byheste / The second Dauyd kyng of Iherusalem / & the thyrd Judas Machabeus of these thre the byble reherceth al theyr no ble hystoryes & actes / And sythe the sayd Incarnacyon haue ben thre noble crysten men stalled and admytted thorugh the vnyuersal world in to the nombre of the ix beste & worthy / of whome was fyrst the noble Arthur / whos noble actes I pur pose to wryte in thys present book here folowyng / The second was Charlemayn or Charles the grete / of whome thystorye is had in many places bothe in frensshe and englysshe / and the thyrd and last was Godefray of boloyn / of whos actes & lyf I made a book vnto the excellent prynce and kyng of noble me morye kyng Edward the fourth / the sayd noble gentylmen instantly requyred me temprynte thystorye of the sayd noble kyng and conquerour kyng Arthur / and of his knyghtes wyth thystorye of the saynt greal / and of the deth and endyng of the sayd Arthur / Affermyng that I ouzt rather tenprynte his actes and noble feates / than of godefroy of boloyn / or

ij

execution by burning. The king at his coronation in the ceremonies of the Church made it his first promise to defend the Church and preserve its privileges. He did this when proceeding against heretics but he considered that his own interests also demanded such action. His sheriffs arrested those who refused to submit to ecclesiastical jurisdiction and detained them until they did so. Royal government was permeated by ecclesiastics, from the prelates who held the highest officers of state and the spiritual lords in parliaments and great councils, to the clerks who wrote the king's letters and kept his accounts. These men belonged to the world of practical affairs, but in their persons they represented the Kingdom that is not of this world. This duality is well exemplified by Bishop Fox, who regularly attended Henry VII as keeper of his privy seal, but on feast days dressed in full pontificals to celebrate mass before the king and his court.[1]

Crown and Church

At the close of the thirteenth century, Pope Boniface VIII advanced extreme claims for the supremacy of the papacy in temporal as well as spiritual affairs. They made little impression in France and England, where royal government was now too well entrenched to be shaken by threats of papal censure. Subsequent popes found it more practicable to make working arrangements with kings than to strive for mastery. In the important question of episcopal appointments, both parties benefited by co-operation. It was a matter of concern to kings that bishops should be personally acceptable, of undoubted political loyalty and preferably useful as councillors; indeed, kings frequently rewarded senior clerical ministers of state by advancing them to bishoprics and would have resented any attempt to debar use of this form of royal patronage. Nominally, however, bishops were elected by cathedral chapters, and although these bodies were generally amenable to royal directives, the possibility of capitular independence could be removed when a bishop was directly appointed by the pope. On his side, the pope gained renewed recognition of his supreme authority in the Church every time a bishop was enthroned by virtue of his letters of provision, and he also obtained the payments that bishop now owed him for his promotion. The pope could not appoint bishops at will, for the king could refuse to allow an unwelcome papal nominee to have possession of the estates of a

G

bishopric. The procedure generally followed whenever a bishopric became vacant, therefore, was for the king to inform the pope of his wishes and for the pope then to provide the royal candidate.

A working arrangement on these lines was reached between the papacy and the English crown in the fourteenth century. Pope Clement VI (1342–52) remarked that if Edward III wished to make a bishop of an ass, he would have to oblige. Later popes occasionally tried to choose their own nominees for English bishoprics, but every time came up against the resistance of royal displeasure. Elsewhere in the fifteenth century, popes and kings made concordats whereby the territorial rulers were allowed specific powers in the regulation of church affairs in their domains. Royal supremacy over the national church was a reality in France and Spain in Henry VII's day. There was little need, from the English king's point of view, to negotiate any formal agreement with the papacy. He was already vested with sufficient customary and statutory powers to exclude any intervention by Rome in English affairs. Parliaments had forced legislation against papal provisions into the statute book in 1351 and 1390. Thereafter popes could only make provisions to benefices in England and Wales with the king's consent which, in practice, was almost entirely confined to episcopal appointments. This unilateral measure ensured the stability of the church establishment. In Ireland, it was effective only within the territories under royal control. Popes continued to provide to benefices in the rest of the country and if their letters were all executed, the results would have been chaotic. Irish priests in Henry's time were frequently making for Rome, accusing incumbents of unseemly conduct, and securing nomination to their churches; some of the allegations were convincing, for the priest accusing a rector of keeping a concubine was sometimes his illegitimate son.[2] The English church was spared the abuses arising from papal provisions at the price of submission to the king.

The papacy naturally objected to the statutes of provisors and pressed the crown to have them annulled. Its efforts were in vain. The commons reacted in 1393 by producing the statute of *Praemunire* to debar litigation in Rome about English church affairs.[3] This extreme measure served an immediate purpose in gaining temporary papal acquiescence to the legislation against provisions. The statute of *Praemunire* was therefore not then enforced, but it remained on record and was invoked in the mid-fifteenth century by Humphrey, duke of Gloucester, in his vendetta against Cardinal Beaufort, and intermittently by other laymen to prevent their citation before church courts for failure to pay tithes. Henry VII imposed fines on clerics for breaches of the statute and prevented some others from going to Rome to pursue litigation. Proceedings under the statute were taken against a canon of Bolton, Yorkshire, who had attempted to depose his prior by litigation in the Roman court.[4] The statute was not forgotten, therefore, and was available as the weapon whereby Henry VIII forced the submission of the clergy.

Whenever the property rights of English subjects were concerned, the courts of common law restricted the jurisdiction of the church courts: they were not allowed to determine ownership of rights of presentation to benefices, and the legitimisation of a bastard by the Church was not accepted as a title to inherit his father's land. The influence of the pope in English affairs was also curtailed. Bishops were required to renounce anything prejudicial to royal authority in their bulls of provision. Henry VII's judges recalled with approval how Edward IV would not admit a papal legate until he promised to do nothing contrary to royal interests, and how Humphrey of Gloucester had flung unacceptable papal bulls into a fire.

Papal taxation of the clergy was universal and organised under regional collectors responsible to the apostolic chamber in Rome. Royal taxation was equally general, and a far more pressing burden.[5] In France and Spain, the kings also took a proportion of the taxes collected for the pope. From the pope's viewpoint, the church in England was a poor source of revenue: the approximate annual total of all payments to Rome, including services and annates due from benefices filled by papal provision, and the traditional Peter's Pence (£199 6s. 8d.), probably did not exceed £4,000. This was less than half of the average yield to the crown in direct taxes alone. These clerical subsidies were granted in meetings of the convocations of Canterbury and York, which were called by their archbishops in compliance with royal commands, generally at the same times as parliaments were held to authorise taxation of the laity. The principle of self-imposition was the only concession to the clergy, for once they had made arrangements for collection, the operation was supervised by the Exchequer. In addition to these clerical subsidies of one-tenth on the assessed value of benefices, clergy were called upon to contribute to benevolences and loans. The temporalities of bishoprics were held for the king's profit during vacancies of sees. The king also required bishops and abbots to provide pensions for his nominees, and made demands on their rights of patronage for the benefit of his servants. Individual prelates were required, like secular subjects, to act on commissions at their own expense. In short, the only sphere of Church life and organisation in which the influence of secular authority was not brought to bear was in the definition of doctrine. Otherwise royal supremacy over the church in England was a fact, even if it had not yet been enshrined in a statutory declaration.

Henry VII and the papacy

The medieval papacy had always been compromised by its position as the secular ruler of a large portion of central Italy. The desperate need for money to finance military operations in defence of the pope's patrimony goes far to explain the extension of provisions, taxation and other aspects of papal government over the Church, and also his readiness to make accommodations with secular rulers which safeguarded his revenues from their clerical subjects. With the invasion of Italy by French, Spanish and Imperial armies, the papacy became directly involved in international diplomacy as an interested party defending its temporal integrity. With these preoccupations and considerations, the popes of Henry VII's time were in no position to strive to recover or defend its spiritual authority in the ecclesiastical polity of so distant a kingdom as England.

Henry's obsessive piety naturally inclined him to establish good relations with Rome; he obviously esteemed the papacy's moral support. On 2 March 1486, Innocent VIII granted a bull of dispensation for Henry's marriage to Elizabeth; the king had presumably applied for this before the arrival of the papal legate who was able to give a dispensation allowing the marriage to take place on 18 January. In confirming the bull, the pope pronounced sentences of excommunication and the greater anathema against all who challenged Henry's possession of the throne. Lest we should doubt the value of this spiritual shield, we might note that contemporaries believed that one ruffian who scorned it straightway turned black in the face and died. Henry had the bull proclaimed throughout the realm, printed as a broadsheet, and confirmed by Alexander VI in 1494. The pope's recognition was probably felt by Henry to be most valuable in his relations with the clergy; he invoked its automatic censures to initiate proceedings against the archbishops of Armagh and Dublin for their part in Lambert Simnel's 'coronation'.[6]

The pope's licence, as has already been noticed, enabled Henry to limit the abuse of sanctuaries, and other papal letters enabled Archbishop Morton to proceed against privileged ecclesiastics in the cause of good order. Morton's cardinalate was granted by Alexander VI after repeated solicitations by the king. He was himself honoured by bestowal of the papal cap and sword of maintenance by successive pontiffs. His scruples—and digestion—were relieved by a papal licence to eat cheese and eggs during Lent.[7] The popes responded benignly to Henry's ardent wish to have Henry VI canonised, but although evidence of miracles through the unfortunate Lancastrian's ghostly intercession were provided in voluminous detail, the Curia procrastinated until Henry VII himself was dead and the matter was then dropped.

This record of continuing papal compliance with Henry's requests for concessions of both national and personal import is evidence of the absence of contention over serious issues. The king preserved the diplomatic niceties in his relations with Rome—an English bishop as resident ambassador, dignified embassies to profer obedience to each new pope, and, of course, payments of fees and gratuities in the transaction of business. Henry sent courteous and circumstantial excuses for his refusal to join in crusades against the Turks. He politely refused permission to burden his subjects with a tax for the same cause. He allowed an indulgence to be proclaimed and, unlike his fellow-monarchs, declined a share of the proceeds: as this yielded only £49, while the collection box at his court only gathered £11 11s.,[8] his self-denial cost him little. In 1501, however, when the pressure of direct royal taxation was no longer falling on his people, Henry authorised subsidies for the Turkish war from the clergy and made a personal contribution of £4,000.

The English episcopate

During the reign, a total of twenty seven new bishops were appointed to English sees, all by papal provision following nomination by the king.[9] Of these, eight were subsequently once translated to other sees, four were moved twice, and one, Richard Fox, three times. In addition, six bishops originally provided under the Yorkist kings were translated. All these translations were to archbishoprics or wealthier sees, and the men concerned were in royal service of some kind. The 'Yorkist' bishops included John Morton, John Alcock and Peter Courtenay, all officers of state under Henry VII, and Thomas Langton, a royal chaplain and ambassador under Edward IV, promoted to the outstandingly wealthy see of Winchester by Henry and his candidate for Canterbury in 1501, when Langton died. The translations were made after intervals of about five years from the first appointments, and obviously came as rewards for continuing good service. Fox's rapid rise (Exeter 1487, Bath and Wells 1492, Durham 1494, Winchester 1501) was the measure of Henry's satisfaction with his keeper of the privy seal.

Henry has been accused of leaving bishoprics vacant for long periods, and adding to the number of vacancies by arranging translations, in order to benefit from royal custody of the temporalities. There were some long vacancies, but the average interval between the death or departure of one bishop and the installation of his successor was twelve months, and this figure applies also to vacancies of the sees of Carlisle and Rochester where the king had no financial stake. Moreover, in nearly a score of cases Henry granted the temporalities to the men designated for the sees months before they were formally instituted, sometimes dating his grant from the beginning of a vacancy.[10] These favours cost him many thousands of pounds over the whole reign. In other respects he undoubtedly had a materialistic approach in dispensing his patronage, in using the Church to pay his ministers, in determining a bishop's suitability for a richer see in the light of his utility to royal government. But this has been the attitude of previous kings and Henry could not have viewed the matter any differently. It is more instructive to consider the quality of the episcopate he created.

The bare biographical details of Henry's bishops make in total an impressive picture and confirm the impression given by his record with temporalities that he exercised his patronage in a conscientious manner. Only one of his promotions was questionable, that of James Stanley (Ely 1506), the father of three illegitimate children and a convicted offender against the laws on retaining, whose chief commendation appears to have been that he was the earl of Derby's son. Stanley was Henry's only baronial nominee to the episcopate. Since the thirteenth century, the religious orders had provided only a small proportion of the bench in England, although many of the appointments to the poor Welsh sees were of monks and friars. The notable Premonstratensian reformer Richard Redman, bishop of St. Asaph since 1471, was advanced to Exeter (1495) and Ely (1501). Henry Dean, after reorganising Llanthony as its prior, was called to royal service as chancellor of Ireland and ultimately appointed archbishop of Canterbury (1501). Two other Benedictines, William Senhouse and John Penny, were first provided to poor sees and therefore allowed to retain their abbeys *in commendam*; Senhouse's services on the northern border won him promotion to Durham (1502). Henry was responsible for the appointment of three Italian bishops, Adrian de Castello, the papal collector in England (Hereford 1502, Bath and Wells 1504) and Giovanni and Silvestro de Giglis, his agents at the papal court (Worcester 1497 and 1498).

The remainder of Henry's bishops were originally secular clerks and were the sons of landed gentry or burgesses. All were graduates, most in canon and civil law, with Oxford men outnumbering those from Cambridge in the ratio of three to one. A few benefitted from having kinsmen already on the bench: Robert Morton (Worcester 1486) was John's nephew, and John (Salisbury 1493) and Geoffrey Blyth (Coventry and Lichfield 1503) were nephews of Archbishop Rotherham of York. Like their fellow bishops, however, all three had been employed in the king's service. Most of these bishops had been engaged in administrative and diplomatic work and were, at least in title, councillors of the king. Robert Morton, John Blyth, William Warham (London 1501, Canterbury 1503), William Barons (London 1503) and Christopher Bainbridge (Durham 1507, York 1508) were successively masters of the rolls of Chancery and had served in embassies and in the hearing of 'poor men's requests'. Thomas Savage (Rochester 1493, London 1496, York 1501), William Smith (Coventry and Lichfield 1493, Lincoln 1496) and Roger Leyburn (Carlisle 1504) were employed in the councils for the north and the Welsh marches. Robert Sherborne (St. Davids 1505, Chichester 1508) had been Cardinal Morton's secretary before serving in royal embassies; while Leyburn and Richard Nykke (Norwich 1501) presumably owed their advancement to Fox, whom they had served in diocesan offices. Henry also gave bishoprics to four of his domestic chaplains: Richard Hill (London 1489) and Thomas Jane (Norwich 1499) were deans of the chapel in the household, and Richard FitzJames (Rochester

1497, Chichester 1504) and Richard Mayhew (Hereford 1504) were the king's almoners; while Hugh Oldham (Exeter 1504) and John Fisher (Rochester 1504) were chaplains of Lady Margaret Beaufort. Royal service was thus the principal, if not the only, avenue to the highest offices in the English church. Other clerical servants of the king prospered if they gave satisfaction. Even if they did not achieve bishoprics, they gathered benefices enough to realise a comfortable income. Henry's secretary Thomas Ruthall, who became bishop of Durham after the king's death in 1509, but probably on his nomination, at that time held the deaneries of Salisbury Cathedral and Wimborne Minster, the archdeaconry of Gloucester, canonries in Lincoln and Exeter Cathedrals, and probably at least one rectory. Pluralism beckoned the royal servant who had taken clerical orders. It was no longer essential, however, for the ambitious man to be a cleric if he hoped to rise in the world by the exercise of non-military talents. The common law had long provided profitable careers for laymen. Royal administration was now equally open to them, and men like Bray, Dudley and Heron had certainly advanced their fortunes. It is likely, therefore, that those of Henry's servants who were in orders had taken them because they had a genuine vocation towards the Church. Of James Stanley alone among Henry's bishops could it be said that he was a layman masquerading as a cleric.

With their doctorates in laws or divinity, Henry's bishops were academically well qualified for their office, and some had earlier experience in diocesan government. Several pursued scholarly interests in the course of their official careers. Fox, Warham, Barons, Bainbridge, Sherborne and Ruthall were attracted to humanism, while FitzJames and Smith tried to counter its influence. Many of these bishops possessed considerable libraries and some were authors. Alcock, FitzJames and Fisher were notable preachers, and the latter was the first Lady Margaret reader in divinity at Cambridge and was to suffer execution for his opposition to Henry VIII's breach with Rome. Of course, even after their consecration, several of these bishops remained immersed in royal business. Cardinal Morton, however, carried out visitations in his province and displayed a vigorous concern for the reform of monastic and clerical shortcomings, and Fox took a direct part in calling the wild Northumbrian clergy to order. The record of benefactions by these bishops is most impressive. They financed works at the cathedrals of Canterbury,

Exeter, Winchester, Durham, Norwich, Salisbury, Bath, Ely and Bangor, and in parish churches and episcopal palaces. Several gave lands, money and books to their colleges. At Oxford, Fox founded Corpus Christi College, and Smith Brasenose, while John Morton completed the Divinity Schools, and at Cambridge, Jesus College was founded by Alcock. Grammar schools were established by Fitz-James at Bruton, Somerset, Fox at Taunton and Grantham, Oldham at Manchester, Smith at Farnworth, Lancashire, and Alcock in Hull. In conclusion, it can be said for Henry VII that he employed his mastery over the English church to give it as distinguished an episcopate as it had possessed since the great era of reform in the thirteenth century.

Royal intervention

The king's interest in the reform of the clergy was disclosed in a statute initiated by royal bill in his first parliament. This declared that it should be lawful for all having episcopal jurisdiction to proceed by canon law against priests, clerks and monks guilty of incontinence, and to imprison those found guilty at discretion. In fact, canon law already empowered bishops to take proceedings against incontinent clergy. What is remarkable here is that Henry authorised a penalty which was not customarily imposed in the church courts. The effect of this measure is not known. It did not curtail ecclesiastical immunities for it specified that bishops should act within the bounds of their jurisdictions.

The privileges of certain monastic houses, whereby bishops were debarred by papal authority from intervening in their affairs, was a long standing grievance of the episcopate, and regarded by them as a serious obstacle to reform. In 1490, Henry obtained a bull from Innocent VIII which empowered Cardinal Morton to visit and reform all religious houses in his province; the king had told the pope that there had been a scandalous decline in the observance of monastic rules. Morton immediately charged the abbot of St. Albans to correct various alleged abuses in his house. This seems to have been as far as the archbishop went, but his actions were more decisive at Folkestone and Northampton, where the priors were removed from office on account of their misgovernment. In 1498, Henry procured another papal bull ordering the archbishop to investigate the country's houses of friars minor, which were said to be at only half strength.

Under Henry, the penetration of royal authority into ecclesiastical affairs took a further step forward. Once he granted a pardon to a knight from all demands against him in church courts.[11] For centuries now, religious houses had supplemented their revenues by the appropriation of parish churches; a monastic house thus became the rector of a church and henceforth assumed all its revenues. The process was regulated by the Lateran Council of 1215 and in consequence bishops, in authorising an appropriation, were required to secure provision of a permanent income for a perpetual vicar who was to exercise the cure of souls pertaining to the church. Later, colleges also took over rectories as endowments. Sometimes the appropriating body obtained its licence from the pope. From 1486, however, Henry began to make grants of licences for appropriations of parish churches, usually with requirements to endow vicarages; these included two parish churches and five chapels which he gave to Westminster Abbey. In the case of a church he allowed to be appropriated to Christ's College, Cambridge, the king specifically excused the college from establishing a vicarage.

The king also gave possession of two priories to other houses and licensed the alienation of a ruinous secular chapel and its endowments to a new house of friars minor at Newark. In 1497, he gave leave to the bishop of Ely to expel the two remaining nuns from the poverty-stricken house of St. Radegund in Cambridge and apply its property to the foundation of Jesus College.[12] This was not the first dissolution of an English convent, there had been other cases in the previous hundred years of small houses attached to continental abbeys being appropriated by new collegiate foundations, but their closure had been authorised by the pope. The king had not enriched himself by these measures, but he had usurped upon the ecclesiastical authorities in making them and created precedents which must have given rise to serious concern.

Clergy and laity

The record of Henry VII's *de facto* supremacy over the ecclesiastical establishment in England accounts in part for the ease with which his son secured the submission of the clergy in 1532. A second important element in the Henrician Reformation was popular antagonism to the clergy. This also had a long history. Anti-clericalism in England arose mainly from practical considerations, from dislike of the church courts and the payment of tithes and other charges. These general grievances were reinforced with complaints about the behaviour of individual clergy, for neglect of duty or moral lapses. The standard of education among the curates and chaplains who carried the main burden of administering church services was, particularly in the towns, no higher and sometimes lower than that of the laymen among whom they lived. The increase of literacy among the laity was bringing the Church into disrepute. Clergy were no longer indispensable for their utility as the only literate section of the population. In fact, the balance was moving in the other direction: not only in the administrative offices of kings and nobles were laymen taking over clerical work, in ecclesiastical organisation also laymen were establishing a foothold as bishops' registrars and summoners. In the parish, churchwardens often did not see eye to eye with their incumbents on the running of the church's business, and their quarrels led to litigation in royal courts of law. Laymen who endowed chantries* sometimes arranged for supervision of the clerical incumbents by secular authorities, and municipal corporations employing chaplains to perform masses dismissed or fined them for misconduct. Here were indications that laymen had no confidence in the ability or willingness of ecclesiastical officials to correct misbehaviour by clergy, and that they would have welcomed an extension of secular jurisdiction over the clerical order.

There is little reason to doubt, however, that the average English layman was habitually devout. Heresy was never extirpated, despite the vigilance of the Church authorities.[13] Nearly a hundred persons are known to have been brought to trial in Henry VII's reign, though a bare half-dozen refused to recant and were sent to the stake. Often enough, the accused appeared only to have uttered unorthodox sentiments in heated moments, generally expressing hostility against the pope or the priesthood or condemning pilgrimages or the venerations of images. In some cases there was a substratum of Lollard doctrine, and the accused possessed English translations of parts of the Bible or some condemned work by John Wycliffe (c. 1330–84). In contrast with this tiny minority, whose origins were generally humble, there is ample evidence of the conventional piety of their contemporaries. The literate Englishman had as many devotional

---

* Small benefices providing enough revenue to employ a priest to celebrate masses for the spiritual benefit of the founder and his other nominees.

books as chronicles and romances, and regularly used pious expressions in his correspondence. Pilgrimages to English shrines were a popular recreation. In the towns, miracle plays and the festivities of gilds gave public expression to religious sentiment. There were legacies to priests and friars in every will, bequests for saying masses and buying candles, while the more affluent gentry and merchants founded chantries in their lifetimes. Most impressive of all is the achievement of Henry's more prosperous subjects in their parish churches, the addition of new parts, and often the entire replacement of old buildings. This lavish testimony of devotion to their religious faith was not incompatible with anti-clerical sentiments. On the contrary, the layman's concern for the well-being of his parish church explains why he was so critical of shortcomings by the clergy.

There is one notable omission in this catalogue of benefactions—the religious orders. Monastic houses had a place apart in late medieval England. Many, of course, were in remote parts of the country. Those which were in towns, however, tended to incur a great deal of popular illwill. When an abbey was the secular lord of a town, as in Reading or Bury St. Edmunds, its jealous preservation of authority clashed harshly with civic ambitions for self-government. In cities like Norwich, where the cathedral priory had privileges excluding secular jurisdiction, there was friction with the municipal authorities. The contribution made by monastic houses to the religious life of urban communities was less conspicuous than their secular role as landlords. The laity had their own parish churches, outside the monastic precincts.* The withdrawal of monks from ordinary life no longer gave cause for admiration to prompt the generosity of laymen. They were considered sufficiently well-endowed already, and indeed there had been talk of plucking them of their riches in parliaments of Richard II and Henry IV. There was only one great benefaction to a religious house in Henry's reign, and that was his own to Westminster Abbey. His wish to reform the monastic orders is a further indication that he harboured no designs to end their existence. Henry's conservatism was their shield, for thirty years after his death neither the laity in general, nor the secular clergy, offered any protest when they were all swept away.

* For an example, see plate 22.

9

Education and the Arts

THE cultural achievements of Henry VII's reign are more impressive in their quantity than in their originality. The number of works surviving from his time is extensive, but they belong to the artistic traditions of the middle ages. The king's effigy and tomb in Westminster Abbey were made by the Italian Torrigiano, and probably the bust* as well, but for his large-scale building works he employed English masons following the traditions of their own country. Likewise in education, the number of new foundations was considerable, but the pattern of teaching they observed was conventional. Although there were now more literate people than ever before in the country, Erasmus recognised a bare half-dozen as being learned according to his standards, at the time of his visits in 1499 and 1505. Throughout the fifteenth century, the only Englishmen to take an interest in the new approach to the study of the classics were those who had spent some time in Italy and had made the acquaintance of humanists there. These men, inevitably, were bishops who went on embassy to the Roman Curia, or clerks who were employed there. The great law school at Bologna drew a small number of English scholars. Those who were infected by the humanists' zeal tended to confine communication about literary studies to small circles of friends. With the exception of Thomas Chandler, warden of New College (1454–79), there was no one in an influential academic position trying to recruit a following for the new learning.

English laymen were notoriously unconcerned with scholarship of any kind. Humphrey, duke of Gloucester (d. 1447), had personal links with Italian humanists and gave his collection of manuscripts

* Plate 8.
193

to Oxford University. John Tiptoft, earl of Worcester (d. 1470), studied at Padua and also patronised scholars. English lords in general, however, and the gentry as well, had little interest in the study of letters. When they did read, their preference was for chronicles and romantic tales of chivalry. Humanistic studies in Italy had their principal following among the urban middle-class, whose civic patriotism was fortified by the example of ancient Rome. It was, in fact, among wealthy Italian laymen that the professional humanists found not only generous patrons but ready pupils. In contrast, the English bourgeoisie took a strictly practical view of education, regarding it as a means towards proficiency in business. The literate English burgess, if he could read in leisure, would also turn to *The Brut* or another popular history, and the keeping of town annals further reveals his interest in the past. From the close of the fourteenth century, these chronicles had been rendered into English, and new works in prose and verse, for business and pleasure, were being written in the vernacular. This is strong evidence of more widespread literacy, but the use of English in preference to Latin or French also heightened the barrier against literary influences from abroad.

Printing

In 1476, thirty or perhaps forty years after the first European printing press had been set up at Mainz, William Caxton returned from Bruges and began printing in Westminster. From the start he enjoyed the patronage of Edward IV, nobles of his court, and wealthy London merchants. Caxton's first book was Earl Rivers' translation of *The Dictes or Sayengs of the Philosophres*, published in 1477. During the next fifteen years he printed 96 editions of books. These included all the major English texts known to us except Langland, and translations from French and Latin, many made by Caxton himself. Nearly half his publications were of a religious or didactic nature, works assured of a ready market; nor did he risk a poor response with most of his other ventures, the poetry of Chaucer, Mallory's *Morte D'Arthur* and other chivalric romances, and *The Chronicles of England*. He commended different books to varying kinds of reader: some were not 'convenient for every rude and simple man', but for lords and gentlemen, or for 'clerks and gentlemen that understand gentleness and science', or for 'ladies and gentlewomen'; while others were commended to 'all good folk' or to 'every Christian man'.* Caxton's business was carried on after his death in 1491 by his German apprentice, Wynkyn de Worde. About the same time, the Norman Richard Pynson took over the London press of William of Malines, which had begun work about 1482; the production of collections of statutes and other legal texts was a speciality of this firm in its earlier years. In 1494, the commercial success of these printers led to the establishment of the first English paper mill at Hertford in Kent.

It has been calculated that by 1500 there were at least 1,700 presses in 300 European towns, a quarter of them in Italy, and that by this date they had produced at least 30,000 editions of books. England's contribution to this total was about one per cent. It cannot be said, either, that the kinds of work produced in the English presses made any original contribution to the development of thought or to furthering the study of classical texts in their original languages. On the other hand, they permitted the growth of a far wider reading public, for in the past only the wealthy could afford to own manuscript volumes. Moreover, books printed abroad were being imported: their sale by foreign merchants in England was authorised in 1484, and in 1485 Henry licensed his stationer, Peter Actoris of Savoy, to import books without paying customs.[1] English scholars who visited Italy returned heavily laden with the books they had bought there. The revolutionary ideas of Erasmus would never have circulated so widely had printing not been available for their dissemination.

Grammar schools

In one respect, education in England was following in the wake of developments overseas, not by imitation but from necessity. This was in its growing secularisation. The influence of the Church on the curriculum remained: pupils were still required to memorise prayers and psalms. Laymen who founded schools regarded it as the first object in education to teach children how to take part in church services. In the fifteenth century, however, the Church's monopoly in providing education was broken by the demands of civic corporations and individuals for more adequate facilities. Cathedral chapters and urban monasteries had supplied schoolmasters, with the principal object of training choristers and prospective recruits for the clergy.

* See also Plate 24, the preface to Caxton's first edition of the *Morte D'Arthur* (1485).

Although such schools were insufficient to cope with the increasing number of children with parents desiring their elementary education, these Church authorities exercised their authority to exclude or regulate 'adulterine' masters. In a test case in 1411, the judges of King's Bench revealed their sympathy with laity striving to set up schools in the face of ecclesiastical opposition. There is no further evidence that the Church again turned to the common law courts to defend its monopoly, although in 1445 the devout Henry VI confirmed it in London. In the following year, a counter-petition pointed to the fewness of teachers in the city, 'where there is a great number of learners'. Subsequently, it appears that both in London and in other towns the Church gave up its attempt to preserve exclusive control.

Few of the fifteenth-century grammar schools were endowed foundations. The master was more often the nominee of a civic corporation or large trade gild, possibly provided with a free house and the sole right to teach within the town or parish. He was generally a priest, often the chaplain of a chantry or gild; this employment left ample time for other work and the fees from pupils (about 8d. a quarter) supplemented his modest stipend. Permanently established schools were rare. The two largest foundations at Winchester (1382) and Eton (1440) were intended to prepare scholars for the associated colleges of New College, Oxford, and King's, Cambridge, whence they would proceed to holy orders; although at both schools provision was made for a small number of extra-collegiate pupils. When smaller schools were endowed elsewhere, it was as part of the foundation for a chantry, the priest being required to teach. Sevenoaks grammar school (1432) was remarkable in that the founder decreed that the master was not to be in orders. By this time, the demand for schoolmasters was seemingly outrunning the supply, a consideration which prompted William Bingham to found Godshouse at Cambridge in 1439 as the first teachers' training college on record. The twenty-four scholars here were to study grammar, not the more advanced disciplines. At Oxford, Magdalen College School (1480) became a centre for teaching grammar by enlightened methods which were carried to other schools, while graduates of its parent college (1458) were to be numbered among the most influential educationalists of the early Tudor period.

In the more affluent years of the later fifteenth century, the pace of endowment of schools quickened. Usually, permanent sources of revenue were settled on schools existing on a hand-to-mouth basis. Thus the gild school at Stratford-on-Avon was firmly established as a free grammar school in 1482. Archbishop Rotherham, who had first gone to school at Rotherham, founded a college of priests there in 1483 and required three of its four members to teach grammar, music and writing; the last was provided for able youths not wishing to be priests so 'that these may be better fitted for the mechanical arts and other concerns of this world'. Secular corporations and merchant benefactors had the same practical approach to education. Some schooling was now being made compulsory in certain trades. The goldsmiths' company, for instance, made a rule that no apprentice was to be accepted unless he could read and write, and scriveners were required to send their apprentices to school if they failed an examination in grammar. The limited objectives of these schools were reached by no less limited methods: the teaching of the alphabet, writing and grammar, was generally by rote, with the master using a textbook fashionable for centuries; other books, if he could afford them, were usually compilations of choice extracts and commentaries rather than original texts.

In 1505, John Colet, a Magdalen graduate and ardent disciple of humanist scholarship, was appointed dean of St. Paul's by the sympathetic bishop of London, William Barons. With the assistance of his friend Erasmus, Colet planned a new kind of school, open to all comers and free from ecclesiastical influence. He committed the charge of his St. Paul's School to the mercers' company, after securing his cathedral chapter's renunciation of its claims to educational control. The schoolhouse was built in 1508, and in 1510 William Lily was instituted as the first highmaster. There were 153 boys, taught free of charge; their division into forms of sixteen, each with its captain, was another novelty. New textbooks were prepared for them, simple grammars in English and Latin, other subjects such as geography and natural history were introduced, and classical authors were studied in their original texts; the adulterated Latin of medieval schoolmen was barred. While the ritual of the contemporary Church was condemned by Colet as mechanical and devoid of real significance, his foremost aim for the pupils of his school was that they should be brought to observe the basic principles of the Christian faith: the purpose of their education was to promote a Christian way of living.

The universities

There were in fact three centres of higher education, the universities of Oxford and Cambridge and the inns of court in London. The latter continued to attract the sons of gentry and merchants who could afford to maintain them in the pursuit of practical and social accomplishments. It is probable that in the legalistic climate of Henry's reign the inns attracted larger numbers than before; the texts of 'readings' to members of the inns survive from this time, and the prosperity of the profession is evidenced by the new buildings then raised by Lincoln's Inn. It is possible, also, that the—to his eyes— more purposeful activity of the inns prompted Edmund Dudley's disparaging observation 'upon your two universities, how famous they have been and in what condition they be now', that is, in 1509. Yet Dudley himself, like some other lawyers, had spent some time at Oxford to learn grammar before entering his inn of court, and his remarks about unlearned prelates and their failure to encourage learning can easily be refuted.

As in the schools, there was no fundamental innovation at the universities before Henry VII's death. Individual scholars espoused humanist studies. William Grocyn, after two years in Italy to improve his knowledge of Greek, returned to Oxford to lecture there. Thomas Linacre, another former fellow of All Souls, studied medicine and classical literature in Italy, and on his return was for some time a teacher in Oxford. The first Oxford college designed to promote humanist studies, however, was Corpus Christi, founded by Bishop Fox in 1517. Like Colet at St. Paul's, Fox eschewed the scholastic theology of the middle ages in order to promote a true understanding of Christian doctrine through the study of works of classical authors and early fathers of the Church. He emphasised the value of a correct understanding of original texts as the basis of true learning, a sharp contrast to the traditional university method of formal disputation, and a challenge to its preoccupation with the works of Duns Scotus. Fifteenth century Oxford had turned to this thirteenth century scholar, the greatest medieval British theologian, on the rebound from its previous obsession with the dialectic of William of Ockham which had led to the heresies of John Wycliffe. While Erasmus mocked the theologians' devotions to 'Dunce', their new preceptor had the merit of making belief in the freedom of the will respectable, and it is arguable that if Ockhamite influence had retained its hold, fewer Oxford graduates would have been inclined to interest themselves in humanist studies.

The full course of study to one of the higher degrees was very long by modern standards; it could be seventeen years in the case of doctors of theology. The age of entry to the university, however, was between thirteen and sixteen. It took four years' study of grammar, logic and rhetoric to achieve the B.A., and another five before a master could begin specialised studies in one of the higher disciplines of theology, canon and civil laws, or medicine. Few of the undergraduates had the means to stay to take degrees. There were about 700 of them at Oxford in the mid-fifteenth century, less at the smaller university of Cambridge. Most lived in small halls, of which there were about sixty at Oxford in 1470, and they had to find their own fees and keep. The graduate students were maintained as fellows of the colleges or as masters of halls. Pious founders in the fifteenth century realised that there was a need for increased provision for students. The threat of heresy, and the increasing literacy among laymen, warned them that the Church was inadequately staffed with educated men. The first college for undergraduates was New College, Oxford (1379), for seventy scholars from Winchester. This model was followed by Henry VI with his double foundation of Eton and King's College, Cambridge. Magdalen College, Oxford, was also planned to house and teach undergraduates. Further provision was made for graduates at Oxford with Lincoln (1429) and All Souls (1438) Colleges, and at Cambridge Queens' (1448), St. Catherine's (1473) and Jesus (1497). The last was the only entirely new university foundation in Henry VII's reign, although Lady Margaret Beaufort re-established Godshouse as Christ's College in 1505 and William Smith began preparations for building Brasenose. Bishop Waynflete's statutes for Magdalen established three university lecturers and this innovation was followed by Lady Margaret's foundations of readerships in divinity at both universities.

Building

The fifteenth century colleges at Oxford and Cambridge, including those founded before 1461, remained incomplete until the later years of the century. The Divinity School at Oxford was first projected in 1426 and gradually the walls and windows were raised, but then the work had to be given up for over twenty years before, in the 1480's, the vault and roof completed the building. The royal Lancastrian foundations nearly suffered the same fate as their patrons. Bishop Waynflete rescued Eton's endowments from Edward's design to give them to his collegiate church at Windsor, and himself largely paid for the erection of the school buildings. Edward ultimately revived work on King's College Chapel, but it was not finished until 1515. Waynflete's own college at Oxford was completed in 1509,* fifty years after its foundation. Political upheavals only partially account for these protracted building programmes. The great works of the later middle ages generally took many years to complete because of an inadequate supply of labour and capital. The shrinking revenues of landowners inevitably retarded their building schemes.

The prosperous years of the later fifteenth century permitted the undertaking of more large-scale operations than had been in hand at any one time since the Black Death. The buildings at Oxford and Cambridge are but a small proportion of the architectural achievement of the years of Edward IV and Henry VII. These kings themselves could afford considerable undertakings: Edward built the hall of Eltham Palace and began St. George's Chapel at Windsor, which Henry completed as well as building palaces at Greenwich and Richmond and his great chapel at Westminster.† Throughout the country, cathedrals, abbeys and parish churches bear witness to England's revived prosperity. There are the central towers of Canterbury‡ and Durham Cathedrals, the vaulted naves or choirs of Bath, Norwich, Oxford, Sherborne and Winchester, the nave of Ripon, the eastern chapels of Peterborough and Gloucester, monastic buildings like the gateway of St. Osyth's in Essex or the Prior's House at Much Wenlock.§ Some of these works were begun in Edward's reign, but nearly all were completed when Henry was on the throne. The amount of building in parish churches dating from this period is immense; more than half the datable examples in the late medieval style belong to this age, with Henry's reign again having the larger share. These attest to the piety and wealth of the middle class, like the clothiers Spring and Branch at Lavenham,¶ or the attorney-general Hobart at Loddon in Norfolk. A wealth of woodwork survives

* Plates 25, 26. *See also* pp. 229–33 for notes on the illustrations.
† Plates 4, 6.   ‡ Plate 10.   § Plate 22.   ¶ Plate 21.

from these years in its richly carved roofs and chancel screens.* In Norfolk and Suffolk alone, about ten of the screens still retaining their decorated panels include Henry VI among the figures shown, which obviously dates them as later than 1485, and where he is accompanied by a Breton saint, as at Litcham or Eye† the association with Henry VII is confirmed.

This great amount of work required improved organisation among the building trades. There were gilds of masons and carpenters in the larger towns, training apprentices and regulating standards. In the larger centres, masons produced details like windows which could be supplied where they were needed; alabaster altars and tombs from Derbyshire were manufactured not only for English clients but also for export. The foremost masons can be traced through their contracts from building to building. John Wastell was employed by Cardinal Morton to build the Bell Harry Tower at Canterbury, then by the king to vault King's College chapel. Some families can be traced, the Janyns in Oxford, Eton and Windsor, the Vertues at Bath, Windsor and Westminster. Continuity also appears in their designs. The late Gothic style in England was native, free of the debt to France revealed in buildings of the twelfth and thirteenth centuries. The pattern for the internal elevations of churches was of lofty piers raising depressed, pointed arches, surmounted by a narrow, decorated stone course beneath vast windows almost filling the upper wall. This design appeared at Canterbury and Winchester at the close of the fourteenth century and was followed in all the church buildings of Henry VII's time. In the parish church, the roof is of timber, the structural requirements receiving decorative treatment—the joints surmounted with carvings, the hammer beams with figures.‡ The greater churches are lightly vaulted in stone with fans of ribs forming cones which fill the entire inner surface of the roof. Fan-vaulting first appeared in the mid-fourteenth century cloisters of Gloucester, but seemingly did not become fashionable until the close of the fifteenth century.§ The towers are another outstanding feature of this period's building, their great height subtly exaggerated by vertical line decoration and by a slight reduction in width after each horizontal division.¶

The secular buildings of this time bear the same evidence of peace and prosperity. Of royal castles in England, the Tower, Dover,

* Plates 28, 29.   † Plate 1.   ‡ Plates 20, 29.   § Plates 6, 25.   ¶ Plates 10, 26.

Windsor, Kenilworth and Nottingham were kept in good repair, but others were tumbling down; in 1489, for instance, the rubble from Gloucester was taken to mend a road.[2] Only on the Scottish border were defensive structures now considered necessary by private owners. The castle of Lord Dacre at Kirkoswald-on-Eden,* described as new in 1486,[3] was probably the last private fortress to be built in England. At Thornbury, in Gloucestershire, the mansion of the duke of Buckingham left unfinished at his death in 1521, the only defensible part was the great tower gateway; the other buildings being raised round three quadrangles were low, with many windows, and designed for amenity, not military strength. Old pictures provide our only views of Henry's palaces at Richmond † and Greenwich. Richmond Palace was built to replace the former royal mansion of Sheen, which was burnt down in 1498. The new palace was sumptuously spacious; the hall was 100 feet in length and 40 wide, the chapel's dimensions were similar, and there was an open gallery 200 feet long adjoining a private garden, with a closed gallery set above it. The building also included a library which, like the galleries, was a new feature in English domestic design.

Richmond was mainly brick built, like large houses in other parts of south-east England raised at this time, such as Oxborough Hall in Norfolk or Layer Marney in Essex; or, in London, the hall and gateway of Lincoln's Inn and Morton's Tower at Lambeth Palace.‡ With smaller buildings, including parish churches, local traditions and materials produced variations in design from district to district. In stoneless East Anglia flint was used from necessity, but exploited decoratively on the external surfaces of churches.§ Stone was given to churches wherever possible, although its treatment varied according to its quality. Northamptonshire stone permitted carving, as Louth spire and Boston Stump show, but the gaunt towers of Devonshire reflect the hardness of its quarries. Where stone was easily available, it might be used for houses of moderate size, as in Dorset at Athelhampton¶ or in Rutland at Lyddington. For most small houses, however, timber frames filled with plaster were the rule.$ The same materials were generally used for building in towns, even for the largest, four-storeyed blocks in London and Bristol.

* Plate 23.   † Plate 4.   ‡ Plate 11.
§ Plate 21.   ¶ Plates 30, 31. $ Plates 17, 32, 33.

Other arts

Time and vandalism by 'reformers' of the sixteenth and seventeenth centuries, and by 'restorers' in the nineteenth, have taken a heavy toll of the lesser arts. The extravagant fan-vaulting of Henry VII's chapel and the carved stonework of chantry chapels* in many churches affirm the skill of English sculptors. Chancel screens, choir stalls at Ripon, Manchester and Westminster, show that what masons did in stone carpenters could imitate in wood. Painted glass has suffered from many hands. Much of this late medieval work was unimaginative, the great frames of the windows being filled by row after row of saintly figures, each occupying its own panel. At Fairford, we can see souls being carried to Hell in a wheelbarrow; here the artist seems to have found inspiration in a morality play. A school of glass-painters flourished at Norwich[4] throughout the fifteenth century and established a tradition for animated pictorial design. Scenes from the lives of Christ and the Virgin appear in East Harling church, the gift of Anne Harling, who died in 1498. There is a figure of her second husband, who died in 1480, but also the arms of her third; she was a lady of landed attractions. The scenes, like the Feast at Cana† provide a record of contemporary costume, though we may doubt if the fare was as meagre at the wedding breakfasts of this time. One of the last products of this Norwich school appears in St. Andrews' church there, which was rebuilt in 1506. At least one window was filled with a representation of the Dance of Death, but all now remaining is a solitary panel showing Death leading away a bishop.

Timor mortis conturbat me. The subject of Death provided a constant theme in the art and literature of the later middle ages. Famine and the Black Death and its decennial reappearances engendered an obsession with mortality. 'Here we have no abiding city' was a stock phrase in wills. Artistic representations of the theme continue into the sixteenth century. John Colet's memorial in Old St. Paul's,‡ destroyed in the Great Fire of London, provided a remarkable picture of the meeting of the waning middle ages with the Renaissance. It was crowned with his bust (by Torrigiano?), an early example for England of a record of individual appearance; but on a lower shelf was a sculptured skeleton. The other outstanding humanist founder of the time, Bishop Fox, is buried in Winchester Cathedral

* Plates 6, 7. † Plate 34. ‡ Plate 27.

under a carving of a naked cadaver, a type of effigy which first appeared in France late in the fourteenth century. Fox's scholarly interests, clearly, did not influence his patronage of the arts. His crozier,* a splendid example of work by the famed English silversmiths, is identical in design with one at least a century older made for his predecessor, William of Wykeham.

At the time of Henry VII's death, the influence of the Italian Renaissance was almost imperceptible in England. His subjects were no less generous than the Italians in patronising the arts they knew; their productivity does not compare unfavourably in terms of quantity. In all the arts but architecture, further comparison would be unkind. The technical skill which achieved fan-vaulting, however, or the quality of design in towers like the Bell Harry or Magdalen's, and in the internal elevations of parish churches, still justify the assurance of their creators; while the king's own chapel at Westminster is one of the great monuments of 'Gothic' Europe.

* Plate 19.

10

The Reckoning

HENRY VII died on 21 April 1509, in his palace at Richmond. His health had been poor for some time, certainly since 1506. He was apparently afflicted with some form of consumption which disabled him about three times a year, particularly in the spring. His life had once been despaired of, in March 1503, when a severe attack of quinsy prevented him from eating and drinking for six days. It has often been said that Henry drove himself to an early grave by his devotion to duty; his unremitting application to the work of government destroyed him. He was, however, aged fifty two when he died, and this was a considerably higher age than the general expectation of life at this time; Henry IV, Henry V and Edward IV had all died through natural causes at earlier ages than he did.

The last years

It is part of the traditional view of Henry VII that his character deteriorated in his last years, from about 1504, that he became obsessed with the desire to amass riches and so turned loose those two 'ravening wolves', Empson and Dudley, to extort money by every conceivable means, legal or otherwise.[1] To the statements to this effect by early Tudor chroniclers could be added the testimony of Henry's dying wishes that his executors should, after investigation, remedy just claims that he had wronged any subject. Thus is Henry supposed to have shown remorse for his exactions. It was, however, quite common for wills to stipulate for the satisfaction of creditors and others injured. The provisions in Henry's will under this head are unusually elaborate, but this was in keeping with his concern for making precise and definitive arrangements; consider, for instance, the elaborate and binding provisions he made with Westminster and other abbeys for the performance of services for his spiritual welfare. Henry was far more than conventionally pious. As he was dying, and knew it, he understandably made extreme protestations of penitence for any act of his life which might have condemned him to purgatory. The last confessions of saints generally dwell on the unworthiness of their own lives, and are not taken as evidence at face-value. Nor can the final utterances of Henry VII be regarded as a commentary on his reign.

The assertions of sixteenth-century chroniclers are another matter. It has been cogently argued that these traditions stem from sources which cannot be considered impartial. Moreover, the record of Henry's government does not sustain a general charge that he embarked, from about 1504, on a programme of increasing revenue by tapping new sources. What it does show is that the organisation of the king's finances was remodelled with the establishment of specialist departments, and that its efficiency was thus improved so that evasion of his proper dues became increasingly difficult. It is hardly surprising that this development aroused feelings of resentment towards a king who already had little hold on his subjects' affections. On the whole, since his demands were based on law and feudal prerogative, it would perhaps be more realistic to regard his fiscal officers in the same light as we look upon diligent inspectors of taxes than to brand them as the extortionate agents of an oppressive despot.

To achieve their aim of fully realising Henry's justifiable dues, however, these officials used methods which enhanced their unpopularity; there was the summary procedure of the council learned, the employment of informers. Expediency doubtless demanded these practices as the only means of discovering and enforcing the king's rights, but this was not an argument likely to placate those thus brought to account. Then there were cases, possibly isolated but widely publicised, of individuals receiving harsh treatment without clearly legal justification. Two sometime mayors of London were condemned to pay fines which appeared excessive in relation to their supposed offences and kept in prison to enforce payment. In contrast, others appear to have received, or expected to receive, the benefit of royal influence in their private litigation by buying the king's goodwill; thus Lord Stafford paid £400 for the king's favour in his dispute with the duke of Buckingham, and others paid the king to write to justices of the peace, presumably ordering them to favour one party in a suit. Dudley indicated that he knew of royal letters being issued to impede the course of justice.

This practice he condemned in 1509 when, a prisoner in the Tower, he saw fit to criticise various abuses of royal power of which he doubtless had first-hand knowledge.[2] Dudley also rebuked royal councillors who prosecuted their master's business 'further than conscience requireth' in order to win his special thanks, or for their own advantage or in pursuit of personal vegeance. In his heyday, Dudley enriched himself as well as the king: he died possessed of lands in thirteen counties and goods worth £5,000. Some of this fortune was honestly earned, but he had not neglected opportunities to gain more. His favour was well worth purchase, and he had bought up estates from men forced to sell them to pay debts or fines to the king. His colleague Empson 'maintained' a suitor in litigation against Sir Robert Plumpton, who was thus deprived of part of his family estates; Empson received a share of the spoil and married his daughter to his client's heir.

In extenuation for Dudley and his like, it must be remembered that the contemporary standard of public morality was not high. All men in positions of influence tried to make profits on the side, and those who wanted their good offices accepted it as being in the order of things that they should proffer gifts. The pursuit of Dudley and Empson in 1509 suggests that they had been unusually successful on their own behalf as well as particularly obnoxious in their service of the late king. The reason for their prosecution has more to it than this. It must be considered in the wider context of the climate of opinion in England after Henry VII's death, when feelings of resentment against his policies burst to the surface. Responsibility for the activities of Dudley and his colleagues rests with Henry himself. He employed them, directed their course of operations, and examined their accounts. He may not have known the full details of how they executed their duties, or what personal advantage they gained; but their general programme of rigorously securing full payment of all the king's legitimate dues was inspired by the king.

Reaction

The second Tudor, Henry VIII, immediately succeeded to the crown amidst great popular rejoicing. The personal attractions and accomplishments of the new monarch were not the sole cause of this welcome. When, to carry out Henry VII's last will, persons with claims of debts and injuries were invited to apply for remedy, the council was overwhelmed by the number which came forward clamouring for the redress of grievances, of extortions and injustices. To still the outcry, Empson and Dudley were placed in the Tower. In June, the new king held a great council.[3] In the following month, he appointed commissions of oyer and terminer, judicial bodies to visit every county to make sworn enquiries about all treasons, crimes and trespasses, and also into all breaches of Magna Carta and any other statute and of the law and custom of the realm. This was a remarkable measure. There was nothing unusual in a commission of oyer and terminer charged to investigate crime and disorder. It had long been the crown's practice to appoint such a body after an outbreak of rebellion or any serious disturbance of the peace. It ensured a speedy visitation of a disaffected area by a high-powered judicial tribunal. The commissions of 1509, however, were not required solely to deal with treason and breaches of the peace. Indeed, there had not been an insurrection demanding such action. The commissions' other terms of reference are therefore the more significant, revealing that their principal purpose was to consider charges of violations of the traditional and statutory liberties of the subject.

Commissions of oyer and terminer had not normally been appointed for this reason in the past. The last occasion when they had been set up for this purpose had been in 1450. Then Henry VI had sent similar commissioners into Kent, Suffolk and Norfolk. In the case of Kent, this was the direct consequence of Cade's rebellion. The Kentishmen had complained of injustices and corrupt practices by local government officials, and the commission's purpose was to still this discontent by receiving specific charges against unpopular individuals. Commissions were sent into East Anglia for the same reason. The king was advised that this was the best course he could take to prevent a dangerous outburst from the victims of oppression and extortion by the duke of Suffolk and his minions. This advice was given to Henry VI by the great council.[4] The parallel with 1509 is inescapable. It would not be unreasonable to presume that Henry VIII's great council was responsible for the appointment of the commissions of oyer and terminer; doubtless its arguments would have been similar to those put to Henry VI in 1450.

The records of proceedings before these commissioners are incomplete, and their enquiries were not exhaustive because they were brought to an end on 26 November following on account of the heavy costs to the parties and juries concerned; the council believed that the most serious cases had then been heard. Many of the surviving indictments have no direct relevance to Henry VII's administration, being concerned with the criminal side of the commissions' terms of reference. There were charges against Dudley, Empson and other officials, often drawn up in a form declaring to be illegal practices which had long been used in conciliar jurisdiction. Thus Sir Robert Sheffield, a councillor, was accused of violating a statute of 1368: he had summoned a man before the council on receipt of an informer's allegation, whereas the statute declared that none need answer in a court of law unless formally accused by a jury.[5] In fact, the information was probably a petition for redress, and the method of summons by writ of privy seal was by now a time-hallowed means of calling a defendant to reply before the council.

The judicial methods of the council learned also came under attack, and further details of the exploits of Empson and Dudley were supplied. Yet if these indictments are themselves tendentious, their judicial context must be taken into account: sessions of oyer and teminer were courts of common law and the phraseology of indictments was regulated by ancient common law practice. The purpose of these commissions was to receive complaints, but they were a very cumbersome means of doing this. They could, as courts of common law, only take cognisance of offences and misdemeanours known in common law. Therefore, all the complaints they received had to be defined in language appropriate to a court and disguised as offences falling within a court's competence.

The magnates in 1509

These records confirm that Henry VII's government was unpopular. What is really interesting about these proceedings, however, is the nature of the influence which set them in motion. The great council of June 1509 was probably responsible. Now, the last time the lords are known to have been called to such a council was in 1496. Yet Henry VIII had thus assembled the peers within two months of his accession. His father's death had left a void at the centre of government, for Henry VII had been his own prime minister; temporarily, the ship of state was without a helmsman. This gave the lords their chance. The earl of Surrey, still treasurer of England, tried to dominate the king's council. The duke of Buckingham, the earl of Northumberland and some other disgruntled magnates associated to bring pressure on the new king; the first was said to have aspired to become protector of the realm, while Northumberland dreamed of restoring his family's bygone supremacy in the north. The young king, naturally, lacked his father's caution; he was at a generous, impressionable age, thirsting for glory and pleasure, ready to embrace the company of the most splendid figures in national society. Consequently the peers' bid to regain recognition of their traditional claim to political consideration met with initial success.

The sudden resurrection of baronial aspirations in 1509 makes it clear that Henry VII had not finally reduced the aristocracy to impotence. He had called it to order, but once his hand had gone the lords felt free to reassert themselves. Each individual peer presumably had reasons of his own for political activity in 1509, but there is a hint that the lords took up a common position. This is the reference to Magna Carta in the commissions of oyer and terminer. Several magnates acted as commissioners, among them Buckingham, Northumberland and Abergavenny. It is possible that, in the great council of June 1509, allegations were made that some features of Henry VII's government were contrary to Magna Carta. It certainly is curious that this traditional cornerstone of English liberties again found its way into public currency in 1509.* It would have been appropriate if it had been the lords who rescued it from limbo, for the charter of 1215 was the outcome of baronial insurrection against an arbitrary king.

There undoubtedly were clauses of Magna Carta which Henry VII might be said to have disregarded. The first guaranteed ecclesiastical liberties. For most of his reign, Henry exercised his mastery of the English church as a conscientious steward, choosing it

---

* Although still often quoted on behalf of individuals in petitions and pleadings in the courts, the charter is not known to have been publicly cited as a general constitutional or 'liberty' document in the second half of the fifteenth century.[6]

distinguished and well-qualified bishops, denying himself a good proportion of his legitimate perquisites at their expense, and promoting attempts at reform. In his final years, however, his standards deteriorated: there was the unworthy choice of James Stanley for Ely in 1506, he accepted—or demanded—payments to advance clerks to cathedral dignities, and he exacted £5,000 from the Cistercian order as the price for a charter merely confirming its ancient privileges and rights to elect its own abbots and priors; while he ceased to remit the revenues due from vacant sees so that his profits from his source rose to a record level. This evidence of a change for the worse in Henry's attitude to the Church does appear to support the traditional view of his decline into avarice. Even when his ecclesiastical policy was more scrupulous, however, the extent of his control cannot have been welcome to the clergy. A bill 'for the liberties of the English church' was introduced in the parliament of 1510, but although the lords approved, it was thereafter lost to view,

The famous thirty-ninth clause of Magna Carta upheld the right of every free man to trial by his peers. There was no jury in conciliar courts. A statute of 1495 permitted justices of the peace to pass sentence without a jury in certain cases; this act was repealed in 1510. The parliament of this year, in fact, provides a number of pointers to features of Henry VII's government which his subjects disliked. Allegations were made that some people had lost possession of their lands by the action of escheators and other royal commissioners in wrongly claiming them for the king. The council learned's search for offenders against penal statutes was another cause for complaint, leading to an act requiring such prosecutions to be made within three years of the offence. It would also seem that there was some disquiet because parliaments had been so rarely held in Henry's last years. The chancellor in his address to the parliament of 1510 held forth on the advantages of regular meetings: they gave subjects an opportunity to ventilate their grievances and seek redress.

The clause of Magna Carta with most relevance for the lords in 1509 was the twenty-first: 'earls and barons shall not be amerced except by their peers, and only in accordance with the nature of their offence'. It had been King John's policy to impose crushing fines on barons who had incurred his wrath as his price for admitting them to his peace and restoring their lands. More, he began to compel such victims of his displeasure to seal deeds which acknowledged that he could seize their lands at will. By such sanctions he hoped to cow opposition,[7] but instead he provoked rebellion. Henry VII had likewise required subjects to seal bonds pledging their loyalty at determined sums of financial liability, and in his final years, as his condition for reducing ruinous fines, compelled a number of lords to acknowledge great debts which were respited during his pleasure. The words of Shakespeare's John of Gaunt could well be applied to England under Henry VII—

> 'bound in with shame,
> With inky blots and rotten parchment bonds.'

These suspended obligations, threatening ruin in the event of royal displeasure, provided Northumberland, Abergavenny and a number of other magnates with a sharp spur to action when Henry died. Their initiative was successful. They persuaded the new king to cancel their recognisances, along with some two score others; in several of Henry VIII's warrants to do this appear statements that these bonds had been made on the unreasonable instigation of certain of Henry VII's councillors, 'against law, right and conscience, to the evident overburdening and danger of our late father's soul'.[8]

Personal decline of Henry VII

The baronial reaction in 1509 was the outcome of the stringent character of Henry's government in his last few years. Bonds to ensure loyalty were understandable enough in times when conspiracy was rife, as at the beginning of the reign and when pretenders were on the warpath. This was no longer the case after 1506, yet it was after this time that Henry embarked on the new policy of putting lords on their best behaviour under threat of ruin. New methods suggest the influence of new men, and it is probable that the council learned devised this programme of muzzling the magnates. The lords had their revenge in 1510, when Dudley and Empson were put to death on trumped up charges of treason.* Yet Henry at the least gave his

---

* There is an interesting parallel with events in France after the death of Philip IV in 1314. There was widespread reaction against his anti-feudal policies and the magnates who gained influence under the new king initiated prosecutions of a number of Philip's 'middle-class' lawyer councillors, and had his chief finance minister put to death. Indeed, the parallel goes further. French historians from the time of the Revolution warmly approved of Philip IV and saw in his councillors the spiritual ancestors of Robespierre and other middle-class destroyers of the aristocracy. One suspects that the enthusiasm of some modern English historians for Henry VII has a similar explanation springing from Victorian liberalism and its belief in 'the rise of the middle class'.

26 Magdalen College, Oxford

25 King's College Chapel, Cambridge

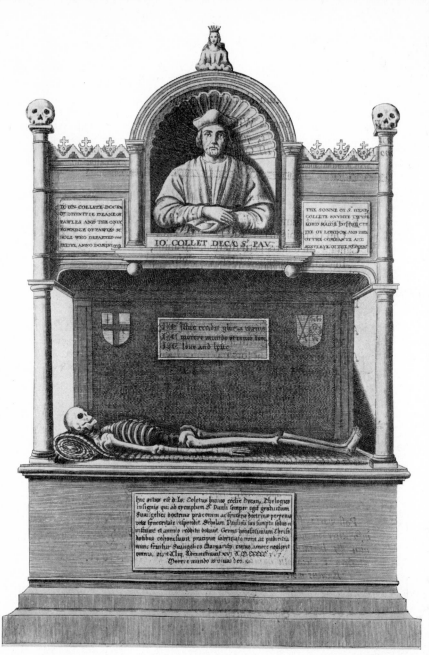

27 John Colet's tomb

approval to their measures. The promptness of the reaction after his death indicates that he had been pressing the lords too hard. Hitherto he had shown his mastery of political craftsmanship in knowing how far he could go; he had respected vested interests, confirmed privileges as long as their possessors met their obligations, and as late as 1504 had gracefully accepted a rebuff from the house of commons. Thereafter, dogged with ill-health and obsessed with the mutations of international diplomacy, it would appear that his judgment was failing him.

The same must be said about his fiscal policy. Without denying that his demands were justifiable in law, public opinion as revealed by protests after his death and recorded in chronicles, indicates that his remorseless exploitation of his subjects was scarcely wise. Perhaps, in mitigation, it might be presumed that Henry felt he required ampler revenues so that he could buy foreign allies; his foundation at Westminster also strained his resources. He was, however, undermining the security of his throne. Wealth would not have saved it in the event of an insurrection on a national scale. Dudley, in his mealy-mouthed political testament, gets at the truth of the matter where he writes, 'The covetous council will show their sovereign his surety standeth much in plenty of treasure, but both these counsels* are but fallible fantasies, for the profit of every Christian king dependeth in the grace of God, which is won by mercy and liberality.' Then, of 'insatiable' kings, 'peradventure of that appetite have there been some other of late time, and were in manner without fault, saving only that. But how such a king shall have the loving hearts of his subjects, late experience may plainly show it.'

It is plain enough that Henry VII did not have his subjects' loving hearts. His death must have been welcomed with relief, not only by the lords, but by all persons holding land; nor would it have brought sorrow to that stronghold of the 'rising middle-class', the city of London, where royal interference in its government, amercements of its corporations, and harsh prosecutions of individuals had recently become grievous burdens. The land rejoiced, wrote Lord Mountjoy to Erasmus; avarice had been banished.[9] Had Henry lived longer, continuing his stringent policies, the pressure of resentment may well have become uncontainable. His death allowed this pressure to be

H   * The other being cruelty.

released, but if he had survived another five years, the consequences to the country might well have been unfortunate. Henry timed his exit as perfectly as his arrival; neither could safely have been deferred.

Henry VII's achievement

Some authorities have concluded that Henry VII has claims to be regarded as the greatest of the Tudors. This is a bold assertion when the achievements of Elizabeth I and Henry VIII are recalled, and it must be reconsidered. The most impressive feature of Henry's career as king is his record in international diplomacy. In comparison, previous kings appear almost parochial in the range of their foreign interests; of none could it have been said by Italians, as it was of him, that he knew the affairs of Italy as well as they did.[10] Moreover, his eventual mastery of the arts of diplomacy was at least equal to that of his fellow-sovereigns. It is true that his treaties were short-lived, but England was outclassed by the super-powers of France and Spain and Henry's diplomacy, conducted on a necessarily hand-to-mouth basis, kept the country free from involvement in European wars without incurring the perils of isolation. It is unlikely that English public opinion applauded his foreign policy; his bellicose son, indeed, received enthusiastic support when he proposed to go to war against France in 1511. After his statesmanship had matured in 1492, however, Henry VII turned his back on the chimera of military glory. He was the last man to be moved by chauvinistic national sentiment; its indulgence was a luxury neither king nor country could afford. In this context, we may properly regard Henry as one of the greatest statesmen to sit on the English throne.

It cannot be said that his domestic record was equally enlightened. There is no case for crediting him with a programme of economic development; although his foreign policy generally facilitated the spontaneous growth of English trade and his reign was, for a variety of other reasons, on balance an age of prosperity and economic growth. Nor does his record as a legislator appear very impressive. Despite the number of his statutes, few give evidence of any policy of legal reform, and they were more concerned with improving the administration of the existing machinery; while, even here, a number of the measures he enacted belong to a programme to promote the office of justice of the peace which had been launched by the parliamentary commons of the Lancastrian period. It may be significant, moreover, that after Cardinal Morton's death there was no more important legislation in the field of public order, with the exception of the statute of 1504 against retaining, nor did the king continue to show an interest in the reform of the clergy.

It must be presumed that Henry's legislation, and his council's oversight of the local law courts, achieved some success in curbing his subjects' propensity for lawlessness and perversion of judicial machinery. Foreigners thought that the English were the least law-abiding of nations, and their reform was an uphill task. Henry VIII soon had to add to the legislation against corrupt juries and extortionate sheriffs. Even the agents on whom the king was forced to rely, the justices of the peace, were not wholly reliable. In one of the best known 'star chamber' cases of the reign, in 1502, charges of instigating an attack on Eynsham abbey by a gang of retainers and corrupt procedure in quarter sessions were made against Sir Robert Harcourt, who was not only a justice of the peace but also an office-holder under the crown. There were disturbances of the peace of sufficient gravity to demand special judicial visitations of Sussex in 1505, the East Midlands in 1506, and Dorset and Rutland in 1508.[11] The number of pardons for felonies annually granted by the king rose from 1501. This is evidence either of an increase in crime or a greater readiness on the king's part to sell his pardon, probably the latter; neither explanation indicates an advance in judicial effectiveness.

Of course we have been told that Henry VII's policies were successful; they must have been, because he was the last of a sequence of kings who won the throne by violence. He was succeeded by his son, and the Tudors retained the crown until their extinction by natural causes. It was fortunate, however, that his heir was eighteen years of age in 1509, so that there was no question of a royal minority. Perhaps it was also fortunate that Henry VIII was his only surviving son. The death of Prince Arthur was a personal disaster to Henry VII, but it prevented the establishment of a cadet branch of the royal family descending from Henry Tudor, duke of York.[12] When we consider what ammunition the various houses descended from Edward III gave to baronial militancy in the fifteenth century, Arthur's death appears less lamentable. Henry (VIII) might have been as dutiful a brother as Richard III, but would he have been a better uncle?* The judicial savagery of his later years makes the prospect a fascinating subject for speculation. What is important here is that the fact of Arthur's death must be taken into account when we assess Henry VII's achievement. So often has it been said that he gave England the benefit of dynastic stability, yet the line of succession to the throne was fashioned by the unforeseeable dispensations of birth and death.

The fact remains that the battle of Stoke was the last contested round in the Wars of the Roses. The nature and causes of these wars, however, have previously been misunderstood, and now that we can see them in proper perspective Henry's emergence as the final victor appears a less remarkable accomplishment. It is quite clear that the wars had not left any legacy of deep partisan division in English society for him to mend; there never had been any extensive polarisation around the banners of York and Lancaster, and the readiness with which men who had held office under Edward IV received the commisisons of Henry VII emphasises that the claims of royal dynasties weighed little with them. The real legacy of the wars was popular indifference to the person who was king for the time being, but this meant that whoever did become king was passively accepted. Henry still had to cope with occasional conspiracies, but the efficiency of his security service, and his own resolution, promptitude and severity crushed these as soon as they were discovered. These were the qualities by which he kept the throne, and he had to employ them throughout his reign. Yet every past king had been on his guard against factious revolt, and only those with courage and determination, if not ruthlessness, had died peacefully; had Henry VI been of this calibre, there would not have been any Wars of the Roses.

The parting of the ways

The reign of Henry VII must still be regarded as one of the great landmarks in England's political development. Historians asking themselves whether he was a 'medieval' or a 'modern' type of king have found their answer by examining the organisation of his administration. This is the wrong yardstick. Henry was not the last king to

* The legend that Henry VIII was originally destined for the Church is without foundation. The last precedent for an ecclesiastical career for a king's son was that of a bastard of Henry II. Henry's creation as duke of York shows that Henry VII intended him to be a layman.

be intimately concerned with the work of government; he may have applied himself more diligently to its details than his successors, but several of his predecessors equally lacked his powers of concentration to business. If previous kings had been less authoritarian and stringent, it was not because they were endowed with fewer prerogatives but rather because their administrative organisations were less efficient or they preferred, or were compelled, to rule with looser reins. Bureaucracy, which freed the king of routine chores, was certainly not a sixteenth-century invention: the Exchequer and all three secretarial departments were established as bureaucratic organs before Henry's accession.

The most characteristic feature of the medieval monarchy was its need for the co-operation of the nobility. It was accepted that the lords as a class were entitled to special consideration in formulating 'the great business of the king and kingdom', they were regarded as the king's 'natural councillors', and this unique political status was given recognition by their periodic assembly in great councils. As we have already noticed, Henry VII held his last great council in 1496. He had summoned these councils only when he required them; he did not hold them as a matter of course. It is obvious that Henry felt himself under no obligations to the nobility on account of their birth. Although he had a preference for noble companions, and admitted individual peers to his council, he showed no favour to the lords as a class; they were as much his subjects as the commoners, bound to obey the same laws and fulfil the same obligations of loyalty and service, nor, he asserted, could they interpose their influence and personal authority between humbler subjects and the crown.

The political resurgence of the peerage in 1509 was short-lived. Other great councils were held in 1511, to discuss the question whether England should join the Holy League, and in 1512 to make plans for the invasion of France.[13] In the king's council, Bishop Fox thwarted Surrey's ambitions, and then himself gave way as Thomas Wolsey established his autocratic domination. Wolsey brought the lords again to heel, destroying Buckingham, reducing the rest to such a state of nerves that they dared not speak to each other about their grievances. Then when Wolsey mismanaged the 'amicable grant' in 1525, a great council was called to propose a remedy. Finally in 1529, Henry VIII opened his attack on the cardinal in another great council.[14] The king had reanimated the peers for the congenial task of overthrowing their oppressor; like his father, he now only called a great council when it served his purpose.

From this time, the institution sank into such obscurity that when its last meeting was called, in 1640, Charles I's advisers believed that no great council had been held since the reign of Edward III.[15] In this context, the reign of Henry VII is the watershed between the old and a new pattern of political life; it divides those centuries when the principal and most constant cause of major disorder had been the aspirations and suspicions of the baronial class from a period which saw the emergence of parties making their stand on issues of religious and constitutional principle.

Bibliographical Note

THIS list is selective and designed to suggest titles for further reading. At the same time, the author wishes to take this opportunity to acknowledge those works which he found particularly helpful. More specialised works are noticed under References. For a fuller bibliography, reference should be made to the *Bibliography of British History: Tudor Period*, 1485–1603, ed. Conyers Read (1959).

Collection of Documents

English Historical Documents, 1485–1558. Ed. C. H. Williams. 1967.
The Reign of Henry VII from Contemporary Sources. Ed. A. F. Pollard. 3 vols. 1913–14.

Medieval Background

Chrimes, S. B. *An Introduction to the Administrative History of Medieval England*. Oxford, 1952.
—— *English Constitutional Ideas in the Fifteenth Century*. Cambridge, 1936.
Fortescue, John. *De Laudibus Legum Anglie*. Ed. with translation by S. B. Chrimes. Cambridge, 1949.
Hay, Denys. *Europe in the Fourteenth and Fifteenth Centuries*. 1966.
Holt, J. C. *Magna Carta*. Cambridge, 1965.
Harriss, G. L. 'Medieval Government and Statecraft', in *Past and Present*, no. 25, 1963.
Kingsford, C. L. *Prejudice and Promise in XVth Century England*. Oxford, 1925.
Lander, J. R. *The Wars of the Roses*. 1965. (This is a collection of contemporary narratives with an introduction.)

McFarlane, K. B. 'The Wars of the Roses', in *Proceedings of the British Academy*, vol. L, 1965.

McKisack, M. *The Fourteenth Century* (Oxford History of England, vol. 5). 1959.

Myers, A. R. 'The Character of Richard III', in *History Today*, vol. IV, 1954.

Scofield, C. L. *The Life and Reign of Edward the Fourth*. 2 vols. 1910.

Storey, R. L. *The End of the House of Lancaster*. 1966.

Biographical and General

The Anglica Historia of Polydore Vergil. A.D. 1485–1537. Ed. with translation by Denys Hay. Royal Historical Society, Camden Series, vol. LXXIV, 1950.

Busch, W. *England under the Tudors: King Henry VII*. Translation by A. M. Todd. 1895.

Mackie, J. D. *The Earlier Tudors, 1485–1558* (Oxford History of England, vol. 7). 1957.

Wernham, R. B. *Before the Armada*. 1966. (A penetrating study of foreign policy, for which Busch and Mackie are also most useful.)

Government

Elton, G. R. 'Henry VII: Rapacity and Remorse', in *Historical Journal*, vol. I, 1958.

Gray, H. L. *The Influence of the Commons on Early Legislation*. Harvard, 1932.

Lander, J. R. 'The Yorkist Council and Administration, 1461 to 1485' in *English Historical Review*, vol. LXXIII, 1958.

—— 'Council, Administration and Councillors, 1461 to 1485', in *Bulletin of the Institute of Historical Research*, vol. XXXII, 1959.

Pickthorn, K. W. H. *Early Tudor Government: Henry VII*. Cambridge, 1949.

Pollard, A. F. *The Evolution of Parliament*. 1938.

Roskell, J. S. *The Commons and their Speakers in English Parliaments, 1376–1523*. Manchester, 1965.

Select Cases in the Council of Henry VII. Ed. C. G. Bayne and W. H. Dunham. Selden Society, vol. 75, 1956.

Wolffe, B. P. 'Henry VII's Land Revenues and Chamber Finance', in *English Historical Review*, vol. LXXIX, 1964.
—— *Yorkist and Early Tudor Government, 1461–1509*. Historical Association Aids for Teachers of History, no. 12, 1966.

Law and Order

Bellamy, J. G. 'Justice under the Yorkist Kings', in *American Journal of Legal History*, vol. 9, 1965.
Plucknett, T. F. T. *A Concise History of the Common Law*. Fifth Edition, 1956.
Putnam, B. H. (ed.) *Early Treatises on the Practice of the Justices of the Peace in the Fifteenth and Sixteenth Centuries* (Oxford Studies in Social and Legal History, vol. VII). 1924.
—— *Proceedings before the Justices of the Peace in the Fourteenth and Fifteenth Centuries*. The Ames Foundation, 1938.
Reid, R. R. *The King's Council in the North*. 1921.
Williams, P. H. *The Council in the Marches of Wales under Elizabeth I*. 1958.

Social and Economic

A Relation of the Island of England. Ed. with translation by C. A. Sneyd. Camden Society, vol. XXXVII, 1847.
Beresford, M. W. *The Lost Villages of England*. 1954.
Bridbury, A. R. *Economic Growth: England in the Later Middle Ages*. 1962.
Carus-Wilson, E. M. *Medieval Merchant Venturers*. 1954.
Clapham, J. H. *A Concise Economic History of Britain to 1750*. Cambridge, 1949.
Darby, H. C. (ed.). *An Historical Geography of England before A.D. 1800*. Cambridge, 1963.
Power, E. *The Wool Trade in English Medieval History*. Oxford, 1941.
—— and M. M. Postan (ed.), *Studies in English Trade in the Fifteenth Century*. 1933.
Russell, J. C. *British Medieval Population*. Albuquerque, 1948.
Saltzmann, L. F. *English Industries in the Middle Ages*. 1913.
Thirsk, Joan (ed.). *The Agrarian History of England and Wales*, vol. IV (1500–1640). Cambridge, 1967.
Williamson, J. A. *The Cabot Voyages and Bristol Discovery under Henry VII*. Hakluyt Society, second series, no CXX, 1962.

The Church

Du Boulay, F. R. H. 'The Fifteenth Century', in *The English Church and the Papacy during the Middle Ages*. Ed. C. H. Lawrence. 1965.

Jenkins, C. 'Cardinal Morton's Register', in *Tudor Studies*. Ed. R. W. Seton-Watson. 1924.

Knowles, M. D. *The Religious Orders in England*. Cambridge, 1950–61. (Vols. II and III.)

Storey, R. L. *Diocesan Administration in the Fifteenth Century*. St. Anthony's Hall Publications, no 16, 1959.

Thompson, A. H. *The English Clergy and their Organization in the Later Middle Ages*. Oxford, 1947.

Wood-Legh, K. L. *Perpetual Chantries in Britain*. Cambridge, 1965.

Woodward, G. W. O. *The Dissolution of the Monasteries*. 1966.

Education

Jacob, E. F. *The Fifteenth Century* (Oxford History of England, vol. 6). 1961. (Chapter XIV.)

Leach, A. F. *English Schools at the Reformation*. 1896.

Rashdall, H. *The Universities of Europe in the Middle Ages*. Ed. F. M. Powicke and A. B. Emden. Oxford, 1936. (Vol. III.)

Simon, Joan. *Education and Society in Tudor England*. 1966.

The Arts

Anderson, M. D. *Looking for History in British Churches*, 1951.

Bennett, H. S. *English Books and Readers, 1475 to 1557*. Cambridge, 1952.

Harvey, J. H. *Gothic England*. 1947.

James, M. R. *Suffolk and Norfolk*. 1930.

Webb, G. *Architecture in Britain in the Middle Ages*, 1956.

References

THESE, again, are selective, only supplied when the information given is not provided in the works listed above. All manuscript sources cited here are preserved in the Public Record Office.

Introduction

1. See below under Chapter 5, note 12, and Chapter 6, note 8.

Chapter 1

1. *Rotuli Parliamentorum* (1783), vol. V, p. 200.
2. *Proceedings and Ordinances of the Privy Council of England*, ed. N. H. Nicolas (Record Commission, 1834–7), vol. III, p. 79; *The Register of Thomas Langley, Bishop of Durham*, ed. R. L. Storey (Surtees Society, 1956– , vol. III, no. 1192.
3. A. L. Brown, 'The Authorisation of Letters under the Great Seal', in *Bulletin of the Institute of Historical Research*, vol. XXXVII, 1964.

Chapter 3

1. D. Williams, 'The Welsh Tudors', in *History Today*, vol. IV, 1954.
2. Exchequer L. T. R.: Foreign Accounts, no. 119, Hanaper 1 Henry VII; *Materials for a History of the Reign of Henry VII*, ed. W. Campbell (Rolls Series, 1873–7), vol. I, p. 226.

For other officers of state, see *The Handbook of British Chronology*, ed. F. M. Powicke and E. B. Fryde (Royal Historical Society, 1961).

3. *Calendar of Papal Letters* (Public Record Office, 1894–), vol. XIV, pp. 14–27.
4. *The English Works of John Fisher*, ed. J. E. B. Mayor (Early English Text Society, extra series, vol. XXVII, 1876), pp. 268–88.
5. *Calendar of State Papers: Spain*, ed. G. A. Bergenroth and others (Public Record Office, 1862–1954), vol. I, pp. 154, 160.

6. *Calendar of Close Rolls* (Public Record Office, 1902–63), *1500–9*, pp. 68, 138–57, 205–6.
7. *Excerpta Historica*, ed. S. Bentley (1831), pp. 89–133 (Privy Purse Expenses of Henry VII); J. Leland, *Collectanea*, ed. T. Hearne (Oxford, 1770), vol. IV, p. 243 (a chronicle of court life 1486–92 by a royal herald).
8. *State Papers: Spain*, I, p. 178.

Chapter 4

1. *Calendar of Patent Rolls* (Public Record Office, 1901–   ), *1485–94*, p. 39; *Cal. Close 1485–1500*, pp. 14, 22.
2. A. H. Burne, *More Battlefields of England* (1952), pp. 157–73. Henry's movements can be traced in his household account (Exchequer K.R.: Various Accounts, box 412, no. 19).
3. *Cal. Patent 1485–94*, pp. 442, 481–508.
4. *Ibid.*, pp. 127, 142.
5. *Cal. Patent 1494–1509*, p. 29. For itinerary, *see* G. Temperley, *Henry VII* (1917), p. 415.

Chapter 5

1. *Cal. Close 1500–9*, p. 21.
2. R. L. Storey, *Thomas Langley and the Bishopric of Durham, 1406–1437* (1961), p. 38.
3. Leland, *Collectanea*, IV, p. 246.
4. *State Papers: Spain*, I, pp. 160, 439.
5. Exchequer of Receipt: Warrants for Issues, box 79, part 2, no 27.
6. Although some of their conclusions require extensive modification in the light of Dr. Wolffe's work, F. C. Dietz, *English Government Finance, 1485–1558* (1921, reprinted 1964), and W. C. Richardson, *Tudor Chamber Administration* (Louisiana State University Press, 1952) remain valuable for detailed information. The latter has an appendix giving the career of Sir Reginald Bray.
7. Exchequer Various Accounts, box 413, no. 2, vol. 1, fo. 36, and vol. 3, fo. 53.
8. *State Papers: Spain*, I, p. 178.
9. G. L. Harriss, 'Aids, Loans and Benevolences', in *Historical Journal*, vol. VI, 1963.
10. Busch, *op. cit.*, pp. 421–2.
11. *The Great Chronicle of London*, ed. A. D. Thomas and I. D. Thornley (1938), pp. 244–5.
12. There are two bundles of these warrants among the unsorted Chancery files in the Public Record Office.
13. *Cal. Patent 1405–8*, pp. 75–9.

14. W. Jay, 'List of Members of the Fourth Parliament of Henry VII', in *Bulletin of the Institute of Historical Research*, vol. III, 1926; *c.f.* J. C. Wedgwood, *History of Parliament* (1936–8), vol. II (Register of Members of the House of Commons).

15. *Relation of England*, p. 36; *State Papers: Spain*, I, p. 178.

16. Scofield, *op. cit.*, vol. II, pp. 377–8.

17. R. R. Steele, *Bibliography of Royal Proclamations of the Tudor and Stuart Period: England and Wales* (vol. V. of Biblioteca Lindesiana, Oxford, 1910), pp. lxxvi–vii.

Chapter 6

1. For legislation, see *Statutes of the Realm*, ed. A. Luders and others (Record Commission, 1810–28), vol. II. Gray (*op. cit.*, chapter VI) identifies the sources of bills and notices commons' bills which were rejected.

2. *Select Cases before the King's Council*, 1243–1482, ed. I. S. Leadam and J. F. Baldwin (Selden Society, vol. 35, 1918), pp. 104–6; Exchequer Warrants, box 55, no. 151.

3. *The Brut*, ed. F. W. D. Brie (Early English Text Society, 1905–8), vol. II, pp. 479, 485; Storey, *End of Lancaster*, pp. 34, 145.

4. There is no evidence of its use before this reign. Dr. Bellamy has misread his source for a supposed case of torture in 1458 (*op. cit.*, p. 145).

5. *Calendar of Letters and Papers, Henry VIII*, ed. J. S. Brewer and others (Public Record Office, 1864–1920), vol. I, part I, p. 195.

6. R. Somerville, 'Henry VII's "Council Learned in the Law" ', in *English Historical Review*, vol. LIV, 1939.

7. *Select Cases in the Court of Requests, 1497–1569*, ed. I. S. Leadam (Selden Society, vol. 12, 1898).

8. There are many files of these writs and returns among the unsorted Chancery files. See *Guide to the Contents of the Public Record Office* (1963), vol. I, pp. 11–12.

9. Plucknett, *op. cit.*, p. 579.

10. R. Sillem, 'Commissions of the Peace, 1380–1485', in *Bulletin of the Institute of Historical Research*, vol. X, 1933.

11. H. C. Johnson, 'The Origin and Office of the Clerk of the Peace', in *The Clerks of the Counties, 1360–1960* (1961).

12. As note 3 above.

13. *Cal. Patent 1476–85*, pp. 553–80; *1485–94*, pp. 481–508.

14. *Ibid.*, pp. 481–508; *1494–1509*, pp. 629–69.

15. *Ibid.*, pp. 500, 611, 632, 654.

16. King's Bench: Plea Rolls, no. 989, Rex, mm. 14, 16.

17. *Cal. Patent 1494–1509*, pp. 446, 501, 504, 519, 527, 535, 539.

18. Exchequer Warrants, boxes 73–77, *passim*.

226 · REFERENCES

19. *List of Sheriffs for England and Wales* (Public Record Office Lists and Indexes, vol. IX, 1898); *c.f.* Wedgwood, *History of Parliament*, vol. II.

20. Exchequer Warrants, boxes 79–86, *passim*.

21. *Cal. Patent 1494–1509*, p. 496.

22. R. L. Storey, 'The Warden of the Marches of England towards Scotland, 1377–1489', in *English Historical Review*, vol. LXXII, 1957.

23. *Cal. Patent 1494–1509*, p. 611.

24. W. Hutchinson, *The History and Antiquities of the County Palatine of Durham* (Newcastle-upon-Tyne), vol. I, pp. 365–85.

25. The most recent special study of this subject is the introduction to W. H. Dunham, *Lord Hastings' Indentured Retainers, 1461–1483* (New Haven, Connecticut, 1955). My disagreement with some of Professor Dunham's arguments appears above and also in my *End of Lancaster*, pp. 10–17, 26–7. *Select Cases in the Council of Henry VII* is also most useful on this topic.

26. J. R. Lander, 'Attainder and Forfeiture, 1453 to 1509', in *Historical Journal*, vol. IV, 1961.

27. *Cal. Close 1485–1500*, pp. 177–8; *1500–9*, pp. 209, 300, 309–11, 357.

Chapter 7

1. Leland, *Collectanea*, IV, p. 254; *Cal. Close 1485–1500*, p. 149; E. Hall, *Chronicle* (1809), pp. 425, 491, 502, 512, 592, 628.

2. Storey, *End of Lancaster*, p. 207; *Tudor Royal Proclamations*, ed. P. L. Hughes and J. F. Larkin, vol. I (1964), p. 27.

3. *Calendar of Charter Rolls* (Public Record Office, 1903–27), vol. VI, pp. 266–74. Further licences appear in *Cal. Patent*.

4. E. M. Carus-Wilson and Olive Coleman, *England's Export Trade, 1275–1547* (Oxford, 1963).

5. Leland, *Collectanea*, IV, p. 200.

6. G. V. Scammell, 'Shipowning in England circa 1450–1550', in *Transactions of the Royal Historical Society*, fifth series, vol. 12, 1962.

7. *Foedera*, ed. T. Rymer (1704–35), vol. XII, pp. 373, 389–90.

8. Exchequer Various Accounts, box 414, no. 6, fo. 207.

9. M. Oppenheim, *A History of the Administration of the Royal Navy* (1896); C. F. Richmond, 'English Naval Power in the Fifteenth Century', in *History*, vol. LII, 1967.

10. Exchequer Warrants, boxes 77, part 3, no. 42; 78, parts 1, nos. 33, 38, and 2, no. 49.

11. *Ibid.*, 79, part 2, no. 22. Oppenheim wrongly gives the size as 600 tuns.

12. *Ibid.*, 79, part 2, no. 26.

Chapter 8

1. Leland, *Collectanea*, IV, p. 246.
2. *Cal. Papal Letters*, XIV, *passim*.
3. W. T. Waugh, 'The Great Statute of Praemunire 1393', in *English Historical Review*, vol. XXXVII, 1922.
4. *Cal. Close 1485–1500*, p. 133.
5. J. J. Scarisbrick, 'Clerical Taxation in England, 1485 to 1547', in *Journal of Ecclesiastical History*, vol. X, 1960.
6. *Cal. Papal Letters*, XIV, pp. 307–8.
7. *Ibid.*, pp. 27–8.
8. *State Papers, Venice*, ed. R. Brown and others (Public Record Office, 1864–1947), vol. I, p. 181.
9. For this biographical information, *c.f.* lists under sees in *Handbook of British Chronology* and A. B. Emden, *A Biographical Register of the University of Oxford to A.D. 1500* (Oxford, 1957–9), 3 vols., and *A Biographical Register of the University of Cambridge to 1500* (Cambridge, 1963).
10. *Cal. Patent 1485–94*, pp. 119, 167, 389; *1494–1509*, pp. 77, 111, 154, 185, 240, 263, 265, 269, 282, 300, 313, 345, 514.
11. *Ibid.*, p. 430.
12. *Cal. Patent 1485–94*, p. 81; *1494–1509*, pp. 72, 196, 200, 226, 270, 303–4, 520, 550, 567, 624–5.
13. J. A. F. Thomson, *The Later Lollards* (Oxford, 1965).

Chapter 9

1. *Cal. Patent 1485–94*, p. 45.
2. *Ibid.*, p. 298.
3. *Calendar of Inquisitions Post Mortem*, second series (Public Record Office, 1898–1956), vol. I, no. 157.
4. C. Woodforde, *The Norwich School of Glass-Painting in the Fifteenth Century* (1950).

Chapter 10

1. Dr. Elton's refutation of this tradition (*Historical Journal*, 1958) was challenged by J. P. Cooper, 'Henry VII's Last Years Reconsidered', in *Ibid.*, vol. II, 1959. Dr. Elton retorted with 'Henry VII: A Restatement', in *Ibid.*, vol. IV, 1961.
2. E. Dudley, *The Tree of Commonwealth*, ed. D. M. Brodie (Cambridge, 1948). *See also* D. M. Brodie, 'Edmund Dudley, Minister of Henry VII', in *Transactions of the Royal Historical Society*, fourth series, vol. XV, 1932.
3. Polydore Vergil, *op. cit.*, pp. 148–9.

4. Storey, *End of Lancaster*, pp. 56, 67.

5. King's Bench: Ancient Indictments, file 453, no. 5.

6. F. Thompson, *Magna Carta* (1948), p. 139.

7. Holt, *Magna Carta*, pp. 110–14.

8. Busch, *op. cit.*, p. 277; *Letters and Papers, Henry VIII*, I, part I, pp. 30, 62, 67, 81, 111, 126, 191, 195, 281.

9. *Letters of Erasmus*, ed. P. S. Allen (Oxford, 1906–58), vol. I, no. 215.

10. *State Papers, Venice*, I, p. 260.

11. *Cal. Patent 1485–94*, p. 405; *1494–1509*, pp. 133, 422, 474, 559, 627, 654.

12. Suggested by K. B. McFarlane, *op. cit.*, p. 95.

13. Polydore Vergil, pp. 160–1, 196–9.

14. Hall, *Chronicle*, pp. 700, 759.

15. S. R. Gardiner, *History of England, 1603–1642* (1894), vol. IX, p. 200.

28 Choir screen of Plymtree Church

29 Angel roof of March Church

30, 31 Athelhampton Hall

32, 33 Gainsborough Old Hall

34 Window of East Harling Church

Notes on the Illustrations

1. Paintings on the choir-screen of the parish church of Eye, Suffolk. There was a cult of Henry VI in the reign of Henry VII, who attempted to have him officially recognised as a saint. St. Ursula, a Breton princess, was believed to have been martyred with 11,000 virgins, some of whom are shown under her cloak.

2, 3. Portraits of Henry VII and Elizabeth of York by Michael Sitium, dated 1505, in the National Portrait Gallery, London.

4. The east view of Henry VII's palace at Richmond, Surrey, in 1727, from the engraving by Samuel and Nathaniel Buck.

5. Illuminated first folio of a volume of ordinances for Henry VII's chantry chapel in Westminster Abbey. The upper edge is indented as these articles were made in the form of an indenture in seven parts (as the text here states), on 16 July 1505. In the initial 'T' the king is shown giving the book of ordinances to the monks of Westminster. In the margins are his arms, supported by a (Welsh) dragon and a greyhound, with his badge of the red rose and Lady Margaret Beaufort's device of a portcullis (gold on blue); both devices frequently appear in the carved decoration of the chapel and other royal buildings of the time.

[PUBLIC RECORD OFFICE: E.33, no.2, fo.1.]

6. The foundation stone of the Lady Chapel of Westminster Abbey—better known as Henry VII's Chapel—was laid on 23 January 1503. The building was completed about 1519.

7. This small chantry chapel of a 'stone-cage' design stands between two piers of the choir of Worcester Cathedral, on the south side of the high altar. It was built, with rich sculptural decoration (by London craftsmen), to hold the tomb of Prince Arthur (d. 1502) and a chaplain celebrating at the altar of the chapel.

8. Bust of Henry VII, presumed to be by Pietro Torrigiano, in the Victoria and Albert Museum, London.

9. This portion of a page of chamber receipts shows how Henry altered the style of his sign-manual in August 1492. The text is as follows:

Master Bray
27 August Item. Received of Master Bray by £108
thands of William Cope of the Reveneuz
of thisle of Wight due at Ester last
passed
Master Bray
28 August Item. Received of Master Bray by £1,382 4s. 3d.
thands of William Coope opon a war-
rant for garnisshing of the king's
salades, shapewex and other
[PUBLIC RECORD OFFICE: E.101, box 413, no. 2, part 2, fo. 36.]

10, 11. Both the central (Bell Harry) tower of Canterbury Cathedral and Morton's Tower at Lambeth Palace, a brick building in the traditional form of a fortified gateway, were raised at the expense of Henry's chancellor, Cardinal Morton.

12. This drawing appears on the first *rotulus*—the 'title page'—of the King's Bench plea roll for Hilary term, 1487. The large figure in the initial 'P' (of *Placita*) is presumably that of the chief justice, while the smaller figures on his right are the two puisne justices of the Bench.
[PUBLIC RECORD OFFICE: KB. 27, no. 902.]

13. This volume of statutes was made for Thomas Pigot, who became a serjeant-at-law in 1503. This plate shows the first folio of the statutes of Henry VII, beginning with the petition to the king to declare his royal title. The initial shows the king in parliament, en-

throned between lords spiritual and temporal. Pigot's arms appear in the bottom margin.

[BODLEIAN LIBRARY: MS. Hatton 10, fo. 336.]

14, 15. These illustrations of country life appear in a herbal and bestiary of the early sixteenth century, apparently made to instruct and amuse children.

[BODLEIAN LIBRARY: MS. Ashmole 1504, ff. 14v., 21v.]

16. The chapel built in 1517 adjoining the nave of Tiverton church, Devon, is decorated on its outer walls with many carvings of ships, anchors and other emblems of the trade of its founder, John Greenaway. As can be seen here, merchant ships might be armed with cannon.

17. Paycockes at Coggeshall, Essex, was built by John Paycocke, wool merchant and butcher, who died in 1505.

18. Northleach, Gloucestershire, was a great centre for wool merchants and the parish church contains many memorials to members of the trade. This rubbing (at the Victoria and Albert Museum) is of the memorial brass of an unknown woolman and his wife of the late fifteenth century; among the details are representations of their four children and his merchant's mark.

19. Silver crozier of Richard Fox, bishop of Winchester, preserved in Corpus Christi College, Oxford. Note Fox's device of a pelican 'in her piety', piercing her breast to feed her young.

20. A number of people contributed to the cost of building Long Melford church, Suffolk. Several men prominent in Edward IV's reign are portrayed in the windows. Inscriptions in the Lady Chapel name various other benefactors, the last being dated 1496 for the chapel itself.

21. Lavenham church, Suffolk, was built between 1486 and 1530 at the expense of the earl of Oxford (the lord of the manor) and the wealthy clothiers Thomas Spring and his son Thomas. In 1523, the father bequeathed £200 for completing the tower. The chapels adjoining the choir were added, after the completion of the church, by Simon Branch and the younger Spring.

22. The Prior's House at Much Wenlock, Shropshire, illustrates the higher demands for domestic comfort from heads of religious houses at the close of the fifteenth century. The outline of the former priory church appears at the right, and of the cloisters and other monastic buildings in the centre. Outside the precincts is the town with its parish church.

23. In 1201, the lord of Kirkoswald, Cumberland, was licensed to build a castle and the remains of his keep can be seen in the centre of this engraving by the Bucks (in 1737). This building was destroyed by the Scots in the fourteenth century, but was presumably repaired between 1470 and 1486 when Humphrey, Lord Dacre, incorporated it as one of the four corners of a much more extensive fortress. (*See* R. L. Storey, 'The Manor of Burgh-by-Sands', in *Transactions of the Cumberland and Westmorland Antiquarian and Archaeological Society*, new series, vol. LIV (1954), p. 121.)

24. The first page of Caxton's preface to his first edition (1485) of Sir Thomas Malory's *Morte D'Arthur*, from the copy in the John Rylands Library, Manchester. Here Caxton refers to his previous publications and how he was urged to produce this book. This plate is a reduction from the original, where the text measures $4\frac{5}{8} \times 7\frac{5}{8}$ inches.

25. Only the foundations and some lower stages of the east end of King's College Chapel were built before the deposition of Henry VI in 1461. Little further progress was made until 1480, when Edward IV was persuaded to make liberal contributions to the building fund. Richard III was also a generous benefactor. His death caused another break in operations until 1506, when Henry VII enabled the remainder of the chapel, including the entire vault, to be erected. The badges of the rose and portcullis are again prominent. The chapel was completed in 1515.

26. The bell tower of Magdalen College, Oxford, was begun in 1492 and completed about 1509.

27. One of Wenceslas Hollar's illustrations for William Dugdale's *History of St. Paul's Cathedral* (1658) which are our principal source of information about the appearance of the cathedral, and its memorials, destroyed in the Great Fire of 1666.

28. The late fifteenth-century screen in Plymtree church is one of the finest examples of the wooden, fan-vaulted Devonshire screens; it extends across both aisles as well as the choir, and most of the panels still have their original painted figures illustrating the Annunciation, Adoration, etc.

29. The double hammer-beam, 'angel roof' of the parish church of March, Cambridgeshire, is one of the best examples of a considerable number of East Anglian roofs dating from about 1500.

30, 31. The central block of Athelhampton Hall, Dorset, was built by William Martin who, somewhat unusually at this date, obtained the king's licence to fortify the house in 1495. Martin was lord mayor of London and a merchant there and at Calais. Although he obviously prospered in trade, he was not, strictly speaking, a 'new man', since his family had been lords of the manor of Athelhampton since the mid-fourteenth century.

The interior view shows the oriel window—one of the newer amenities in domestic architecture—and linen-fold panelling typical of the early Tudor period.

32, 33. Gainsborough Old Hall, Lincolnshire, was built to replace a house destroyed in 1470. It belonged to Sir Thomas Burgh (d. 1489) who earned various distinctions for successive services to Edward IV, Richard III and Henry VII.

34. Window illustrating the Feast at Cana in East Harling church, Suffolk (see p. 203).

Index